Fodor's Second E

KU-477-486

Denmark

The complete guide, thoroughly up-to-date

Packed with details that will make your trip

The must-see sights, off and on the beaten path

What to see, what to skip

Mix-and-match vacation itineraries

City strolls, countryside adventures

Smart lodging and dining options

Essential local do's and taboos

Transportation tips, distances and directions

Key contacts, savvy travel tips

When to go, what to pack

Clear, accurate, easy-to-use maps

Books to read, videos to watch

Excerpted from *Fodor's Scandinavia*

Fodor's Travel Publications • New York, Toronto, London, Sydney, Auckland
www.fodors.com

Fodor's Denmark

EDITORS: Andrew Collins, Tania Inowlocki

Editorial Contributors: Lauren Myers, Karina Porcelli
Editorial Production: Brian Vitunic
Maps: David Lindroth, *cartographer;* Rebecca Baer, Bob Blake, *map editors*
Design: Fabrizio La Rocca, *creative director;* Guido Caroti, *art director;* Jolie Novak, *photo editor*
Cover Design: Pentagram
Production/Manufacturing: Robert Shields
Cover Photograph: Bob Krist

Copyright

ISBN 0–679–00401–7

ISSN 1520–7765

2nd Edition

Special Sales

Fodor's Travel Publications are available at special discounts for bulk purchases for sales promotions or premiums. Special editions, including personalized covers, excerpts of existing guides, and corporate imprints, can be created in large quantities for special needs. For more information, contact your local bookseller or write to Special Markets, Fodor's Travel Publications, 201 East 50th Street, New York, NY 10022. Inquiries from Canada should be directed to your local Canadian bookseller or sent to Random House of Canada, Ltd., Marketing Department, 2775 Matheson Boulevard East, Mississauga, Ontario L4W 4P7. Inquiries from the United Kingdom should be sent to Fodor's Travel Publications, 20 Vauxhall Bridge Road, London, England SW1V 2SA.

PRINTED IN THE UNITED STATES OF AMERICA

10 9 8 7 6 5 4 3 2 1

Important Tip

Although all prices, opening times, and other details in this book are based on information supplied to us at press time, changes occur all the time in the travel world, and Fodor's cannot accept responsibility for facts that become outdated or for inadvertent errors or omissions. So **always confirm information when it matters,** especially if you're making a detour to visit a specific place.

CONTENTS

Maps

ON THE ROAD WITH FODOR'S

THE TRIPS YOU TAKE this year and next are going to be significant trips, if only because they'll be your first in the new millennium. For that reason, if there was ever a time you needed excellent travel information, it's now. So we've pulled out all stops in preparing *Fodor's Denmark* and scoured all corners of the country. Our goals: To discover the places that are truly worth your time and money and to unearth the fascinating facts that will help you view what you've traveled to see in a rich new light.

About Our Writer

Our success in helping to make your trip the best of all possible vacations is a credit to the hard work of our Denmark writer and our editors.

Long-time Fodor's contributor, writer, and editor **Karina Porcelli** has been living, working, and raising a family in Copenhagen since 1989. She has written for a number of international newspapers and magazines, including *National Geographic Traveler, Travel & Leisure, Saveur,* and *El Pais,* and has interviewed great Danes ranging from the country's prime ministers and politicians to its rock stars and literati.

Don't Forget to Write

We love feedback—positive and negative—and follow up on all suggestions. So contact the Denmark editor at editors@fodors.com or c/o Fodor's, 201 East 50th Street, New York, New York 10022. Have a wonderful trip!

Karen Cure

Karen Cure
Editorial Director

VI

Copenhagen

Denmark

North
Sea

Skagerrak

TO
GREENLAND

TO
FAROE ISLANDS

Skagen

Hirtshals

Frederikshavn

Hjørring

Sæby

Brønderslev

Læsø

Hanstholm

Aalborg

Limfjord

Thisted

*Lim-
fjord*

*Aalborg
Bugt*

Kattegat

Nykøbing

Hadsund

Lemvig

Skive

Anholt

Struer

Viborg

Holstebro

Randers

Grenå

Jylland

Silkeborg

Ringkøbing

Herning

Skanderborg

Århus

Ebeltoft

Grindsted

Horsens

Samsø

Tisvildeleje

Hornbæk

Skjern

Vejle

Nykøbing

Helsingør

Billund

Frederikssund

Hillerød

Esbjerg

Holsted

Fredericia

Kalundborg

Holbæk

Fanø

Kolding

Middelfart

*Store-
bælt*

Jyderup

Roskilde

Copenhagen

Ribe

Vojens

Assens

Odense

Kerteminde

Slagelse

Ringsted

Amager

Rømø

Haderslev

Fyn

Halsskov

Korsør

Køge

*Køge
Bugt*

Skærbæk

Åbenrå

Nyborg

Næstved

St.
Heddinge

Tønder

Fåborg

Karrebæksminde

Sønderborg

Als

Svendborg

Langeland

Vordingborg

Lillebælt

Troense

Tranekær

Stege

Møn

Ærøskøbing

Rudkøbing

Nakskov

Marstal

Ærø

Nykøbing

Rødby

Maribo

Falster

Lolland

Nysted

TO
BORNHOLM

Ostsee

GERMANY

N

0   50 miles

0   75 km

SWEDEN

SWEDEN

*Baltic
Sea*

Bornholm

Rønne

Scandinavia

World Time Zones

Numbers below vertical bands relate each zone to Greenwich Mean Time (0 hrs.).
Local times frequently differ from these general indications,
as indicated by light-face numbers on map.

Algiers, **29**	Berlin, **34**	Delhi, **48**	Jerusalem, **42**
Anchorage, **3**	Bogotá, **19**	Denver, **8**	Johannesburg, **44**
Athens, **41**	Budapest, **37**	Dublin, **26**	Lima, **20**
Auckland, **1**	Buenos Aires, **24**	Edmonton, **7**	Lisbon, **28**
Baghdad, **46**	Caracas, **22**	Hong Kong, **56**	London
Bangkok, **50**	Chicago, **9**	Honolulu, **2**	(Greenwich), **27**
Beijing, **54**	Copenhagen, **33**	Istanbul, **40**	Los Angeles, **6**
	Dallas, **10**	Jakarta, **53**	Madrid, **38**
			Manila, **57**

Mecca, **47**
Mexico City, **12**
Miami, **18**
Montréal, **15**
Moscow, **45**
Nairobi, **43**
New Orleans, **11**
New York City, **16**

Ottawa, **14**
Paris, **30**
Perth, **58**
Reykjavík, **25**
Rio de Janeiro, **23**
Rome, **39**
Saigon (Ho Chi Minh
City), **51**

San Francisco, **5**
Santiago, **21**
Seoul, **59**
Shanghai, **55**
Singapore, **52**
Stockholm, **32**
Sydney, **61**
Tokyo, **60**

Toronto, **13**
Vancouver, **4**
Vienna, **35**
Warsaw, **36**
Washington, D.C., **17**
Yangon, **49**
Zürich, **31**

SMART TRAVEL TIPS A TO Z

Basic Information on Traveling in Denmark, Savvy Tips to Make Your Trip a Breeze, and Companies and Organizations to Contact

AIR TRAVEL

BOOKING YOUR FLIGHT

When you book **look for nonstop flights** and **remember that "direct" flights stop at least once.** Try to avoid connecting flights, which require a change of plane.

CARRIERS

Aer Lingus flies direct from Dublin. British Airways offers connecting flights via London from Atlanta, Baltimore, Boston, Charlotte, Chicago, Dallas, Denver, Detroit, Houston, Los Angeles, Miami, New York, Orlando, Philadelphia, Phoenix, Pittsburgh, San Diego, San Francisco, Seattle, Tampa, and Washington, D.C.; they fly nonstop from Heathrow, Gatwick, Birmingham, and Manchester. Finnair has service through Helsinki from Miami, New York, and—between May and September—San Francisco. Go Fly Ltd. has very cheap flight between London's Stanstead airport and Copenhagen. Icelandair makes connecting flights via Reykjavík from Baltimore, Fort Lauderdale, New York, and Orlando. Mærsk Air flies nonstop from Gatwick to Billund and Copenhagen. Scandinavian Airlines System (SAS), the main carrier, makes nonstop flights from Chicago, Newark, and Seattle and from Heathrow, Manchester, and Glasgow. Virgin Airlines is also inexpensive and flies between London's Gatwick and Stanstead airports via Brussels to Copenhagen.

➤ MAJOR AIRLINES: Aer Lingus (☎ 0161/832–5771 in the U.K.). American (☎ 800/433–7300). British Airways (☎ 800/247–9297 in the U.S., ☎ 020/7491–4989 in the U.K.). Delta (☎ 800/221–1212). Finnair (☎ 800/950–5000). Go Fly Ltd. (☎ 0845/6054–321 in the U.K.). Icelandair (☎ 800/223–5500). Mærsk Air (☎ 020/7333-0066 in the U.K, ☎ 32/31–45–45 in Denmark). Scandinavian Airlines (SAS) (☎ 800/221–2350 in the U.S., ☎ 020/7706–8832 in the U.K., and ☎ 32/32–00–00 in Denmark). Virgin Airlines (☎ 020/7744–00046 in the U.K.).

CHECK-IN & BOARDING

Assuming that not everyone with a ticket will show up, airlines routinely overbook planes. When that happens, airlines ask for volunteers to give up their seats. In return these volunteers usually get a certificate for a free flight and are rebooked on the next flight out. If there are not enough volunteers, the airline must choose who will be denied boarding. The first to get bumped are passengers who checked in late and those flying on discounted tickets, so **get to the gate and check in as early as possible,** especially during peak periods.

Always **bring a government-issued photo I.D. to the airport.** You may be asked to show it before you are allowed to check in.

CUTTING COSTS

The least-expensive airfares to Denmark must usually be purchased in advance and are nonrefundable. It's smart to **call a number of airlines, and when you are quoted a good price, book it on the spot**—the same fare may not be available the next day. Always **check different routings** and look into using different airports. Travel agents, especially low-fare specialists (☞ Discounts & Deals, *below*), are helpful.

Consolidators are another good source. They buy tickets for scheduled international flights at reduced rates from the airlines, then sell them at prices that beat the best fare available directly from the airlines, usually without restrictions. Sometimes you can even get your money back if you need to return the ticket. Carefully read the fine print detailing penalties for changes and cancellations, and **confirm your consolidator reservation with the airline.**

When you **fly as a courier** you trade your checked-luggage space for a ticket deeply subsidized by a courier service. There are restrictions on when you can book and how long you can stay.

➤ CONSOLIDATORS: **Cheap Tickets** (☎ 800/377–1000). **Up & Away Travel** (☎ 212/889–2345). **Discount Airline Ticket Service** (☎ 800/576–1600). **Unitravel** (☎ 800/325–2222). **World Travel Network** (☎ 800/409–6753).

ENJOYING THE FLIGHT

For more legroom **request an emergency-aisle seat.** Don't sit in the row in front of the emergency aisle or in front of a bulkhead, where seats may not recline. If you have dietary concerns, **ask for special meals when booking.** These can be vegetarian, low-cholesterol, or kosher, for example. On long flights, try to maintain a normal routine, to help fight jet lag. At night **get some sleep.** By day **eat light meals, drink water** (not alcohol), and **move around the cabin** to stretch your legs.

FLYING TIMES

Flying time from New York to Copenhagen is 7¾ hours. From Los Angeles to Copenhagen, flying time is 9¾ hours. From London to Copenhagen the flight takes 1 hour, 55 minutes. Flight times within the country are all less than one hour.

HOW TO COMPLAIN

If your baggage goes astray or your flight goes awry, complain right away. Most carriers require that you **file a claim immediately.**

➤ AIRLINE COMPLAINTS: U.S. Department of Transportation **Aviation Consumer Protection Division** (✉ C-75, Room 4107, Washington, DC 20590, ☎ 202/366–2220). **Federal Aviation Administration Consumer Hotline** (☎ 800/322–7873).

WITHIN SCANDINAVIA

Scandinavia is larger than it looks on a map, and many native travelers choose to fly between the capital cities, using trains and buses for domestic travel.

If you are traveling from south to north in Norway, Sweden, or Finland, flying is often a necessity: Stavanger in southern Norway is as close to Rome, Italy, as it is to the northern tip of Norway.

For international travelers, one or two stopovers can often be purchased more cheaply along with an international ticket. With SAS, the least expensive tickets (Jackpot) are round-trip, must include a Saturday night, and can be bought only within Scandinavia from 7 to 14 days ahead. Ask about low rates for hotels and car rental in connection with Jackpot tickets. Weekend Jackpot tickets can be bought right up to flight time. SAS also gives couples who travel together a discount off some tickets and significant discounts on SAS hotels and car rentals. Low-priced round-trip weekend excursions from one Scandinavian capital to another (minimum three-day stay) can be bought one day in advance from SAS.

Intra-Scandinavian travel is usually expensive. If you want to economize, **look into the Visit Scandinavia Fare.** One coupon costs about $85; six about $510, but they vary greatly depending on routing and destination—generally, the cost rises the farther north the destination. The coupons are valid for destinations within Denmark, Sweden, Norway, and also between Sweden and Finland. They are sold only in the United States and only to non-Scandinavians. Coupons can be used year-round for a maximum of three months and must be purchased in conjunction with transatlantic flights.

AIRPORTS

Kastrup International Airport, the hub of Scandinavian air travel, is 10 km (6 mi) southeast of Copenhagen.

➤ AIRPORT INFORMATION: **Kastrup International Airport** (☎ 011–45–32/54–17–01).

BIKE TRAVEL

Biking is a way of life in Denmark, with more people biking to work than driving. Biking vacations in Denmark are popular, as they are easy for all ages due to the flat landscape.

BIKES IN FLIGHT

Most airlines accommodate bikes as luggage, provided they are dismantled and boxed. For bike boxes, often free at bike shops, you'll pay about $5 (at least $100 for bike bags) from airlines. International travelers can sometimes substitute a bike for a piece of checked luggage at no charge; otherwise, the cost is about $100. Domestic and Canadian airlines charge $25–$50.

BOAT & FERRY TRAVEL

Taking a ferry isn't only fun, it's often necessary in Scandinavia. Many companies arrange package trips, some offering a rental car and hotel accommodations as part of the deal.

Ferry crossings often last overnight. The trip between Copenhagen and Oslo, for example, takes approximately 16 hours, most lines leaving at about 5 PM and arriving about 9 the next morning. The direct cruise between Stockholm and Helsinki takes 12 hours, usually leaving at about 6 PM and arriving the next morning at 9. The shortest ferry route runs between Helsingør, Denmark, and Helsingborg, Sweden; it takes only 25 minutes.

From the United Kingdom, **Scandinavian Seaways Ferries (DFDS)** sail from Harwich to Esbjerg (20 hours) on Jylland's west coast. Schedules in both summer and winter are very irregular. There are many discounts, including 20% for senior citizens and people with disabilities, and 50% for children between the ages of 4 and 16.

FARES & SCHEDULES

➤ BOAT & FERRY INFORMATION: **Color Line** (⊠ Box 30, DK–985O Hirsthals, Denmark, ☎ 45/99–56–20–00, FAX 45/99–56–20–20; Hjortneskaia, Box 1422 Vika, N–0115 Oslo, Norway, ☎ 47/22–94–44–00, FAX 47/22–83–04–30; c/o Bergen Line, Inc., 405 5th Ave., New York, NY 10022, ☎ 800/323–7436, FAX 212/983–1275; Tyne Commission Quay, North Shields NE29 6EA, Newcastle, England, ☎ 091/296–1313, FAX 091/296–1540). **Scandinavian Seaways Ferries (DFDS)** (⊠ Sankt Annæ Plads 30, DK–1295 Copenhagen). **Scand-Lines** (⊠ Box 1, DK–300O Helsingør, Denmark, ☎ 45/33–15–15–15, FAX 45/33–15–10–20; Knutpunkten 44, S–252 78 Helsingborg, Sweden, ☎ 46/42–18–61–00, FAX 46/42–18–74–10).

➤ MAJOR OPERATOR: **Scandinavian Seaways Ferries (DFDS)** (⊠ Sankt Annae Plads 30, DK–1295 Copenhagen, Denmark, ☎ 45/33–15–63–00, ☎ 45/33–42–30–00, FAX 45/33–42–33–41; DFDS Travel Centre, 15 Hanover St., London W1R 9HG, ☎ 020/7409–6060, FAX 020/7409–6035; DFDS Seaways USA Inc., 6555 NW 9th Ave., Suite 207, Fort Lauderdale, FL 33309, ☎ 800/533–3755, FAX 305/491–7958; Box 8895, Scandiahamnen, S–402 72 Göteborg, Sweden, ☎ 46/31–650–610).

PLYING SCANDINAVIAN WATERS

Connections from Denmark to Norway and Sweden are available through DFDS and the Stena Line. Fjord Line sails along the magnificent west coast of Norway. Connections to the Faroe Islands from Norway and Denmark are available through the Smyril Line. Silja Line and Viking Line offer a variety of cruises to Finland, with departures from Stockholm to Mariehamn in the Åland archipelago, lTurku (Åbo) and Helsinki (Helsingfors), and a crossing from Umeå to Vaasa.

➤ MAJOR OPERATORS: **DFDS Seaways** (☞ *above*). **Stena Line** (⊠ Trafikhamnen, DK–9900 Frederikshavn, Denmark, ☎ 45/96–20–02–00, FAX 45/96–20–02–80; Jernbanetorget 2, N–0154 Oslo 1, Norway, ☎ 47/23–17–90–00, FAX 47/23–17–90–60; Scandinavia AB, S–405 19 Göteborg, Sweden, ☎ 46/31–704–0000, FAX 46/31–241–038). **Fjord Line** (⊠ Skoltegrunnskaien, Box 7250, N–5020 Bergen, Norway, ☎ 47/55–54–88–00, FAX 47/55–54–86–01). **Smyril Line** (☞ DFDS Seaways, *above*; or J. Brocksgøta 37, Box 370, FO–110 Tórshavn, Faroe Islands, ☎ 298/31–59–00, FAX 298/31–57–07; Slottsgate 1, Box 4135 Dreggen, N–5023 Bergen, Norway, ☎ 47 /55–32–09–70, FAX 47/55–96–02–72). **Silja Line** (⊠ Kungsgatan 2, S–111 43 Stockholm, Sweden, ☎ 46/8–666–3512, FAX 46/8–611–9162; c/o Scandinavian Seaways, Parkeston Quay Scand. House, Harwich, Essex, England CO12 4QG, ☎ 44/255–240–240, FAX 44/255–244–382).

CAR FERRIES

Travel by car in Scandinavia often necessitates travel by ferry. Some well-known vehicle and passenger ferries run between Dragør, Denmark (just south of Copenhagen), and Limhamn, Sweden (just south of Malmö); between Helsingør, Denmark, and Helsingborg, Sweden; and between Copenhagen and Göteborg, Sweden. On the Dragør/Limhamn ferry (ScandLines), taking a car one-way costs SKr 395 (about $60 or £39). The Helsingør/Helsingborg ferry (ScandLines also) takes only 25 minutes; taking a car along one-way costs SKr 330 (about $50 or £33). Fares for round-trip are cheaper, and on weekends the Öresund Runt pass (for crossing between Dragoør and Limhamn one way and Helsingborg and Helsingoør the other way) costs only SKr 495 (about $75 or £49).

➤ MAJOR OPERATORS: **DSB Rederi** (☎ 33/15–15–15 in the U.K.). **Stena Line** (Sweden, ☎ 46–31/775–00–00). **ScandLines** (☞ *above*).

BUS TRAVEL

Traveling by bus or train is easy because DSB and a few private companies cover the country with a dense network of services, supplemented by buses in remote areas. Bus tickets are usually sold on buses. Children under five travel free, and those between five and twelve travel for half-price. Ask about discounts for senior citizens and groups of three or more.

Not particularly comfortable or fast, bus travel from the United Kingdom is inexpensive. Eurolines travels from London's Victoria Station on Saturday at 2:30 PM, crossing the North Sea on the Dover-Calais ferry, and arrives in Copenhagen about 22 hours later.

➤ BUS OPERATOR: **DSB** (☎ 70/13–14–15, in Denmark). **Eurolines** (✉ 52 Grosvenor Gardens SWI London, ☎ 020/7730–8235, ✉ Reventlowsg. 8, Copenhagen DK–1651, ☎ 33/25–12–44).

BUSINESS HOURS

BANKS

Banks in Copenhagen are open week-days 9:30 to 4 and Thursdays until 6. Several *bureaux de change,* including the ones at Copenhagen's central station and airport, stay open until 10 PM. Outside Copenhagen, banking hours vary.

MUSEUMS

A number of Copenhagen's museums hold confounding hours, so always call first to confirm. As a rule, however, most museums are open 10 to 3 or 11 to 4 and are closed on Monday. In winter, opening hours are shorter, and some museums close for the season. Check the local papers or ask at tourist offices for current schedules.

SHOPS

Though many Danish stores are expanding their hours, sometimes even staying open on Sundays, most shops still keep the traditional hours: weekdays 10 to 5:30, until 7 on Thursday and Friday, until 1 or 2 on Saturday—though the larger department stores stay open until 5. Everything except bakeries, kiosks, flower shops, and a handful of grocers are closed on Sunday, and most bakeries take Monday off. The first and last Saturday of the month are Long Saturdays, when even the smaller shops, especially in large cities, stay open until 4 or 5. Grocery stores stay open until 8 PM on weekdays, and kiosks until much later.

CAMERAS & PHOTOGRAPHY

➤ PHOTO HELP: **Kodak Information Center** (☎ 800/242–2424). *Kodak Guide to Shooting Great Travel Pictures,* available in bookstores or from Fodor's Travel Publications (☎ 800/533–6478; $16.50 plus $4 shipping).

EQUIPMENT PRECAUTIONS

Always **keep your film and tape out of the sun.** Carry an extra supply of batteries, and **be prepared to turn on your camera or camcorder** to prove to security personnel that the device is real. Always **ask for hand inspection of film,** which becomes clouded after successive exposures to airport X-ray machines, and **keep videotapes away from metal detectors.**

CAR RENTAL

Major international car-rental agencies are represented throughout Denmark. In Copenhagen, most car-rental agencies are located near the Vesterport Station.

Rates begin at $110 a day and $210 a week for an economy car without air-conditioning, and with a manual transmission and unlimited mileage.

Europcar (✉ Copenhagen Airport, ☎ 32/50–30–90). **Budget-Pitzner Auto** (✉ Copenhagen Airport, ☎ 32/50–90–65).

➤ MAJOR AGENCIES: **Alamo** (☎ 800/522–9696; 020/8759–6200 in the U.K.). **Avis** (☎ 800/331–1084; 800/879–2847 in Canada; 02/9353–9000 in Australia; 09/525–1982 in New Zealand). **Budget** (☎ 800/527–0700; 0144/227–6266 in the U.K.). **Dollar** (☎ 800/800–6000; 020/8897–0811 in the U.K., where it is known as Eurodollar, 02/9223–1444 in Australia). **Hertz** (☎ 800/654–3001; 800/263–0600 in Canada; 0990/90–60–90 in the U.K.; 02/9669–2444 in Australia; 03/358–6777 in New Zealand). **National InterRent** (☎ 800/227–3876; 0345/222525 in the U.K., where it is known as Europcar InterRent).

CUTTING COSTS

To get the best deal **book through a travel agent who will shop around.** Do **look into wholesalers,** companies that do not own fleets but rent in bulk from those that do and often offer better rates than traditional car-rental operations. Payment must be made before you leave home.

➤ WHOLESALERS: **Auto Europe** (☎ 207/842–2000 or 800/223–5555, FAX 800–235–6321). **Europe by Car** (☎ 212/581–3040 or 800/223–1516, FAX 212/246–1458). **DER Travel Services** (✉ 9501 W. Devon Ave., Rosemont, IL 60018, ☎ 800/782–2424, FAX 800/282–7474 for information; 800/860–9944 for brochures). **Kemwel Holiday Autos** (☎ 914/825–3000 or 800/678–0678, FAX 914/381–8847).

INSURANCE

When driving a rented car you are generally responsible for any damage to or loss of the vehicle. Before you rent see what coverage your personal auto-insurance policy and credit cards already provide.

Collision policies that car-rental companies sell for European rentals usually do not include stolen-vehicle coverage. Before you buy it, check your existing policies—you may already be covered.

REQUIREMENTS & RESTRICTIONS

Ask about age requirements: Several countries require drivers to be over 20 years old, but some car-rental companies require that drivers be at least 25. In Scandinavia your own driver's license is acceptable for a limited time; check with the country's tourist board before you go. An International Driver's Permit is a good idea; it's available from the American or Canadian automobile association, or, in the United Kingdom, from the Automobile Association or Royal Automobile Club.

SURCHARGES

Before you pick up a car in one city and leave it in another **ask about drop-off charges or one-way service fees,** which can be substantial. Note, too, that some rental agencies charge extra if you return the car before the time specified in your contract. To avoid a hefty refueling fee **fill the tank just before you turn in the car,** but be aware that gas stations near the rental outlet may overcharge.

CAR TRAVEL

The only part of Denmark that is connected to the European continent is Jylland, via the E45 highway from Germany. The E20 highway then leads to Middelfart on Fyn and east to Knudshoved. From there a ferry crosses to Korsør on Sjælland and E20 leads east to Copenhagen.

The **Storebæltsbro Bridge,** connecting Fyn and Sjælland via the E20 highway, has greatly reduced the travel time between the islands. The **Storebæltsbro railway link** has also cut train travel time sharply.

Another option is to take the 1½-hour car ferry from Århus directly to Kalundborg in western Sjælland. From there, Route 23 leads to Copenhagen. Make reservations for the ferry in advance through the DSB Rederi (☞ Car Ferries, *above*). (*Note:* During the busy summer months, passengers without reservations for their vehicles can wait hours.)

Excellent, well-marked roads make driving a great way to explore Scandinavia—but beware that gasoline costs more than $1 per liter of lead-free gas, roughly four times the typical U.S.

price. Ferry costs can be steep, and reservations are vital. Tolls on some major roads add to the expense, as do the high fees for city parking; tickets for illegal parking are painfully costly.

Also be aware that there are relatively low legal blood-alcohol limits and tough penalties for driving while intoxicated in Scandinavia. Penalties include suspension of the driver's license and fines or imprisonment and are enforced by random police road-blocks in urban areas on weekends. In addition, an accident involving a driver with an illegal blood-alcohol level usually voids all insurance agreements, so the driver becomes responsible for his own medical bills and damage to the cars.

In a few remote areas, especially in Iceland and northern Norway, Sweden, and Finland, road conditions can be unpredictable, and careful planning is required for safety's sake. It is wise to **use a four-wheel-drive vehicle** and to **travel with at least one other car** in these areas.

Keep your headlights on at all times; this is required by law in most of Scandinavia. Also by Scandinavian law, everyone, including infants, must **wear seat belts.**

EMERGENCY ASSISTANCE

Before leaving home, consult your insurance company. Members of organizations affiliated with Alliance International de Tourisme (AIT) can get technical and legal advice from the Danish Motoring Organization, open 10–4 weekdays. All highways have emergency phones, and you can call the rental company for help. If you cannot drive your car to a garage for repairs, the rescue corps Falck can help anywhere, anytime. In most cases they charge for assistance.

AUTO CLUBS

➤ IN AUSTRALIA: **Australian Automobile Association** (☎ 02/6247–7311).

➤ IN CANADA: **Canadian Automobile Association (CAA,** ☎ 613/247–0117).

➤ IN DENMARK: **Danish Motoring Organization (FDM,** ✉ Firskovvej 32, 2800 Lyngby, ☎ 45/27–07–07). Falck (☎ 70/10–20–30)

➤ IN NEW ZEALAND: **New Zealand Automobile Association** (☎ 09/377–4660).

➤ IN THE U.K.: **Automobile Association (AA,** ☎ 0990/500–600). **Royal Automobile Club (RAC,** ☎ 0990/722–722 for membership; 0345/121–345 for insurance).

➤ IN THE U.S.: **American Automobile Association** (☎ 800/564–6222).

PARKING

You can usually park on the right-hand side of the road in Denmark, though not on main roads and highways. Signs reading PARKERING/STANDSNING FORBUNDT mean no parking or stopping, though you are allowed a three-minute grace period for loading and unloading. In town, parking disks are used where there are no automatic ticket-vending machines. Get disks from gas stations, post offices, police stations, or tourist offices, and set them to show your time of arrival. For most downtown parking, you must buy a ticket from an automatic vending machine and display it on the dash. Parking costs about Dkr 10 or more per hour.

RULES OF THE ROAD

To drive in Denmark you need a valid driver's license, and if you're using your own car, it must have a certificate of registration and national plates. A triangular hazard-warning sign is compulsory in every car and is provided with rentals. Motorcyclists must wear helmets and use low-beam lights as well.

Drive on the right and give way to traffic—*especially to bicyclists*—on the right. A red-and-white YIELD sign or a line of white triangles across the road means you must yield to traffic on the road you are entering. Do not turn right on red unless there is a green arrow indicating that this is allowed. Speed limits are 50 kph (30 mph) in built-up areas; 100 kph (60 mph) on highways; and 80 kph (50 mph) on other roads. If you are towing a trailer, you must not exceed 70 kph (40 mph). Speeding is treated severely; Americans and other foreign tourists must pay fines on the spot.

SMART TRAVEL TIPS A TO Z

CHILDREN IN DENMARK

In Scandinavia children are to be seen *and* heard and are genuinely welcome in most public places. If you are renting a car don't forget to **arrange for a car seat** when you reserve.

DISCOUNTS

Children are entitled to discount tickets (often as much as 50% off) on buses, trains, and ferries throughout Scandinavia, as well as reductions on special City Cards. Children under 12 pay half-price and children under 2 pay 10% on SAS and Linjeflyg round-trips. The only restriction on this discount is that the family travel together and return to the originating city in Scandinavia at least two days later. With the Scanrail Pass (☞ Cutting Costs *in* Train Travel, *below*)—good for rail journeys throughout Scandinavia—children under 4 (on lap) travel free; those 4–11 pay half-fare and those 12–25 can get a Scanrail Youth Pass, providing a 25% discount off of the adult fare.

FLYING

If your children are two or older **ask about children's airfares.** As a general rule, infants under two not occupying a seat fly at greatly reduced fares or even for free. When booking **confirm carry-on allowances** if you're traveling with infants. In general, for babies charged 10% of the adult fare, you are allowed one carry-on bag and a collapsible stroller; if the flight is full the stroller may have to be checked or you may be limited to less.

Experts agree that it's a good idea to use safety seats aloft for children weighing less than 40 pounds. Airlines set their own policies: U.S. carriers usually require that the child be ticketed, even if he or she is young enough to ride free, since the seats must be strapped into regular seats. Do **check your airline's policy about using safety seats during takeoff and landing.** And since safety seats are not allowed just everywhere in the plane, get your seat assignments early.

When reserving, **request children's meals or a freestanding bassinet** if you need them. But note that bulkhead seats, where you must sit to use the bassinet, may lack an overhead bin or storage space on the floor.

LODGING

Most hotels in Denmark allow children under a certain age to stay in their parents' room at no extra charge, but others charge for them as extra adults; be sure to **find out the cutoff age for children's discounts.**

SIGHTS & ATTRACTIONS

Places that are especially good for children are indicated by a rubber duckie icon in the margin.

CONSUMER PROTECTION

Whenever shopping or buying travel services in Denmark, **pay with a major credit card** so you can cancel payment or get reimbursed if there's a problem. If you're doing business with a particular company for the first time, **contact your local Better Business Bureau and the attorney general's offices** in your state and the company's home state, as well. Have any complaints been filed? Finally, if you're buying a package or tour, always **consider travel insurance** that includes default coverage (☞ Insurance, *below*).

➤ LOCAL BBBs: **Council of Better Business Bureaus** (✉ 4200 Wilson Blvd., Suite 800, Arlington, VA 22203, ☎ 703/276–0100, ℻ 703/525–8277).

CUSTOMS & DUTIES

If you are 21 or older, have purchased goods in a country that is a member of the European Union (EU), and pay that country's value-added tax (V.A.T.) on those goods, you may import duty-free 1½ liters of liquor; 300 cigarettes or 150 cigarillos or 75 cigars or 400 grams of tobacco. If you are entering Denmark from a non-EU country or if you have purchased your goods on a ferryboat or in an airport not taxed in the EU, you must pay Danish taxes on any amount of alcoholic beverages greater than 1 liter of liquor or 2 liters of strong wine, plus 2 liters of table wine. For tobacco, the limit is 200 cigarettes or 100 cigarillos or 50 cigars or 250 grams of tobacco. You are also allowed 50 grams of perfume. Other articles (including beer) are allowed up to a maximum of Dkr 1,350.

When shopping, **keep receipts** for all purchases. Upon reentering the country, **be ready to show customs officials**

what you've bought. If you feel a duty is incorrect or object to the way your clearance was handled, note the inspector's badge number and ask to see a supervisor. If the problem isn't resolved, write to the appropriate authorities, beginning with the port director at your point of entry.

IN DENMARK

Limits on what you can bring in duty-free vary from country to country. **Check with individual country tourist boards for limits on alcohol, cigarettes, and other items.** Also be careful to check before bringing food of any kind into Iceland.

IN AUSTRALIA

Australia residents who are 18 or older may bring home $A400 worth of souvenirs and gifts (including jewelry), 250 cigarettes or 250 grams of tobacco, and 1,125 ml of alcohol (including wine, beer, and spirits). Residents under 18 may bring back $A200 worth of goods. Prohibited items include meat products. Seeds, plants, and fruits need to be declared upon arrival.

➤ INFORMATION: **Australian Customs Service** (Regional Director, ✉ Box 8, Sydney, NSW 2001, ☎ 02/9213–2000, FAX 02/9213–4000).

IN CANADA

Canadian residents who have been out of Canada for at least 7 days may bring home C$500 worth of goods duty-free. If you've been away less than 7 days but more than 48 hours, the duty-free allowance drops to C$200; if your trip lasts 24–48 hours, the allowance is C$50. You may not pool allowances with family members. Goods claimed under the C$500 exemption may follow you by mail; those claimed under the lesser exemptions must accompany you. Alcohol and tobacco products may be included in the 7-day and 48-hour exemptions but not in the 24-hour exemption. If you meet the age requirements of the province or territory through which you reenter Canada, you may bring in, duty-free, 1.14 liters (40 imperial ounces) of wine or liquor *or* 24 12-ounce cans or bottles of beer or ale. If you are 16 or older you may bring in, duty-free, 200 cigarettes and 50 cigars. Check ahead of time with Revenue Canada or the Department of Agriculture for policies regarding meat products, seeds, plants, and fruits.

You may send an unlimited number of gifts worth up to C$60 each duty-free to Canada. Label the package UNSOLICITED GIFT—VALUE UNDER $60. Alcohol and tobacco are excluded.

➤ INFORMATION: **Revenue Canada** (✉ 2265 St. Laurent Blvd. S, Ottawa, Ontario K1G 4K3, ☎ 613/993–0534; 800/461–9999 in Canada).

IN NEW ZEALAND

Homeward-bound residents 17 or older may bring back $700 worth of souvenirs and gifts. Your duty-free allowance also includes 4.5 liters of wine or beer; one 1,125-ml bottle of spirits; and either 200 cigarettes, 250 grams of tobacco, 50 cigars, or a combination of the three up to 250 grams. Prohibited items include meat products, seeds, plants, and fruits.

➤ INFORMATION: **New Zealand Customs** (Custom House, ✉ 50 Anzac Ave., Box 29, Auckland, New Zealand, ☎ 09/359–6655, FAX 09/359–6732).

IN THE U.K.

If you are a U.K. resident and your journey was wholly within the European Union (EU), you won't have to pass through customs when you return to the United Kingdom. If you plan to bring back large quantities of alcohol or tobacco, check EU limits beforehand. From countries outside the EU, including Iceland, Norway, and Sweden, you may import, duty-free, 200 cigarettes or 50 cigars; 1 liter of spirits or 2 liters of fortified or sparkling wine or liqueurs; 2 liters of still table wine; 60 milliliters of perfume; 250 milliliters of toilet water; plus £136 worth of other goods, including gifts and souvenirs.

➤ INFORMATION: **HM Customs and Excise** (✉ Dorset House, Stamford St., Bromley Kent BR1 1XX, ☎ 020/7202–4227).

IN THE U.S.

U.S. residents who have been out of the country for at least 48 hours (and who have not used the $400 allowance or any part of it in the past 30 days) may bring home $400 worth of foreign goods duty-free. U.S. residents 21 and older may bring back 1 liter of alcohol duty-free. In addition, regardless of your age, you are allowed 200 cigarettes and 100 non-Cuban cigars. Antiques, which the U.S. Customs Service defines as objects more than 100 years old, enter duty-free, as do original works of art done entirely by hand, including paintings, drawings, and sculptures.

You may also send packages home duty-free: up to $200 worth of goods for personal use, with a limit of one parcel per addressee per day (and no alcohol or tobacco products or perfume worth more than $5); label the package PERSONAL USE and attach a list of its contents and their retail value. Do not label the package UNSOLICITED GIFT or your duty-free exemption will drop to $100. Mailed items do not affect your duty-free allowance on your return.

➤ INFORMATION: **U.S. Customs Service** (inquiries, ✉ 1300 Pennsylvania Ave. NW, Washington, DC 20229, ☎ 202/927–6724; complaints, ✉ Office of Regulations and Rulings, 1300 Pennsylvania Ave. NW, Washington, DC 20229; registration of equipment, ✉ Registration Information, 1300 Pennsylvania Ave. NW, Washington, DC 20229, ☎ 202/927–0540).

DINING

Denmark's major cities offer a full range of dining choices, from traditional to international restaurants. Restaurants in smaller towns stick to traditional local fare. Local dishes can be very good, especially in the seafood and game categories, but bear in mind that northern climes beget exceptionally hearty, and heavy, meals. Sausage appears in a thousand forms, likewise potatoes. Some particular northern tastes can seem very different, such as the fondness for pickled and fermented fish—to be sampled carefully at first—and a universal obsession with sweet pastries, ice cream, and chocolate. Other novelties for the visitor might be the use of fruit in main dishes and soups, or sour milk on breakfast cereal, or preserved fish paste as a spread for crackers, or the prevalence of tasty, whole-grain crisp breads and hearty rye breads. The Swedish *smörgåsbord* and its Danish

cousins are often the traveling diner's best bet, providing you find an authentic sampling. They include fresh fish and vegetables alongside meat and starches, and are also among the lower-priced menu choices.

Restaurant meals are a big-ticket item throughout Denmark, but there are ways to keep the cost of eating down. Take full advantage of the large, buffet breakfast usually included in the cost of a hotel room. At lunch, look for the "menu" that offers a set two- or three-course meal for a set price, or limit yourself to a hearty appetizer. Some restaurants now include a trip to the salad bar in the dinner price. At dinner, pay careful attention to the price of wine and drinks, since the high tax on alcohol raises these costs considerably. For more information on affordable eating, *see* Money Matters *below*.

Properties indicated by an ✕⌑ are lodging establishments whose restaurant warrants a special trip.

RESERVATIONS & DRESS

Reservations are always a good idea: we mention them only when they're essential or are not accepted. Book as far ahead as you can, and reconfirm as soon as you arrive. We mention dress only when men are required to wear a jacket or a jacket and tie.

DISABILITIES & ACCESSIBILITY

Facilities for travelers with disabilities in Scandinavia are generally good, and most of the major tourist offices offer special booklets and brochures on travel and accommodations.

LODGING

Best Western offers properties with wheelchair-accessible rooms in Helsinki, Oslo, Stockholm, and just outside Copenhagen. If wheelchair-accessible rooms are not available, ground-floor rooms are provided.

When discussing accessibility with an operator or reservations agent **ask hard questions.** Are there any stairs, inside *or* out? Are there grab bars next to the toilet *and* in the shower/tub? How wide is the doorway to the room? To the bathroom? For the most extensive facilities meeting the latest legal specifications **opt for newer accommodations.**

➤ WHEELCHAIR-FRIENDLY CHAIN: **Best Western** (☎ 800/528–1234).

TRANSPORTATION

➤ COMPLAINTS: **Disability Rights Section** (✉ U.S. Department of Justice, Civil Rights Division, Box 66738, Washington, DC 20035-6738, ☎ 202/514–0301; 800/514–0301; 202/514–0301 TTY; 800/514–0301 TTY, 🖷 202 /307–1198) for general complaints. **Aviation Consumer Protection Division** (☞ Air Travel, *above*) for airline-related problems. **Civil Rights Office** (✉ U.S. Department of Transportation, Departmental Office of Civil Rights, S-30, 400 7th St. SW, Room 10215, Washington, DC 20590, ☎ 202/366–4648, 🖷 202/366–9371) for problems with surface transportation.

TRAVEL AGENCIES

In the United States, although the Americans with Disabilities Act requires that travel firms serve the needs of all travelers, some agencies specialize in working with people with disabilities.

➤ TRAVELERS WITH MOBILITY PROBLEMS: **Access Adventures** (✉ 206 Chestnut Ridge Rd., Rochester, NY 14624, ☎ 716/889–9096), run by a former physical-rehabilitation counselor. **Accessible Journeys** (✉ 35 W. Sellers Ave., Ridley Park, PA 19078, ☎ 610/521–0339 or 800/846–4537, 🖷 610/521–6959). **CareVacations** (✉ 5-5110 50th Ave., Leduc, Alberta T9E 6V4, ☎ 780/986–6404 or 877/478–7827, 🖷 780/986–8332) has group tours and is especially helpful with cruise vacations. **Flying Wheels Travel** (✉ 143 W. Bridge St., Box 382, Owatonna, MN 55060, ☎ 507/451–5005 or 800/535–6790, 🖷 507/451–1685). **Hinsdale Travel Service** (✉ 201 E. Ogden Ave., Suite 100, Hinsdale, IL 60521, ☎ 630/325–1335, 🖷 630/325–1342).

DISCOUNTS & DEALS

Be a smart shopper and **compare all your options** before making decisions. A plane ticket bought with a promotional coupon from travel clubs, coupon books, and direct-mail offers may not be cheaper than the least expensive fare from a discount ticket agency. And always keep in mind that what you get is just as important as what you save.

DISCOUNT RESERVATIONS

To save money **look into discount-reservations services** with toll-free numbers, which use their buying power to get a better price on hotels, airline tickets, even car rentals. When booking a room, always **call the hotel's local toll-free number** (if one is available) rather than the central reservations number—you'll often get a better price. Always ask about special packages or corporate rates.

When shopping for the best deal on hotels and car rentals **look for guaranteed exchange rates,** which protect you against a falling dollar. With your rate locked in, you won't pay more, even if the price goes up in the local currency.

➤ AIRLINE TICKETS: ☎ 800/FLY–4–LESS.

➤ HOTEL ROOMS: **International Marketing & Travel Concepts** (☎ 800/790–4682). Steigenberger Reservation Service (☎ 800/223–5652). **Travel Interlink** (☎ 800/888–5898).

PACKAGE DEALS

Don't confuse packages and guided tours. When you buy a package, you travel on your own, just as though you had planned the trip yourself. Fly/drive packages, which combine airfare and car rental, are often a good deal. If you **buy a rail/drive pass** you may save on train tickets and car rentals. All Eurail- and Europass holders get a discount on Eurostar fares through the Channel Tunnel. Also check rates for Scanrail Passes (☞ Cutting Costs *in* Train Travel, *below*).

ELECTRICITY

To use your U.S.-purchased electric-powered equipment **bring a converter and adapter.** The electrical current in Denmark is 220 volts, 50 cycles alternating current (AC); wall outlets take Continental-type plugs, with two round prongs.

If your appliances are dual-voltage you'll need only an adapter. Don't use 110-volt outlets, marked FOR SHAVERS

ONLY, for high-wattage appliances such as blow-dryers. Most laptops operate equally well on 110 and 220 volts and so require only an adapter.

EMBASSIES

➤ U.S. EMBASSY: ✉ Dag Hammarskjölds Allé 24, DK–2100 Copenhagen Ø, ☎ 35/55–31–44.

➤ CANADA EMBASSY: ✉ Kristen Bernikows G. 1, DK–1105 Copenhagen Ø, ☎ 33/12–22–99.

➤ U.K. EMBASSY: ✉ Kastesvej 40, DK–2100 Copenhagen Ø, ☎ 35/44–52–00.

EMERGENCIES

Ambulance, fire, and police assistance is available 24 hours in Scandinavia. The general emergency number throughout Denmark is ☎ 112.

GAY & LESBIAN TRAVEL

➤ GAY- AND LESBIAN-FRIENDLY TRAVEL AGENCIES: **Different Roads Travel** (✉ 8383 Wilshire Blvd., Suite 902, Beverly Hills, CA 90211, ☎ 323/651–5557 or 800/429–8747, FAX 323/651–3678). **Kennedy Travel** (✉ 314 Jericho Turnpike, Floral Park, NY 11001, ☎ 516/352–4888 or 800/237–7433, FAX 516/354–8849). **Now Voyager** (✉ 4406 18th St., San Francisco, CA 94114, ☎ 415/626–1169 or 800/255–6951, FAX 415/626–8626). **Skylink Travel and Tour** (✉ 1006 Mendocino Ave., Santa Rosa, CA 95401, ☎ 707/546–9888 or 800/225–5759, FAX 707/546–9891), serving lesbian travelers.

INSURANCE

The most useful travel insurance plan is a comprehensive policy that includes coverage for trip cancellation and interruption, default, trip delay, and medical expenses (with a waiver for preexisting conditions).

Without insurance you will lose all or most of your money if you cancel your trip, regardless of the reason. Default insurance covers you if your tour operator, airline, or cruise line goes out of business. Trip-delay covers expenses that arise because of bad weather or mechanical delays. Study the fine print when comparing policies.

If you're traveling internationally, a key component of travel insurance is coverage for medical bills incurred if you get sick on the road. Such expenses are not generally covered by Medicare or private policies. U.K. residents can buy a travel-insurance policy valid for most vacations taken during the year in which it's purchased (but check pre-existing-condition coverage). Always **buy travel policies directly from the insurance company**; if you buy it from a cruise line, airline, or tour operator that goes out of business you probably will not be covered for the agency or operator's default, a major risk. Before you make any purchase **review your existing health and homeowner's policies** to find what they cover away from home.

➤ TRAVEL INSURERS: In the U.S. Access America (✉ 6600 W. Broad St., Richmond, VA 23230, ☎ 804/285–3300 or 800/284–8300), **Travel Guard International** (✉ 1145 Clark St., Stevens Point, WI 54481, ☎ 715/345–0505 or 800/826–1300). In Canada **Voyager Insurance** (✉ 44 Peel Center Dr., Brampton, Ontario L6T 4M8, ☎ 905/791–8700; 800/668–4342 in Canada).

➤ INSURANCE INFORMATION: In the U.K. the **Association of British Insurers** (✉ 51–55 Gresham St., London EC2V 7HQ, ☎ 020/7600–3333, FAX 020/7696–8999). In Australia the **Insurance Council of Australia** (☎ 03/9614–1077, FAX 03/9614–7924).

LANGUAGE

Despite the fact that four of the five Scandinavian tongues are in the Germanic family of languages, it is a myth that someone who speaks German can understand Danish. English is widely spoken in Scandinavia. German is the most common third language. English becomes rarer outside major cities, and it's a good idea to **take along a dictionary or phrase book.** Even here, however, anyone under the age of 50 is likely to have studied English in school.

Characters special to these three languages are the Danish "ø" and the Swedish "ö," pronounced a bit like a very short "er," similar to the French "eu"; "æ" or "ä," which sounds like the "a" in "ape" but with a glottal stop, or the "a" in "cat," depending on the region, and the "å" (also written "aa"), which sounds like the "o" in "ghost." The important thing about these characters isn't that you pronounce them correctly—foreigners usually can't—but that you know to look for them in the phone book at the very end. Mr. Søren Åstrup, for example, will be found after "Z." Æ or Ä and q or Ö follow.

LANGUAGES FOR TRAVELERS

A phrase book and language-tape set can help get you started.

LODGING

The lodgings we list are the cream of the crop in each price category. We always list the facilities that are available—but we don't specify whether they cost extra: When pricing accommodations, always ask what's included and what costs extra.

In the larger cities, lodging ranges from first-class business hotels run by SAS, Sheraton, and Scandic to good-quality tourist-class hotels, such as RESO, Best Western, Scandic Budget, and Sweden Hotels, to a wide variety of single-entrepreneur hotels. In the countryside, look for independently run inns and motels. In Denmark they're called *kroer;* in Norway, *fjellstuer* or *pensjonat;* in Finland, *kienvari;* and elsewhere, guest houses. "Mökki" holidays, in summer cottages or farmhouses, have become popular with foreign visitors to Finland. Before you leave home, **ask your travel agent about discounts** (☞ Hotels, *below*), including summer hotel checks for Best Western, Scandic, and Inter Nor hotels, a summer Fjord pass in Norway, and enormous year-round rebates at SAS hotels for travelers over 65. All EuroClass (business class) passengers can get discounts of at least 10% at SAS hotels when they book through SAS.

Two things about hotels usually surprise North Americans: the relatively limited dimensions of Scandinavian beds and the generous size of Scandinavian breakfasts. Scandinavian double beds are often about 60 inches wide or slightly less, close in size to the U.S. queen size. King-size beds (72 inches wide) are difficult to find and, if available, require special reservations.

Older hotels may have some rooms described as "double," which in fact have one double bed plus one foldout sofa big enough for two people. This arrangement is occasionally called a combi-room but is being phased out.

Many older hotels, particularly the country inns and independently run smaller hotels in the cities, do not have private bathrooms. Ask ahead if this is important to you.

Scandinavian breakfasts resemble what many people would call lunch, usually including breads, cheeses, marmalade, hams, lunch meats, eggs, juice, cereal, milk, and coffee. Generally, the farther north you go, the larger the breakfasts become. Breakfast is usually included in hotel rates.

Make reservations whenever possible. Even countryside inns, which usually have space, are sometimes packed with vacationing Europeans.

Ask about high and low seasons when making reservations, since different countries define their tourist seasons differently. Some hotels lower prices during tourist season, whereas others raise them during the same period.

Assume that hotels operate on the European Plan (EP, with no meals) unless we specify that they use the Continental Plan (CP, with a Continental breakfast daily), Modified American Plan (MAP, with breakfast and dinner daily), or the Full American Plan (FAP, with all meals).

CAMPING

If you plan to camp in one of Denmark's 500-plus approved campsites, you'll need an International Camping Carnet or Danish Camping Pass (available at any campsite and valid for one year).

➤ INFORMATION: **Campingrådet** (✉ Hesseløg. 16, DK–2100 Copenhagen Ø, ☎ 39/27–88–44).

APARTMENT & VILLA RENTALS

If you want a home base that's roomy enough for a family and comes with cooking facilities **consider a furnished rental.** These can save you money, especially if you're traveling with a group. Home-exchange directories sometimes list rentals as well as exchanges. A simple house with room

SMART TRAVEL TIPS A TO Z

for four will cost from Dkr 2,500 per week and up.

➤ CONTACT: **DanCenter** (✉ Søtorv 5, DK–1371 Copenhagen, ☎ 70/13–00–00).

If you would like to exchange your home for someone else's **join a home-exchange organization,** which will send you its updated listings of available exchanges for a year and will include your own listing in at least one of them. It's up to you to make specific arrangements.

HOME EXCHANGES

➤ EXCHANGE CLUBS: **HomeLink International** (✉ Box 650, Key West, FL 33041, ☎ 305/294–7766 or 800/638–3841, FAX 305/294–1448; $93 per year). **Intervac U.S.** (✉ Box 590504, San Francisco, CA 94159, ☎ 800/756–4663, FAX 415/435–7440; $83 for catalogues).

HOSTELS

No matter what your age you can **save on lodging costs by staying at hostels.** In some 5,000 locations in more than 70 countries around the world, Hostelling International (HI), the umbrella group for a number of national youth-hostel associations, offers single-sex, dorm-style beds and, at many hostels, couples rooms and family accommodations. Membership in any HI national hostel association, open to travelers of all ages, allows you to stay in HI-affiliated hostels at member rates (one-year membership is about $25 for adults; hostels run about $10–$25 per night). Members also have priority if the hostel is full; they're eligible for discounts around the world, even on rail and bus travel in some countries.

With an HI card, the average cost is Dkr 70 to Dkr 85 per person. Without the card, there's a surcharge of Dkr 25. The hostels fill up quickly in summer, so make your reservations early. Most hostels are particularly sympathetic to students and will usually find them at least a place on the floor. Bring your own linens or sleep sheet, though these can usually be rented at the hostel. Sleeping bags are not allowed. Contact Danhostel Danmarks Vandrehjem, which charges for information. You can get a free brochure, *Camping/Youth and*

Family Hostels, from the Danish Tourist Board.

➤ ORGANIZATIONS: **Australian Youth Hostel Association** (✉ 10 Mallett St., Camperdown, NSW 2050, ☎ 02/9565–1699, FAX 02/9565–1325). **Danhostel Danmarks Vandrehjem** (✉ Vesterbrog. 39, DK–1620, Copenhagen V, ☎ 33/31–36–12, FAX 33/31–36–26). **Hostelling International— American Youth Hostels** (✉ 733 15th St. NW, Suite 840, Washington, DC 20005, ☎ 202/783–6161, FAX 202/783–6171). **Hostelling International—Canada** (✉ 400–205 Catherine St., Ottawa, Ontario K2P 1C3, ☎ 613/237–7884, FAX 613/237–7868). **Youth Hostel Association of England and Wales** (✉ Trevelyan House, 8 St. Stephen's Hill, St. Albans, Hertfordshire AL1 2DY, ☎ 01727/855215 or 01727/845047, FAX 01727/844126). **Youth Hostels Association of New Zealand** (✉ Box 436, Christchurch, New Zealand, ☎ 03/379–9970, FAX 03/365–4476). Membership in the U.S. $25, in Canada C$26.75, in the U.K. £9.30, in Australia $44, in New Zealand $24.

B&B'S

Contact Dansk Kroferie to order a free catalogue of B&B inns, but choose carefully: the organization includes some chain hotels that would be hard-pressed to demonstrate a modicum of inn-related charm. The price of an inn covers one overnight stay in a room with bath, breakfast included. Note that some establishments tack an additional Dkr 125 surcharge onto the price of a double. You can save money by investing in Inn Checks, valid at 84 inns. Each check costs Dkr 640 per couple. Family checks (Dkr 720–Dkr 800) are also available.

➤ CONTACTS: **Dansk Kroferie** (✉ Vejlevej 16, DK–8700 Horsens, ☎ 75/64–87–00).

HOTELS

Make your reservations well in advance, especially in resort areas near the coasts. Many places offer summer reductions to compensate for the slowdown in business travel and conferences.

Many Danes prefer a shower to a bath, so if you particularly want a bath, ask for it, but be prepared to pay more. Taxes are usually included in prices, but check when making a reservation. As time goes on, it appears that an increasing number of hotels are eliminating breakfast from their room rates; even if it is not included, breakfast is usually well worth its price.

The very friendly staff at the hotel booking desk at Wonderful Copenhagen can help find rooms in hotels, hostels, and private homes, or even at campsites in advance of a trip. If you find yourself in Copenhagen without a reservation, head for the tourist office's hotel booking desk, which is open May–August, Monday–Saturday 9–8 and Sunday 10–8; September–April, weekdays 9–4:30 and Saturday 9–1:30. Prebooking in private homes and hotels must be done two months in advance, but last-minute (as in same-day) hotel rooms booked at the tourist office can save you 50% off the normal price.

All five Scandinavian countries offer Inn Checks, or prepaid hotel vouchers, for accommodations ranging from first-class hotels to country cottages. These vouchers, which must be purchased from travel agents or from the Scandinavian Tourist Board (☞ Visitor Information, below) before departure, are sold individually and in packets for as many nights as needed and offer savings of up to 50%. Most countries also offer summer bargains for foreign tourists. For further information about Scandinavian hotel vouchers, contact the Scandinavian Tourist Board.

ProSkandinavia checks can be used in 430 hotels across Scandinavia (excluding Iceland) for savings up to 50%, for reservations made usually no earlier than 24 hours before arrival, although some hotels allow earlier bookings. One check costs about $40 U.S. Two checks will pay for a double room at a hotel, one check for a room in a cottage. The checks can be bought at many travel agencies in Scandinavia or ordered from **ProSkandinavia**. All hotels listed have private bath unless otherwise noted.

➤ CONTACT: **ProSkandinavia** (⊠ Nedre Slottsgate 13, N-0157 Oslo, Norway, ☎ 47–22/42–50–06, ℻ 47–22/42–06–57). **Wonderful Copenhagen** (⊠ Gammel Kongevej 1, DK–1610 Copenhagen K, ☎ 33/25–38–44).

➤ TOLL-FREE NUMBERS: **Adams Mark** (☎ 800/444/2326). **Baymont Inns** (☎ 800/428–3438). **Best Western** (☎ 800/528–1234). **Choice** (☎ 800/221–2222). **Clarion** (☎ 800/252–7466). **Colony** (☎ 800/777–1700). **Comfort** (☎ 800/228–5150). **Days Inn** (☎ 800/325–2525). **Doubletree and Red Lion Hotels** (☎ 800/222–8733). **Embassy Suites** (☎ 800/362–2779). **Fairfield Inn** (☎ 800/228–2800). **Forte** (☎ 800/225–5843). **Four Seasons** (☎ 800/332–3442). **Hilton** (☎ 800/445–8667). **Holiday Inn** (☎ 800/465–4329). **Howard Johnson** (☎ 800/654–4656). **Hyatt Hotels & Resorts** (☎ 800/233–1234). **Inter-Continental** (☎ 800/327–0200). **La Quinta** (☎ 800/531–5900). **Marriott** (☎ 800/228–9290). **Le Meridien** (☎ 800/543–4300). **Nikko Hotels International** (☎ 800/645–5687). **Omni** (☎ 800/843–6664). **Quality Inn** (☎ 800/228–5151). **Radisson** (☎ 800/333–3333). **Ramada** (☎ 800/228–2828). **Renaissance Hotels & Resorts** (☎ 800/468–3571). **Ritz-Carlton** (☎ 800/241–3333). **Sheraton** (☎ 800/325–3535). **Sleep Inn** (☎ 800/753–3746). **Westin Hotels & Resorts** (☎ 800/228–3000). **Wyndham Hotels & Resorts** (☎ 800/822-4200).

FARM VACATIONS

There's a minimum stay of three nights for most farm stays. Bed-and-breakfast costs Dkr 150; half-board, around Dkr 245. Lunch and dinner can often be purchased for Dkr 25 to Dkr 35, and full board can be arranged.

➤ CONTACTS: **Ferie på Landet** (Holiday in the Country, ⊠ Søndergade 26, DK–8700 Horsens, Jylland, ☎ 70/10–41–90).

MAIL

POSTAL RATES

Airmail letters and postcards to the United States cost Dkr 5.50 for 20 grams. Letters and postcards to the United Kingdom and EU countries cost Dkr 4.50. You can buy stamps at post offices or from shops selling postcards.

RECEIVING MAIL

You can arrange to have your mail sent general delivery, marked *poste*

SMART TRAVEL TIPS A TO Z

restante, to any post office, hotel, or inn. The address for the main post office in Copenhagen is Tietgensgade 37, DK–1704 KBH.

MONEY MATTERS

Costs are high in Denmark, where so many things must be imported. Sales taxes can be very high, but foreigners can get some refunds by shopping at tax-free stores (☞ Taxes, *below*). City cards can save you transportation and entrance fees in many of the larger cities.

You can **reduce the cost of food by planning.** Breakfast is often included in your hotel bill; if not, you may wish to buy fruit, sweet rolls, and a beverage for a picnic breakfast. Electrical devices for hot coffee or tea should be bought abroad, though, to conform to the local current. **Opt for a restaurant lunch instead of dinner,** since the latter tends to be significantly more expensive. Instead of beer or wine, **drink tap water**—liquor can cost four times the price of the same brand in a store—but do specify tap water, as the term "water" can refer to soft drinks and bottled water, which are also expensive. Throughout Scandinavia, the tip is included in the cost of your meal. Service is included in bills for hotels and bars, as well. Taxi drivers round up the fare to the next krone but expect no tip. The exception is hotel porters, who receive about Dkr 5 per bag.

In most of Scandinavia, liquor and strong beer (over 3% alcohol) can be purchased only in state-owned shops, at very high prices, during weekday business hours, usually 9:30 to 6 and in some areas on Saturdays until midafternoon. Denmark takes a less restrictive approach, with liquor and beer available in the smallest of grocery stores, open weekdays and Saturday mornings—but Danish prices, too, are high. (When you visit relatives in Scandinavia, a bottle of liquor or fine wine bought duty-free on the trip over is often much appreciated.) Weaker beers and ciders are usually available in grocery stores in Scandinavia.

Prices throughout this guide are given for adults. Substantially reduced fees are almost always available for children, students, and senior citizens. For information on taxes, *see* Taxes, *below.*

SAMPLE PRICES

Denmark's economy is stable, and inflation remains reasonably low. Although lower than Norway's and Sweden's, the Danish cost of living is nonetheless high, especially for cigarettes and alcohol. Prices are highest in Copenhagen, lower elsewhere in the country. Some sample prices: cup of coffee, Dkr 14–Dkr 25; bottle of beer, Dkr 15–Dkr 30; soda, Dkr 10–Dkr 15; ham sandwich, Dkr 25–Dkr 40; 1-mi taxi ride, Dkr 35–Dkr 50, depending on traffic.

ATMS

➤ ATM LOCATIONS: Cirrus (☎ 800/ 424–7787).

CREDIT CARDS

Throughout this guide, the following abbreviations are used: AE, American Express; DC, Diner's Club; MC, MasterCard; and V, Visa.

Most major credit cards are accepted in Denmark. Traveler's checks can be exchanged in banks and at many hotels, restaurants, and shops.

CURRENCY

The monetary unit in Denmark is the krone (Dkr), divided into 100 øre. At press time (winter 2000), the krone stood at 7.33 to the dollar, 11.94 to the pound sterling, and 5.03 to the Canadian dollar. New 50, 100, 200, 500, and 1,000 kroner notes, featuring great Danes like authoress Karen Blixen and physicist Niels Bohr, are to be issued in the years up to the millennium, as the old notes are phased out. **Since rates fluctuate daily, you should check them at the time of your departure.**

CURRENCY EXCHANGE

For the most favorable rates, **change money through banks.** Although ATM transaction fees may be higher abroad than at home, ATM rates are excellent because they are based on wholesale rates offered only by major banks. You won't do as well at exchange booths in airports or rail and bus stations, in hotels, in restaurants, or in stores. To avoid lines at airport exchange booths **get a bit of local currency before you leave home.**

➤ EXCHANGE SERVICES: International Currency Express (☎ 888/842–0880 on East Coast; 888/278–6628 on West Coast). **Thomas Cook Currency Services** (☎ 800/287–7362 for telephone orders and retail locations).

TRAVELER'S CHECKS

Do you need traveler's checks? It depends on where you're headed. If you're going to rural areas and small towns, go with cash; traveler's checks are best used in cities. Lost or stolen checks can usually be replaced within 24 hours. To ensure a speedy refund, buy your own traveler's checks—don't let someone else pay for them: irregularities like this can cause delays. The person who bought the checks should make the call to request a refund.

OUTDOOR ACTIVITIES AND SPORTS

BIKING

Bicycles can be sent as baggage between most train stations and can also be carried onto most trains and ferries; contact DSB for information. All cabs must be able to take bikes and are equipped with racks (they add a modest fee).

Most towns have rentals, but check with local tourism offices for referrals. For more information, contact the Danish Cyclist Federation. The Danish Tourist Board also publishes bicycle maps and brochures.

Copenhagen-based BikeDenmark combines the flexibility of individual tours with the security of an organized outing. Choose from seven preplanned 5- to 10-day tours, which include bikes, maps, two fine meals per day, hotel accommodations, and hotel-to-hotel baggage transfers.

➤ CONTACTS: **BikeDenmark** (✉ Åboulevarden 1, ☎ 35/36–41–00 or 48/48–58–00). **Borton Oversees** (✉ 5516 Lyndale Ave. S, Minneapolis, MN 55419, ☎ 800/843–0602). **Danish Cyclist Federation** (✉ Rømersg. 7, DK–1362 KBH K, ☎ 33/32–31–21). **DSB** (☎ 70/13–14–15). **Gerhard's Bicycle Odysseys** (✉ Box 757, Portland, Oregon, 97207, ☎ 503/223-2402. **Nordique Tours** (✉ 5250 W. Century Blvd., Suite 626, Los Angeles, CA 90045, ☎ 800/995–

7997). **Scanam World Tours** (✉ 933 Rte. 23, Pompton Plains, NJ 07444, ☎ 800/545–2204).

FISHING AND ANGLING

Licenses are required for fishing along the coasts; requirements vary from one area to another for fishing in lakes, streams, and the ocean. Licenses generally cost around Dkr 100 and can be purchased from any post office. Remember—it is illegal to fish within 1,650 ft of the mouth of a stream.

PACKING

Bring a folding umbrella and a lightweight raincoat, as it is common for the sky to be clear at 9 AM, rainy at 11 AM, and clear again in time for lunch. **Pack casual clothes,** as Scandinavians tend to dress more casually than their Continental brethren. If you have trouble sleeping when it is light or are sensitive to strong sun, **bring an eye mask and dark sunglasses;** the sun rises as early as 4 AM in some areas, and the far-northern latitude causes it to slant at angles unseen elsewhere on the globe. **Bring bug repellent** if you plan to venture away from the capital cities; large mosquitoes can be a real nuisance on summer evenings throughout Scandinavia.

In your carry-on luggage **bring an extra pair of eyeglasses or contact lenses** and **enough of any medication you take** to last the entire trip. You may also want your doctor to write a spare prescription using the drug's generic name, since brand names may vary from country to country. In luggage to be checked, **never pack prescription drugs or valuables.** To avoid customs delays, carry medications in their original packaging. And don't forget to copy down and carry addresses of offices that handle refunds of lost traveler's checks.

CHECKING LUGGAGE

How many carry-on bags you can bring with you is up to the airline. Most allow two, but not always, so make sure that everything you carry aboard will fit under your seat, and get to the gate early. Note that if you have a seat at the back of the plane, you'll probably board first, while the overhead bins are still empty.

If you are flying internationally, note that baggage allowances may be determined not by piece but by weight—generally 88 pounds (40 kilograms) in first class, 66 pounds (30 kilograms) in business class, and 44 pounds (20 kilograms) in economy.

Airline liability for baggage is limited to $1,250 per person on flights within the United States. On international flights it amounts to $9.07 per pound or $20 per kilogram for checked baggage (roughly $640 per 70-pound bag) and $400 per passenger for unchecked baggage. You can buy additional coverage at check-in for about $10 per $1,000 of coverage, but it excludes a rather extensive list of items, shown on your airline ticket.

Before departure **itemize your bags' contents** and their worth, and label the bags with your name, address, and phone number. (If you use your home address, cover it so that potential thieves can't see it readily.) Inside each bag **pack a copy of your itinerary.** At check-in **make sure that each bag is correctly tagged** with the destination airport's three-letter code. If your bags arrive damaged or fail to arrive at all, file a written report with the airline before leaving the airport.

PASSPORTS & VISAS

When traveling internationally **carry a passport even if you don't need one** (it's always the best form of ID), and **make two photocopies of the data page** (one for someone at home and another for you, carried separately from your passport). If you lose your passport promptly call the nearest embassy or consulate and the local police.

ENTERING SCANDINAVIA

All U.S. citizens, even infants, need only a valid passport to enter any Scandinavian country for stays of up to three months.

PASSPORT OFFICES

The best time to apply for a passport or to renew is during the fall and winter. Before any trip, check your passport's expiration date, and, if necessary, renew it as soon as possible.

➤ AUSTRALIAN CITIZENS: **Australian Passport Office** (☎ 131–232).

➤ CANADIAN CITIZENS: **Passport Office** (☎ 819/994–3500 or 800/567–6868).

➤ NEW ZEALAND CITIZENS: **New Zealand Passport Office** (☎ 04/494–0700 for information on how to apply; 04/474–8000 or 0800/225–050 in New Zealand for information on applications already submitted).

➤ U.K. CITIZENS: **London Passport Office** (☎ 0990/210–410) for fees and documentation requirements and to request an emergency passport.

➤ U.S. CITIZENS: **National Passport Information Center** (☎ 900/225–5674; calls are 35¢ per minute for automated service, $1.05 per minute for operator service).

SENIOR-CITIZEN TRAVEL

To qualify for age-related discounts **mention your senior-citizen status up front** when booking hotel reservations (not when checking out) and before you're seated in restaurants (not when paying the bill). When renting a car ask about promotional car-rental discounts, which can be cheaper than senior-citizen rates.

TRAIN TRAVEL

Travelers over 60 can buy a **Senior-Rail Card** for DKr150 (about $27) in Denmark. It gives 30% discounts on train travel in 21 European countries for a whole year from purchase.

➤ EDUCATIONAL PROGRAMS: **Elderhostel** (✉ 75 Federal St., 3rd fl., Boston, MA 02110, ☎ 877/426–8056, FAX 877/426–2166). **Interhostel** (✉ University of New Hampshire, 6 Garrison Ave., Durham, NH 03824, ☎ 603/862–1147 or 800/733–9753, FAX 603/862–1113).

SHOPPING

Prices in Scandinavia are never low, but quality is high, and specialties are sometimes less expensive here than elsewhere. Danish Lego blocks and furniture are just a few of the items to look for. Keep an eye out for sales, called *udsalg* in Danish.

STUDENTS IN SCANDINAVIA

➤ STUDENT IDs & SERVICES: **Council on International Educational Exchange** (CIEE, ✉ 205 E. 42nd St., 14th fl., New York, NY 10017, ☎

212/822–2600 or 888/268–6245, FAX 212/822–2699) for mail orders only, in the U.S. **Travel Cuts** (✉ 187 College St., Toronto, Ontario M5T 1P7, ☎ 416/979–2406 or 800/667–2887) in Canada.

TAXES

VALUE-ADDED TAX (V.A.T.)

One way to beat high prices is to **take advantage of tax-free shopping.** Throughout Scandinavia, you can make major purchases free of tax if you have a foreign passport. Ask about tax-free shopping when you make a purchase for $50 (about £32) or more. When your purchases exceed a specified limit (which varies from country to country), you receive a special export receipt. Keep the parcels intact and take them out of the country within 30 days of purchase. When you leave the last EU country visited, you can obtain a refund of the V.A.T. (what the Danes call *moms*) in cash from a special office at the airport, or, upon arriving home, you can send your receipts to an office in the country of purchase to receive your refund by mail. Citizens of EU countries are not eligible for the refund. V.A.T. is 25%; non-EU citizens can obtain an 18% refund.

All hotel, restaurant, and departure taxes and V.A.T. are automatically included in prices. The more than 1,500 shops that participate in the tax-free scheme have a white TAX FREE sticker on their windows. Purchases must be at least Dkr 300 per store and must be sealed and unused in Denmark. At the shop, you'll be asked to fill out a form and show your passport. The form can then be turned in at any airport or ferry customs desk, where you can choose a cash or charge-card credit. Keep all your receipts and tags; occasionally, customs authorities do ask to see purchases, so pack them where they will be accessible.

Note: Tax-free sales of alcohol, cigarettes, and other luxury goods has been abolished among EU countries, with the Scandinavian countries among the last to adopt these regulations. The Aland islands, however, are not part of the EU customs union and allows tax-free sales for ferries in transit through its ports. All Sweden–Finland ferry routes now pass through the islands, de facto continuing the extremely popular tax-free sales for tourists. Air travel to the Scandinavia EU member states (Sweden, Finland, Denmark), as well as Norway, no longer allows tax-free sales.

Europe Tax-Free Shopping is a V.A.T. refund service that makes getting your money back hassle-free. E.T.S. is Europe-wide and has 90,000 affiliated stores. In participating stores, **ask for the E.T.S. refund form** (called a Shopping Cheque). As is true for all customs forms, when leaving the European Union you get them stamped by the customs official. Then you take them to the E.T.S. counter and they will refund your money right there in cash, by check, or a refund to your credit card. All that convenience will cost you 20%—but then it's done.

➤ VAT REFUNDS: **Global Refund** (✉ 707 Summer St., Stamford, CT 06901, ☎ 800/566–9828).

TELEPHONES

Telephone exchanges throughout Denmark were changed over the past couple of years. If you hear a recorded message or three loud beeps, chances are the number you are trying to reach has been changed. **KTAS** information (☎ 118) can always find current numbers.

COUNTRY & AREA CODES

The country code for Denmark is 45. When dialing a Scandinavian number from abroad, drop the initial 0 from the local area code. The country code is 1 for the U.S. and Canada, 61 for Australia, 64 for New Zealand, and 44 for the U.K.

DIRECTORY ASSISTANCE AND OPERATOR INFORMATION

Most operators speak English. For national directory assistance, dial ☎ 118; for an international operator, dial ☎ 113; for a directory-assisted international call, dial ☎ 115.

INTERNATIONAL CALLS

Dial ☎ 00, then the country code (1 for the United States and Canada, 44 for Great Britain), the area code, and the number. It's very expensive to telephone or fax from hotels, although the regional phone companies

SMART TRAVEL TIPS A TO Z

offer a discount after 7:30 PM. It's more economical to make calls from either the Copenhagen main rail station or the airports.

LOCAL CALLS

Phones accept 1-, 5-, 10-, and 20-kroner coins. Pick up the receiver, dial the number, always including the area code, and wait until the party answers; then deposit the coins. You have roughly a minute per krone, so you can make another call on the same payment if your time has not run out. When it does, you will hear a beep and your call will be disconnected unless you deposit another coin. Dial the eight-digit number for calls anywhere within the country. For calls to the Faroe Islands (☎ 298) and Greenland (☎ 299), dial ☎ 00, then the three-digit code, then the five-digit number. It may be more economical and less frustrating, however, to buy a phone card from a kiosk; coin-operated phones are becoming increasingly rare.

LONG-DISTANCE SERVICES

AT&T, MCI, and Sprint access codes make calling long distance relatively convenient, but you may find the local access number blocked in many hotel rooms. First ask the hotel operator to connect you. If the hotel operator balks ask for an international operator, or dial the international operator yourself. One way to improve your odds of getting connected to your long-distance carrier is to travel with more than one company's calling card (a hotel may block Sprint, for example, but not MCI). If all else fails call from a pay phone.

➤ ACCESS CODES: **AT&T USADirect** (☎ 8001/0010 Denmark).

MCI Call USA (☎ 8001/0022 Denmark).

Sprint Express (☎ 800/10877 Denmark).

TOURS & PACKAGES

On a prepackaged tour or independent vacation everything is prearranged so you'll spend less time planning—and often get it all at a good price.

BOOKING WITH AN AGENT

Travel agents are excellent resources. But it's a good idea to collect brochures from several agencies because some agents' suggestions may be influenced by relationships with tour and package firms that reward them for volume sales. If you have a special interest **find an agent with expertise in that area**; ASTA (☞ Travel Agencies, *below*) has a database of specialists worldwide.

Make sure your travel agent knows the accommodations and other services of the place they're recommending. Ask about the hotel's location, room size, beds, and whether it has a pool, room service, or programs for children, if you care about these. Has your agent been there in person or sent others whom you can contact?

Do some homework on your own, too: Local tourism boards can provide information about lesser-known and small-niche operators, some of which may sell only direct.

BUYER BEWARE

Each year consumers are stranded or lose their money when tour operators—even large ones with excellent reputations—go out of business. So **check out the operator.** Ask several travel agents about its reputation, and try to **book with a company that has a consumer-protection program.** (Look for information in the company's brochure.) In the United States, members of the National Tour Association and United States Tour Operators Association are required to set aside funds to cover your payments and travel arrangements in case the company defaults. It's also a good idea to choose a company that participates in the American Society of Travel Agents' Tour Operator Program (TOP); ASTA will act as mediator in any disputes between you and your tour operator.

Remember that the more your package or tour includes the better you can predict the ultimate cost of your vacation. Make sure you know exactly what is covered, and **beware of hidden costs.** Are taxes, tips, and transfers included? Entertainment and excursions? These can add up.

➤ TOUR-OPERATOR RECOMMENDATIONS: **American Society of Travel Agents** (☞ Travel Agencies, *below*). **Copenhagen Excursions** (☎ 32/54–06–06 in Denmark). **National Tour**

Association (NTA, ✉ 546 E. Main St., Lexington, KY 40508, ☎ 606/226–4444 or 800/682–8886). **United States Tour Operators Association** (USTOA, ✉ 342 Madison Ave., Suite 1522, New York, NY 10173, ☎ 212/599–6599 or 800/468–7862, FAX 212/599–6744).

TRAIN TRAVEL

Trains within Europe are well connected to Denmark, with Copenhagen serving as the main hub; however, it's often little cheaper than flying, especially if you make your arrangements from the United States. Scanrail Passes offer discounts on train, ferry, and car transportation in Denmark, Finland, Sweden, and Norway (☞ Cutting Costs, *below*). EurailPasses, purchased only in the United States, are accepted by the Danish State Railways and on some ferries operated by DSB (☞ *below*). DSB also accepts Interail passes on all its trains. From London, the crossing by train takes 18 hours, including ferry; call the British Rail European Travel Center or Wasteels.

DSB and a few private companies cover the country with a dense network of services, supplemented by buses in remote areas. Hourly intercity trains connect the main towns in Jylland and Fyn with Copenhagen and Sjælland, using high-speed diesels, called IC-3, on the most important stretches. All these trains make one-hour ferry crossings of the Great Belt. You can reserve seats on intercity trains, and you *must* have a reservation if you plan to cross the Great Belt. Buy tickets at stations.

➤ FROM THE UNITED KINGDOM: **British Rail European Travel Center** (✉ Picadilly 179, London W1, ☎ 099/084–8848). **DSB** (☎ 33/14–11–26 in Denmark). **Wasteels** (✉ 121 Wilton Rd., London SW1, ☎ 020/7834–7066).

CUTTING COSTS

The Scanrail Pass is available for travel in Denmark, Sweden, Norway, and Finland for both first- and second-class train travel; it also affords restricted ferry passage in and beyond Scandinavia. You may have five days of unlimited travel in a 15-day period ($222 first-class/$176 second-class); 10 days of unlimited travel in a

month ($354/$248); or one month of consecutive day unlimited train travel ($516/$414). With the Scanrail Pass, you also enjoy travel bonuses, including free or discounted ferry, boat, and bus travel and a Hotel Discount Card that allows 10–30% off rates for select hotels June–August. Passengers 12–25 can **buy Scanrail Youth Passes** ($167 first-class/$132 second-class, five travel days in 15 days; $266/$213 for 10 travel days in a month; $387/$311 for one month of unlimited travel). Those over 55 can **take advantage of the Scanrail 55+** Pass, which offers the travel bonuses of the Scanrail Pass and discounted travel ($198 first-class/$157 second-class, five days; $315/$253 10 days; $459/$368 one month). Buy Scanrail passes through Rail Europe and travel agents.

For car and train travel, price the Scanrail'n Drive Pass: in 15 days you can get five days of unlimited train travel and three days of car rental (choice of three car categories) with unlimited mileage in Denmark, Finland, Norway, and Sweden. You can purchase extra car rental days and choose from first- or second-class train travel. Rates for two adults (compact car $315 first-class/$275 second-class), are considerably lower (about 25%) than for single adults. You may want to wait to buy the pass until you get to Scandinavia; unlike the EurailPass, which is cheaper in the United States, the ScanRail Pass is cheaper in Scandinavia. Double-check prices before you leave home. No matter where you get it though, various discounts are offered to holders of the pass by hotel chains and other organizations; ask DER, Rail Europe, or your travel agent for details.

In Scandinavia, you can **use Eurail-Passes,** which provide unlimited first-class rail travel, in all of the participating countries, for the duration of the pass. If you plan to rack up the miles, get a standard pass. These are available for 15 days ($522), 21 days ($678), one month ($838), two months ($1,188), and three months ($1,468). Eurail- and EuroPasses are available through travel agents and Rail Europe.

In addition to standard EurailPasses, **ask about special rail-pass plans.**

Among these are the Eurail YouthPass (for those under age 26), the Eurail SaverPass (which gives a discount for two or more people traveling together), a Eurail FlexiPass (which allows a certain number of travel days within a set period), the Euraildrive Pass, and the EuroPass Drive (which combines travel by train and rental car).

Many travelers assume that rail passes guarantee them seats on the trains they wish to ride. Not so. You need to **book seats ahead even if you are using a rail pass;** seat reservations are required on some European trains, particularly high-speed trains, and are a good idea on trains that may be crowded—particularly in summer on popular routes. You will also need a reservation if you purchase sleeping accommodations.

➤ WHERE TO BUY RAIL PASSES: **Rail Europe** (✉ 226–230 Westchester Ave., White Plains, NY 10604, ☎ 914/682–5172 or 800/438–7245; 2087 Dundas East, Suite 105, Mississauga, Ontario L4X 1M2, ☎ 416/602–4195). **DER Tours** (✉ Box 1606, Des Plaines, IL 60017, ☎ 800/782–2424, FAX 800/282–7474). **CIT Tours Corp.** (✉ 342 Madison Ave., Suite 207, New York, NY 10173, ☎ 212/697–2100 or 800/248–8687, or 800/248–7245 in western U.S.).

TRANSPORTATION AROUND SCANDINAVIA

Vast distances between cities and towns make air transportation a cost-efficient mode of travel in Scandinavia. SAS is Scandinavia's major air carrier; it also operates domestic lines in Norway, Sweden, and Denmark. SAS offers discount packages for travel among the Scandinavian capitals, as well as reduced domestic fares in the summer. Finnair is also expanding its routes in Scandinavia.

Trains—comfortable, clean, and fast—are good for covering large distances in Scandinavia. Remember to ask for a smoking or nonsmoking seat or compartment. You should inquire with your travel agent about Scanrail Passes for travel within the region.

Another means of getting around Scandinavia's countries is to go by ferry. These huge vessels offer a combination of efficient travel (you sleep aboard and wake up in your destination the next morning) and amenities approaching what you might expect on a cruise ship: luxury dining, gambling, a sauna and pool, and entertainment. Travelers should beware, however, that the noise level may be high and the crowd is usually very lively.

If you prefer the freedom of planning an itinerary and traveling at your own pace, a rental car is a good, albeit expensive, alternative. Most major car rental companies operate in Scandinavia. Roads are generally good, but allow plenty of time for navigating the region's winding highway network. Scandinavia enforces some of the most strict drinking-and-driving laws in the world—a drunk driver could end up in jail after one offense.

Public transportation in Scandinavia's cities is safe, fast, and inexpensive. Some cities, including the capitals, offer day passes reducing the cost of buses and train travel.

Taxis in Scandinavia are safe, clean, *and* expensive. All taxis should be clearly marked and have a meter inside; unmarked taxis—usually operated illegally by unlicensed drivers—are not recommended. A 10% tip is a friendly gesture, but by no means necessary. Most taxis accept major credit cards and cash.

TRAVEL AGENCIES

A good travel agent puts your needs first. Look for an agency that has been in business at least five years, emphasizes customer service, and has someone on staff who specializes in your destination. In addition **make sure the agency belongs to a professional trade organization.** The American Society of Travel Agents (ASTA), with 27,000 agents in some 170 countries, is the largest and most influential in the field. Operating under the motto "Integrity in Travel," it maintains and enforces a strict code of ethics and will step in to help mediate any agent-client disputes if necessary. ASTA also maintains a Web site that includes a directory of agents. Note that if a travel agency is also acting as your tour operator, *see* Buyer Beware *in* Tours & Packages, *above.*

► LOCAL AGENT REFERRALS: American Society of Travel Agents (ASTA, ☎ 800/965–2782 24-hr hot line, FAX 703/684–8319, www.astanet.com). Association of British Travel Agents (✉ 68–271 Newman St., London W1P 4AH, ☎ 020/7637–2444, FAX 020/7637–0713). Association of Canadian Travel Agents (✉ 1729 Bank St., Suite 201, Ottawa, Ontario K1V 7Z5, ☎ 613/521–0474, FAX 613/521–0805). Australian Federation of Travel Agents (✉ Level 3, 309 Pitt St., Sydney 2000, ☎ 02/9264–3299, FAX 02/9264–1085). Travel Agents' Association of New Zealand (✉ Box 1888, Wellington 10033, ☎ 04/499–0104, FAX 04/499–0786).

VISITOR INFORMATION

► SCANDINAVIAN TOURIST BOARD: U.S.: Scandinavian Tourist Board (✉ 655 3rd Ave., New York, New York 10017-5617, ☎ 212/949–2333 or 212/8859700, FAX 212/983–5260 or 212/6970835).

► TOURIST BOARDS: Danish Tourist Board (✉ 655 3rd Ave., New York, NY 10017, ☎ 212/949–2333; ✉ 55 Sloane St., London SW1 X9SY, ☎ 020/7259–5959).

Danmarks Turistråd (Danish Tourist Board ✉ Vesterbrogade 6D, DK–1620 Copenhagen V, ☎ 33/11–14–15).

► U.S. GOVERNMENT ADVISORIES: U.S. Department of State (✉ Overseas Citizens Services Office, Room 4811 N.S., 2201 C St. NW, Washington, DC 20520; ☎ 202/647–5225 for interactive hot line; 301/946–4400 for computer bulletin board; FAX 202/647–3000 for interactive hot line); enclose a self-addressed, stamped, business-size envelope.

WEB SITES

Do **check out the World Wide Web** when you're planning. You'll find everything from up-to-date weather forecasts to virtual tours of famous cities. Fodor's Web site, www.fodors.com, is a great place to start your online travels.

FERRY OPERATORS

Color Line (www.colorline.com), **Fjord Line** (www.fjordline.com), **ScandLines** (www.scandlines.com), **Scandinavian Seaways** (www.scansea.com), **Silja Line** (www.silja.com), **Smyril Line** (www.smyril-line.fo), **Stena Line** (www.stenaline.dk), **Viking Line** (www.vikingline.fi)

DANISH RESOURCES

Tourism information (general, www.dt.dk; oriented toward North American visitors, www.visitdenmark.dt.dk; oriented toward British and Irish visitors, www.dtb.dt.dk).

WHEN TO GO

The Scandinavian tourist season peaks in June, July, and August, when daytime temperatures are often in the 70s (21°C to 26°C) and sometimes rise into the 80s (27°C to 32°C). In general, the weather is not overly warm, and a brisk breeze and brief rainstorms are possible anytime. Nights can be chilly, even in summer.

Visit in summer if you want to experience the delightfully long summer days. In June, the sun rises in Copenhagen at 4 AM and sets at 11 PM and daylight lasts even longer farther north, making it possible to continue your sightseeing into the balmy evenings. Many attractions extend their hours during the summer, and many shut down altogether when summer ends. Fall, spring, and even winter are pleasant, despite the area's reputation for gloom. The days become shorter quickly, but the sun casts a golden light not seen farther south. On dark days, fires and candlelight will warm you indoors.

The Gulf Stream warms Denmark, the western coast of Norway, and Iceland, making winters in these areas similar to those in London. Even the harbor of Narvik, far to the north in Norway, remains ice-free year-round. Away from the protection of the Gulf Stream, however, northern Norway, Sweden, and Finland experience very cold, clear weather that attracts skiers; even Stockholm's harbor, well south in Sweden but facing the Baltic Sea, freezes over completely.

CLIMATE

The following are average daily maximum and minimum temperatures for Copenhagen.

SMART TRAVEL TIPS A TO Z

➤ FORECASTS: Weather Channel Connection (☎ 900/932–8437), 95¢ per minute from a Touch-Tone phone.

COPENHAGEN

Jan.	36F	2C	May	61F	16C	Sept.	64F	18C
	28	– 2		46	8		52	11
Feb.	36F	2C	June	66F	19C	Oct.	54F	12C
	27	– 3		52	11		45	7
Mar.	41F	5C	July	72F	22C	Nov.	45F	7C
	30	– 1		57	14		37	3
Apr.	52F	11C	Aug.	70F	21C	Dec.	39F	4C
	37	3		57	14		34	1

FESTIVALS AND SEASONAL EVENTS

➤ MAR.: The **Ice Sculpture Festival** takes place in Nuuk, Greenland; the **Nuuk Marathon** draws a hardy crowd of runners.

➤ APR.: In Greenland, the **Arctic Circle Race** begins in Kangangerlussuaq and ends in Sisimiut. At the beginning of the month The **Drambui Ice Golf World Championships** take place in Uumannaq—with a red ball on the frozen fjord—with about 35 participants, including some of the world's best.

➤ APR. 16: The **Queen's Birthday** is celebrated with the royal guard in full ceremonial dress as the royal family appears before the public on the balcony of Amalienborg.

➤ MAY: **Copenhagen Carnival** includes boat parades in Nyhavn and costumed revelers in the streets.

➤ MAY–AUG.: **Tivoli** in Copenhagen twinkles with rides, concerts, and entertainment.

➤ MAY–SEPT.: **Legoland,** a park constructed of 45 million Lego blocks, is open in Billund, Jylland.

➤ JUNE: The **Around Fyn Regatta** starts in Kerteminde. The **Round Zealand Regatta,** one of the largest yachting events in the world, starts and ends in Helsingø. The **Aalborg Jazz Festival** fills the city with four days of indoor and outdoor concerts, many of them free. The **Viking Festival** in Frederikssund includes open-air performances of a Viking play. On **Midsummer's Night,** Danes celebrate the longest day of the year with bonfires and picnics.

➤ JUNE 21: **Greenland National Day** celebrates the anniversary of Home Rule.

➤ JUNE–JULY: The **Roskilde Festival,** the largest rock concert in northern Europe, attracts dozens of bands and more than 75,000 fans.

➤ JULY: The **Copenhagen Jazz Festival** gathers international and Scandinavian jazz greats for a week of concerts, many of them free.

➤ JULY 4: The **Fourth of July** celebration in Rebild Park, near Aalborg, sets off the only American Independence Day festivities outside the United States.

➤ MID-JULY: The **Århus Jazz Festival** gathers European and other world-renowned names, with indoor and outdoor concerts. The **Images of the World Festival,** organized by the Copenhagen International Theater, fills the city with performances.

➤ AUG.: Between the 7th and 10th, the **Cutty Sark Tall Ship Race** brings more than 100 ships to the Copenhagen harbor.

➤ MID-AUG.: The annual **Copenhagen Water Festival** celebrates the city's ties to the sea with concerts, exhibits, and plenty of outdoor activities.

➤ SEPT.: The **Århus Festival,** Denmark's most comprehensive fête, fills the city with concerts, sports, and theater. The **Golden Days Festival** celebrates the 19th-century cultural blossoming of Denmark through exhibits, readings, and performances.

➤ MID-SEPTEMBER: Until the end of the year, **Cultural Bridge** celebrates the common and unique legacies of Denmark and Sweden, now linked by the new Øresund Bridge. This is a biennial festival of the visual arts, design, dance, theater, and music.

➤ NEW YEAR'S EVE: **Fireworks** at the Town Hall Square are set off by local revelers.

1 DESTINATION: DENMARK

FAIRY TALES AND FJORDS

THE KINGDOM OF DENMARK dapples the Baltic Sea in an archipelago of some 450 islands and the crescent of one peninsula. Measuring 43,069 square km (17,028 square mi) and with a population of 5.1 million, it is the geographical link between Scandinavia and Europe. Half-timber villages and tidy agriculture rub shoulders with provincial towns and a handful of cities, where pedestrians set the pace, not traffic. Mothers safely park baby carriages outside bakeries while outdoor cafés fill with cappuccino-sippers, and lanky Danes pedal to work in lanes thick with bicycle traffic. Clearly this is a land where the process of life is the greatest reward.

While in Denmark, visitors pinch themselves in disbelief and make long lists of resolutions to emulate the natives. The Danes' lifestyle is certainly enviable, not yet the pressure-cooked life of some other Western countries. Long one of the world's most liberal countries, Denmark has a highly developed social-welfare system. Hefty taxes are the subject of grumbles and jokes, but Danes remain proud of their state-funded medical and educational systems and high standard of living. They enjoy monthlong vacations, 7½-hour workdays, and overall security.

Educated, patriotic, and keenly aware of their tiny international stance, most Danes travel extensively and have a balanced perspective of their nation's benefits and shortfalls. As in many other provincial states, egalitarianism is often a constraint for the ambitious. In Denmark, the Jante law, which refers to a literary principle penned in the early 20th century by Axel Sandemose, essentially means "Don't think you're anything special"—and works as an insidious cultural barrier to talent and aspiration. On the other hand, free education and state support give refugees, immigrants, and the underprivileged an opportunity to begin new, often prosperous lives.

The history of the little country stretches back 250,000 years, when Jylland was inhabited by nomadic hunters, but it wasn't until AD 500 that a tribe from Sweden, called the Danes, migrated south and christened the land Denmark. The Viking expansion that followed was based on the country's strategic position in the north. Struggles for control of the North Sea with England and western Europe, for the Skagerrak (the strait between Denmark and Norway) with Norway and Sweden, and for the Baltic Sea with Germany, Poland, and Russia ensued. With high-speed ships and fine-tuned warriors, intrepid navies navigated to Europe and Canada, invading and often pillaging, until, under King Knud (Canute) the Great (995–1035), they captured England by 1018.

After the British conquest, Viking supremacy declined as feudal Europe learned to defend itself. Internally, the pagan way of life was threatened by the expansion of Christianity, introduced under Harald Bluetooth, who in AD 980 "baptized" the country, essentially to avoid war with Germany. For the next several hundred years, the country tried to maintain its Baltic power with the influence of the German Hanseatic League. Under the leadership of Valdemar IV (1340–1375), Sweden, Norway, Iceland, Greenland, and the Faroe Islands became a part of Denmark. Sweden broke away by the mid-15th century and battled Denmark for much of the next several hundred years, whereas Norway remained under Danish rule until 1814, Iceland until 1943. Greenland and the Faroe Islands are still self-governing Danish provinces.

Denmark prospered again in the 16th century, thanks to the Sound Dues, a levy charged to ships crossing the Øresund, the slender waterway between Denmark and Sweden. Under King Christian IV, a construction boom crowned the land with what remain architectural gems today, but his fantasy spires and castles, compounded with the Thirty Years' War in the 17th century, led to state bankruptcy.

By the 18th century, absolute monarchy had given way to representative democracy, and culture flourished. Then—in a fatal mistake—Denmark sided with France and refused to surrender its navy to the English during the Napoleonic Wars. In a less than valiant episode of British history, Lord Nelson turned his famous blind eye to the destruction and bombed Copenhagen to bits. The defeated King Frederik VI handed Norway to Sweden. Denmark's days of glory were over.

Though Denmark was unaligned during World War II, the Nazis invaded in 1940. Against them, the Danes used the only weapons they had: a cold shoulder and massive underground resistance. After the war, Denmark focused inward, refining its welfare system and concentrating on its main industries of agriculture, shipping, and financial and technical services. It is an outspoken member of the European Union (EU), championing environmental responsibility and supporting development in emerging economies. It was one of the only countries to forgive a considerable amount of third world debt during the World Summit in Copenhagen in 1995. Expensive as it is, Denmark is in many ways less pricey than the rest of Scandinavia.

Copenhagen fidgets with its modern identity as both a Scandinavian–European link and cozy capital. The center of Danish politics, culture, and finance, it copes through balance and a sense of humor with a taste for the absurd. Stroll the streets and you'll pass classic architecture painted in candy colors, businessmen clad in jeans and T-shirts.

Sjælland's surrounding countryside is not to be missed. Less than an hour away, fields and half-timber cottages checker the land. Roskilde, to the east, has a 12th-century cathedral, and in the north, the Kronborg Castle of *Hamlet* fame crowns Helsingør. Beaches, some chic, some deserted, are powdered with fine white sand.

Fyn rightly earned its storybook reputation by making cuteness a local passion. The city of Odense, Hans Christian Andersen's birthplace, is cobbled with crooked old streets and Lilliputian cottages. Jylland's landscape is the most severe, with Ice Age–chiseled fjords and hills, sheepishly called mountains by the Danes. In the cities of Århus and Aalborg you'll find museums and nightlife rivaling Copenhagen's.

The best way to discover Denmark is to strike up a conversation with an affable and hospitable Dane. Hyggelig defies definition but comes close to meaning a cozy and charming hospitality. A summertime beach picnic can be as hyggelig as tea on a cold winter's night. The only requirement is the company of a Dane.

—By Karina Porcelli

NEW AND NOTEWORTHY

Copenhagen's massive infrastructure projects should be finished in mid- to late 2000, making travel here much simpler. The first of these colossal projects, the Storebæltsbro (the Great Belt) rail and automobile link between Fyn and Sjælland has reduced crossing times by at least an hour and eliminated, for better or worse, many of the enormous ferries that used to ply the Danish waters. By June 2000, the construction of the Øresund bridge between Copenhagen and Malmö, Sweden, will be completed, linking the two countries and creating what many hope will be a new binational metropolis.

Plans to celebrate this union include the Cultural Bridge, a three-and-a-half-month celebration that kicks off September 15 on both sides of the sound, with a flurry of activities—including concerts, theater, and expositions—in the Lund-Malmö-Copenhagen-Skåne region. Streamlined travel between Copenhagen Airport and the city center should serve as a primer for urban planners everywhere: Not accounting for traffic delays, cars can zip from city center to the airport on the new highway in 10 minutes; the newest subway of the city train system can get you between the airport and the city's main train station in about 12 minutes. As transportation becomes easier, hotel capacity is increasing: In the center of town, just next door to Tivoli, a four-star First Hotel was opened in May 1999 with 403 rooms. Among the biggest new projects underway, Copenhagen will be graced by a new four-star 375-room Hilton hotel, which will be completed in 2000 next door to the Copenhagen Airport's Air Rail Terminal. Finally, Marriott is building its first Scandinavian hotel in Copenhagen. The five-star, 395-room harbor-front property is due to be completed in summer 2001.

WHAT'S WHERE

The Kingdom of Denmark dapples the Baltic Sea in an archipelago of some 450 islands and the arc of one peninsula. Measuring 43,069 square km (16,628 square mi), with a population of 5.1 million, it is the geographical link between Scandinavia and Europe.

The island of Sjælland, the largest of the Danish isles, is the most popular tourist destination. Here you'll find Copenhagen, Scandinavia's largest city (population 1.5 million), Denmark's capital, and the seat of the oldest kingdom in the world. If there's such as a thing as a cozy city, this is it: Bicycles spin alongside cars in the narrow streets, and a handful of skyscrapers are tucked away amid cafés, museums, and quaint old homes. To the north of the city are royal castles (including Helsingør's Kronborg of *Hamlet* fame) and ritzy beach towns. To the west, Roskilde holds relics of medieval Denmark. And to the west and south, rural towns and farms edge up to beach communities and fine white beaches, often surrounded by forests.

Fyn (Funen), the smaller of the country's two main islands, is the site of Denmark's third-largest city, Odense, the birthplace of Hans Christian Andersen. It's no wonder this area inspired many fairy tales: 1,120 km (700 mi) of coastline and lush stretches of vegetable and flower gardens are punctuated by manor houses, beech glades, castles, swan ponds, and thatched houses.

Jylland, Denmark's western peninsula, shares its southern border with Germany. At the northern tip lies Skagen, a luminous, dune-covered point, and just below it are Århus and Aalborg, respectively Denmark's second- and fourth-largest cities. The heart of the peninsula, mostly lakeland and beech forests, is dotted with castles and parklands and is home to the famed Legoland. Along the east coast, deep fjords are rimmed by forests. The south holds marshlands, gabled houses, and Ribe, Denmark's oldest town.

Finally, there's the island of Bornholm, 177 km (110 mi) southeast of Sjælland, with a temperate climate that distinguishes it from the rest of Denmark. Bornholm's natural beauty and winsomely rustic towns have earned it the title of Pearl of the Baltic.

PLEASURES AND PASTIMES

Beaches

In this country of islands, coastline, and water, beaches come in many breeds. In Sjælland, a series of chic strands stretches along Strandvejen—the old beach road—pinned down by a string of lovely old seaside towns; here is where young people go to strut and preen. Fyn's gentle, golden beaches are less a showplace than a quiet getaway for a largely northern European crowd. Windswept Jylland has the country's most expansive and dramatic beaches—at its tip you can even see the line in the waves where the Kattegat meets the Skaggerak Sea.

Biking

Without a doubt, Denmark is one of the best places for biking. More than half of the population pedals along city streets that effectively coordinate public transportation and cycle traffic and along the country paths laced through Jylland and the island of Bornholm.

Boating and Sailing

Well-marked channels and nearby anchorages make sailing and boating easy and popular along the 7,300-km (4,500-mi) coastline. Waters range from the open seas of the Kattegat and the Baltic to Smålandshavet (between Sjælland, Lolland, and Falster) and the calm Limsfjord in Jylland. The country's calm streams are navigable for canoes and kayaks. In Copenhagen, the historic harbors of Christianshavn and Nyhavn and scores of marinas bristling with crisp, white sails are lined with old wooden houseboats, motorboats, yachts, and their colorful crews. And it's not only the well-heeled taking up this pastime: Tousle-haired parents and babes, partying youths, and leathery pensioners tend to their boats and picnics, lending a festive, community spirit to the marinas.

Danish Design

Danish design has earned an international reputation for form and function. The best sales take place after Christmas until February, when you can snatch up glassware, stainless steel, pottery, ceramics, and fur for good prices. Danish antiques and silver are also much cheaper here than in the United States. For major purchases—Bang & Olufsen products, for example—check prices stateside first so you can spot a good price.

Dining

From the hearty meals of Denmark's fishing heritage to the inspired creations of a new generation of chefs, Danish cuisine combines the best of tradition and novelty. Though the country has long looked to the French as a beacon of gastronomy, chefs have proudly returned to the Danish table, emphasizing fresh, local ingredients and combining them with fusion trends. Sample fresh fish and seafood from the Baltic, beef and pork from Jylland, and more exotic delicacies, such as reindeer, caribou, seal meat, and whale from Greenland. Denmark's famed dairy products—sweet butter and milk among them—as well as a burgeoning organic foods industry, all contribute to the freshness of the modern Danish kitchen.

Lunchtime is reserved for smørrebrød. You'll find the best, most traditional sampling of these open-face sandwiches in modest family-run restaurants that focus on generous portions—though never excessive—and artful presentation. If you fix your gaze on tender mounds of roast beef topped with pickles or baby shrimp marching across a slice of French bread, you are experiencing a slice of authentic Danish culture. Another specialty is wienerbrød, a confection far superior to anything billed as "Danish pastry" elsewhere. All Scandinavian countries have versions of the cold table, but Danes claim that theirs, det store kolde bord, is the original and the best.

On the liquid refreshment front, slowly the ubiquitous Carlsberg and Tuborg are facing international competition. You can't do better than to stick with the Danish brands, which happily complement the traditional fare better than high-priced wine. If you go for the harder stuff, try the famous snaps, the aquavit traditionally savored with cold food.

CATEGORY	COPENHAGEN*	OTHER AREAS*
$$$$	over Dkr 400	over Dkr 350
$$$	Dkr 200– Dkr 400	Dkr 200– Dkr 350
$$	Dkr 120– Dkr 200	Dkr 100– Dkr 200
$	under Dkr 120	under Dkr 100

*per person for a three-course meal, including taxes and service charge and excluding wine

Lodging

Accommodations in Denmark range from spare to resplendent. Luxury hotels in the city or countryside offer rooms of a high standard, and in a manor-house hotel you may find yourself sleeping in a four-poster bed. Even inexpensive hotels are well designed with good materials and good, firm beds—and the country's 100 youth and family hostels and 500-plus campgrounds are among the world's finest. Usually for all of July, conference hotels often lower prices and offer weekend specials.

Farmhouses and kroer (old stagecoach inns) offer a terrific alternative to more traditional hotels. Perhaps the best way to see how the Danes live and work, farm stays allow you to share meals with the family and maybe even help with the chores. If you prefer a more independent setup, consider renting a summer home in the countryside.

CATEGORY	COPENHAGEN*	OTHER AREAS*
$$$$	over Dkr 1,300	over Dkr 950
$$$	Dkr 800– Dkr 1,300	Dkr 700– Dkr 950
$$	Dkr 670– Dkr 800	Dkr 450– Dkr 700
$	under Dkr 670	under Dkr 450

*Prices are for two people in a double room and include service and taxes and usually breakfast.

GREAT ITINERARIES

Denmark is divided into three regions: the two major islands of Sjælland and

Fyn, and the peninsula of Jylland. To the east, Sjælland is Denmark's largest and most populated island, with Copenhagen its focal point. Denmark's second largest island, Fyn, is a pastoral, undulating land dotted with farms and summer-house beach villages, with Odense as its one major town. To the west, the relatively vast Jylland connects Denmark to the European continent; here you'll find the towns of Århus and Aalborg.

If You Have 3 Days

Take at least two days to explore and enjoy **Copenhagen**. The last day, head north of the city, first to **Rungsted** to see Karen Blixen's manor house and the lush garden surrounding it, then to the Louisiana modern art museum in **Humlebæk**.

If You Have 5 Days

After two days and nights in **Copenhagen**, head north to **Rungsted** and **Humlebæk**; then spend the night in **Helsingør**. The next day, visit the castles of Helsingør and **Hillerød**, and spend the night in medieval **Roskilde**. Day five, venture southeast to enjoy the dramatic nature and history of **Møn** and the villages and beaches of Lolland and Falster. An alternative last-day tour is to head west to Hans Christian Andersen's birthplace of **Odense**, on Fyn.

If You Have 7 Days

In a week you can see Copenhagen and environs and explore Fyn and Jylland. Rent a car for the latter—it's the quickest way to make it from the historic cities of **Århus** and **Aalborg** to the blond beaches of **Skagen**, with time left over to meander through a couple of smaller villages. Keep in mind that to take in Greenland or the Faroe Islands in addition to seeing mainland Denmark, you'll need more than a week—ideally two.

When to Tour Denmark

Summertime—when the lingering sun of June, July, and August brings out the best in the climate and the Danes—is the best time to visit. In summer, Bornholm tends to stay warmer and sunnier longer than elsewhere; this is also the best time to visit Greenland and the Faroe Islands. The jazz festival season gets underway in Copenhagen and Aalborg in June and in Århus in July. In July most Danes flee to their summer homes or go abroad.

Winter is dark and rainy, but it's a great time to visit museums, libraries, and the countless atmospheric meeting places in which the Danes take refuge. The weeks preceding Christmas are a prime time to experience Tivoli. Although the experience is radically different from the flower-filled summertime park, the winter park has a charm all its own. Much of Tivoli is closed during these weeks, but you can still experience some of the shops, restaurants, a handful of rides, an "elf house," and some theater in Danish.

FODOR'S CHOICE

Flavors

★ **Kommandanten.** The ever-changing menu here is inventive and fresh with unusual combinations such as oxtail and lobster stew as well as pigeon on a vegetable and fava bean bed. $$$$

Comforts

★ **D'Angleterre, Copenhagen.** This grande dame has hosted everyone from royalty to rock stars. $$$$

★ **Falsled Kro, Millinge.** Once a smuggler's hideaway, this utterly romantic 500-year-old staying place is now one of Scandinavia's most elegant inns. $$$$

★ **Vandrehjem (youth hostels), anywhere in Denmark.** More than 100 excellent youth hostels welcome travelers of all ages. $

Castles and Churches

★ **Christianborg Slot, Copenhagen.** The queen still receives guests in this 12th-century castle.

★ **Kronborg Slot, Helsingør, Sjælland.** William Shakespeare never saw this fantastic castle, but that didn't stop him from using it as the setting for *Hamlet*.

★ **Rosenborg Slot, Copenhagen.** The only castle that is still passed down from monarch to monarch, Rosenborg Slot is home to the crown jewels.

Museums

★ **Louisiana, Copenhagen.** A half-hour drive from the city, this world-class modern art collection displays the likes of Warhol and Picasso.

⭐ **Nationalmuseet, Copenhagen.** Brilliantly restored and regarded as one of the best national museums in Europe, this institution curates exhibits chronicling Danish cultural history.

⭐ **Ny Carlsberg Glyptotek.** The best collection of Etruscan art outside Italy, and Europe's finest collection of Roman portraits are housed here along with an impressive pre-Impressionist collection including rare works by Gaugin and Rodin.

Special Moments

⭐ Dogsledding on a frozen fjord in Uummannaq, Greenland

⭐ Walking through Tivoli at dusk

⭐ Watching a bonfire on Skt. Hansaften, the longest day of the year

2 COPENHAGEN

COPENHAGEN—KØBENHAVN IN DANISH—has no glittering skylines, few killer views, and only a handful of meager skyscrapers. Bicycles glide alongside manageable traffic at a pace that's utterly human. The early morning air in the pedestrian streets of the city's core, Strøget, is redolent of freshly baked bread and soap-scrubbed storefronts. If there's such a thing as a cozy city, this is it.

Extremely livable and relatively calm, Copenhagen is not a microcosm of Denmark, but rather a cosmopolitan city with an identity of its own. Denmark's political, cultural, and financial capital is inhabited by 1.5 million Danes, a fifth of the national population, as well as a growing immigrant community. Filled with museums, restaurants, cafés, and lively nightlife, it has its greatest resource in its spirited inhabitants. The imaginative, unconventional, and affable Copenhageners exude an egalitarian philosophy that embraces nearly all lifestyles and leanings.

The town was a fishing colony until 1157, when Valdemar the Great gave it to Bishop Absalon, who built a castle on what is now Christianborg. It grew as a center on the Baltic trade route and became known as *købmændenes havn* (merchants' harbor) and eventually København. In the 15th century it became the royal residence and the capital of Norway and Sweden. A hundred years later, Christian IV, a Renaissance king obsessed with fine architecture, began a building boom that crowned the city with towers and castles, many of which still exist. They are almost all that remain of the city's 800-year history; much of Copenhagen was destroyed by two major fires in the 18th century and by Lord Nelson's bombings during the Napoleonic Wars.

Despite a tumultuous history, Copenhagen survives as the liveliest Scandinavian capital. With its backdrop of copper towers and crooked rooftops, the venerable city is humored by playful street musicians and performers, soothed by one of the highest standards of living in the world, and spangled by the thousand lights and gardens of Tivoli.

EXPLORING COPENHAGEN

The sites in Copenhagen rarely jump out at you; its elegant spires and tangle of cobbled one-way streets are best sought out on foot, and lingered over. Excellent bus and train systems can come to the rescue of weary legs. It is not divided into single-purpose districts; people work, play, shop, and live throughout the central core of this multilayered, densely populated capital.

Be it sea or canal, Copenhagen is surrounded by water. A network of bridges and drawbridges connects the two main islands—Sjælland and Amager—that Copenhagen is built on. The seafaring atmosphere is indelible, especially around Nyhavn and Christianshavn.

You might wonder why so many Copenhagen sites, especially churches, keep such peculiar, and often short, hours. It's a good idea to call and confirm opening times, especially in fall and winter.

Numbers in the text correspond to numbers in the margin and on the Copenhagen map.

Rådhus Pladsen, Christiansborg Slot, and Strøget

In 1728, and again in 1795, fires broke out in central Copenhagen with devastating effect. Disaster struck again in 1801, when Lord Nelson bombed the city—*after* the Danes had surrendered and *after* he was

10

Copenhagen

Dag Hammarskjölds Al.
Krishaniag.
Langeliniebrd.
Krishaniag.
Østbaneg.
Stockholmsg.
Østport Station
Oslo Plads
Folke Bernadottes Al.
Forbindelsesv
Langelinie
Yderhavn
Østbaneg.
Øster Anlæg
Churchill-parken
25
26
27
34
Rigensg.
NYBODER
St. Kongensg.
24
Esplanaden
Sølvg.
Fredericiag.
Bredgade
23
Amalieg.
32
Kongens Have
Store Kongensg.
22
Bredgade
21
Toldbodg.
Kronprincessg.
Dronningens Tværg.
Adelg.
Borgerg.
Amalieg.
Amalieg.
Sankt Annæ Plads
Gammelmel.
Gothersg.
Ny Østerg.
Kongens Nytorv
17
19
Nyhavn
Kvæsthusbroen
Inderhavn
HOLMEN
lestræde
Kr. Berniks
Bremerholm
18
Nyhavn Canal
20
14
Østerg.
16
Højbro Plads
Heibergsg.
Holbergsg.
OLMEN
magertorv
æderstr.
Holmenskanal
Tordenskjolds.
Havnegade
Gammel Strand
Holmenskanal
12
6
Christiansborg Slotsplads
11
Chr. IV's Bro
Bodsmands- sstræde
CHRISTIANSHAVN
5
9
Børsg.
Knippelsbro
Bodsmandsstræde
8
Tøjhusgade
Strandg.
Wildersg.
Sankt Annæ
Christiania
10
7
Toryg.
13
Christians Brygge
Fredericholms
Kanal
oldg.
Langebro
Langerbrog.
Dronningensg.
Princessg.
Christianshavns Voldg.
Amagerbrog.
Vermlandsg.
Amager Blvd.
Christianshavns Voldg.
Stadsgraven

ordered to stop, he feigned ignorance and turned his famed blind eye
to the command. These events still shape modern Copenhagen, which
was rebuilt with wide, curved-corner streets—making it easier for fire
trucks to turn—and large, four-sided apartment buildings centered
with courtyards. Arguably the liveliest area of the city, central Copenhagen is packed with shops, restaurants, businesses, and apartment buildings, as well as the crowning architectural achievements of Christian
IV—all of it aswarm with Danes and visitors. Copenhagen's central
spine consists of the five consecutive pedestrian strands known as
Strøget and the surrounding tangle of roads and courtyards—less than
a mile square in total. Across the capital's main harbor is the smaller,
17th-century Christianshavn. In the early 1600s, this area was mostly
a series of shallows between land, which were eventually dammed. Today
Christianshavn's colorful boats and postcard maritime character make
it one of the toniest parts of town.

A Good Walk

The city's heart is the Rådhus Pladsen, home to the Baroque-style
Rådhus ① and its clock tower. On the right side of the square is the
landmark **Lurblæserne** ②. Off the square's northeastern corner is Frederiksberggade, the first of the five pedestrian streets that make up
Strøget ③, Copenhagen's shopping district. Walk past the cafés and
trendy boutiques to the double square of Gammeltorv and Nytorv.

Down Rådhusstræde toward Frederiksholms Kanal, the **Nationalmuseet** ④ contains an amazing collection of Viking artifacts. Cross Frederiksholms Kanal to Christiansborg Slotsplads, a small atoll divided
by the canal and dominated by the burly **Christiansborg Slot** ⑤. North
of the castle is **Thorvaldsen Museum** ⑥, devoted to the works of one
of Denmark's most important sculptors, Bertel Thorvaldsen. On the
south end of Slotsholmen is the three-story Romanesque-style **Kongelige
Bibliotek** ⑦, edged by carefully tended gardens and tree-lined avenues.
To the south, on the harbor side of the royal library, is its new glass
and granite annex, nicknamed the "Black Diamond." Back on the south
face of Christiansborg are the **Teatermuseum** ⑧ and the **Kongelige
Stald** ⑨ and its new annex, the "Black Diamond," just next door.

On the street that bears its name is the **Tøjhusmuseet** ⑩, and a few steps
away is the architecturally marvelous **Børsen** ⑪ and the **Holmens
Kirken** ⑫. To the east is **Christianshavn,** connected to Slotsholmen by
the drawbridge Knippelsbro. Farther north, the former shipyard of Holmen is marked by expansive venues and several departments of the
Københavns Universitet.

From nearly anywhere in the area, you can see the green-and-gold spire
of **Vor Frelsers Kirken** ⑬. Across the Knippels Torvegade Bridge, under
a mile down Børgsgade through Højbroplads, is Amagertorv, one of
Strøget's five streets. On the left is **W. Ø. Larsens Tobakmuseet** ⑭, and
farther down the street and to the left is the 18th-century **Helligånds
Kirken** ⑮. On Strøget's Østergade, the massive spire of **Nikolaj Kirken** ⑯
looks many sizes too large for the tiny cobbled streets below.

TIMING

The walk itself takes about two hours. Typically, Christiansborg Slot
and its ruins and the Nationalmuseet both take at least an hour and a
half to see—even more for Viking fans. Expect to spend more than an
hour if you want to see a film at the Omnimax Theater at the Tycho
Brahe Planetarium. The hundreds of shops along Strøget are enticing,
so plan extra shopping and café time—at least as much as your wal-
let can spare. Note that many sites in this walk are closed Sunday or
Monday, and some have odd hours; always call ahead.

Sights to See

⑪ **Børsen** (Stock Exchange). Believed to be the oldest stock exchange still in use, this masterpiece of fantasy and architecture is topped by a spire of three intertwined dragons' tails—said to have been twisted by its builder, King Christian IV. Built between 1619 and 1640, it was originally used as a sort of medieval mall, filled with shopping stalls. With its steep roofs, tiny windows, and gables, the treasured building is used only for special occasions. ⊠ *Christiansborg Slotspl.* ⊙ *Not open to the public.*

★ ⑤ **Christiansborg Slot** (Christiansborg Castle). Surrounded by canals on three sides, the massive granite castle is where the queen officially receives guests. From 1441 until the fire of 1795, it was used as the royal residence. Even though the first two castles on the site were burned, Christiansborg remains an impressive Baroque compound, even by European standards: there's the **Folketinget** (Parliament House) (☎ 33/ 37–55–00, ⛀ free, ⊙ May–Sept., Mon.–Sat., tours hourly (except noon) 10–4; Oct.–Apr., Tues., Thurs., and Sat., tours hourly (except noon) 10–4); the **Kongelige Repræsantationlokaler** (Royal Reception Chambers), where you'll be asked to don slippers to protect the floors (⊙ guided tours only): May and Sept., Tues.–Sun., English tours at 11 and 3; June–Aug., Tues.–Sun., tours at 11, 1, and 3; Oct.–Dec. and Feb.– Apr., Tues., Thurs., and Sun., tours at 11 and 3); and the **Højesteret** (Supreme Court), on the site of the city's first fortress and built by Bishop Absalon in 1167. The guards at the entrance are knowledgeable and friendly; call them first to double-check the complicated opening hours.

While the castle was being rebuilt at the turn of the century, the Nationalmuseet (☞ *below*) excavated the **ruins** beneath it. This dark, subterranean maze contains fascinating models and architectural relics (☎ 33/92–64–92, ⛀ Dkr 15, ⊙ May–Sept., daily 9:30–3:30, Oct.–Apr., Tues., Thurs, and weekends 9:30–3:30).

Wander around **Højbro Plads** and the delightful row of houses that border the northern edge of Slotsholmen. The quays were long Copenhagen's fish market, but today a lone early-morning fisherwoman hawking fresh fish, marinated herring, and eel is the sole fishmonger you'll see carrying on the tradition. ⊠ *Christiansborg. Ruins,* ☎ *33/ 92–64–92. Folketinget,* ☎ *33/37–55–00.* ⛀ *Ruins Dkr 15; reception chambers Dkr 30; Folketinget free.* ⊙ *Ruins: May–Sept., daily 9:30– 3:30; Oct.–Apr., Tues., Thurs., and weekends 9:30–3:30. Reception chambers (guided tours only): May and Sept., Tues.–Sun., English tours at 11 and 3; June–Aug., Tues.–Sun., tours at 11, 1, and 3; Oct.– Dec. and Feb.–Apr., Tues., Thurs., and Sun., tours at 11 and 3. Folketinget: May–Sept., Mon.–Sat., tours hourly (except noon) 10–4; Oct.–Apr., Tues., Thurs., Sat., tours hourly (except noon) 10–4.*

Christianshavn. This tangle of cobbled avenues, antique street lamps, and Left Bank charm makes up one of the oldest neighborhoods in the city. Even the old system of earthworks—the best preserved of Copenhagen's original fortification walls—still exists. In the 17th century, King Christian IV offered what were patches of partially flooded land for free, and with additional tax benefits; in return, takers would have to fill them in and construct sturdy buildings for trade, commerce, housing for the shipbuilding workers, and defense against sea attacks. Gentrified today, the area harbors restaurants, cafés, and boutiques, and its ramparts are edged with green areas and walking paths, making it the perfect neighborhood for an afternoon or evening amble.

CHRISTIANIA – If you are nostalgic for the '60s counterculture, head to this anarchists' commune on Christianshavn. Founded in 1971, when students occupied army barracks, it is now a peaceful community of nonconformists who run a number of businesses, including a bike shop, bakery, rock club, and communal bathhouse. Wall cartoons preach drugs and peace, but the inhabitants are less fond of cameras—picture-taking is forbidden. ⊠ *Prinsesseg. and Badsmandsstr.*

HOLMEN – Previously isolated (indeed closed) from central Copenhagen, this former navy base just north of Christianshavn produced ships and ammunition until the 1980s. It was formally opened as the sight of the 1995 United Nations Summit on Human Development and played an important role as a cultural area during Copenhagen's 1996 reign as the Cultural Capital of Europe. Today, among its several cultural venues is the city's biggest performance space, the Torpedo Hall, where torpedoes were actually produced. You'll also find the Danish Art Academy's Architecture School, the National Theater School, the Rhythmic Music Conservatory, and the Danish Film School, which all host special activities.

⑮ Helligånds Kirken (Church of the Holy Ghost). This 18th-century church was founded as an abbey of the Holy Ghost and is still one of the city's oldest places of worship. Its choir contains a font by the sculptor Thorvaldsen, and more modern art is found in the large exhibition room—once a hospital—that faces Strøget. ⊠ *Niels Hemmingseng. 5, Amagertorv section,* ☎ *33/12–95–55.* 🎟 *Free.* ☉ *Weekdays 9–1, Sat. 10–noon.*

⑫ Holmens Kirken (Islet's Church). Two of the country's most revered naval heroes are buried here: Niels Juel crushed the Swedish fleet at Køge in 1677. Peder Tordenskjold defeated Charles XII of Sweden during the Great Northern War in the early 18th century. ⊠ *Holmens Kanal,* ☎ *33/13–61–78.* 🎟 *Free.* ☉ *May 15–Sept. 15, weekdays 9–2, Sat. 9–noon; Sept. 16–May 14, Mon.–Sat. 9–noon.*

❼ Kongelige Bibliotek (Royal Library). The Royal Library houses the country's largest collection of books, newspapers, and manuscripts. Among the more than 2 million volumes are accounts of Viking journeys to America and Greenland and original manuscripts by Hans Christian Andersen and Karen Blixen (a.k.a. Isak Dinesen). If you happen to be in the area anyway and are craving a literary encounter, ramble around the statue of philosopher Søren Kierkegaard (1813–55), formal gardens, and tree-lined avenues surrounding the scholarly building. The library's massive glass-and-granite annex, called the Black Diamond, opened in late 1999 and looms between the current building and the waterfront. ⊠ *Christians Brygge 8,* ☎ *33/47–47–47.* ☉ *Call for hrs.*

☾ ❾ Kongelige Stald (Royal Stables). Between 9 and noon, time stands still while riders elegantly clad in breeches and jackets exercise the horses. The vehicles, including coaches and carriages, and harnesses on display have been used by the Danish monarchy from 1778 to the present. ⊠ *Christiansborg Ridebane 12,* ☎ *33/40–10–10.* 🎟 *Dkr 10.* ☉ *May–Sept., Fri.–Sun. 2–4; Oct.–Apr., weekends 2–4.*

❷ Lurblæserne (Lur Blower Column). Topped by two Vikings blowing an ancient trumpet called a *lur,* this column displays a good deal of artistic license—the lur dates from the Bronze Age, 1500 BC, whereas the Vikings lived a mere 1,000 years ago. City tours often start at this important landmark, which was erected in 1914. ⊠ *East side of Rådhus Pl.*

★ ☾ ❹ Nationalmuseet (National Museum). This brilliantly restored 18th-century royal residence, peaked by massive overhead windows, has housed what is regarded as one of the best national museums in Europe since the 1930s. Extensive collections chronicle Danish cultural history from prehistoric to modern times—included is one of the largest collections of Stone Age tools in the world—and Egyptian, Greek, and Roman antiquities are on display. The children's museum, with replicas of period clothing and all sorts of touchable items, transforms history into something kids under 12 can relate to. ⊠ *Ny Vesterg. 10,* ☎ *33/13–44–11.* 🎟 *Dkr 40.* ☉ *Tues.–Sun. 10–5.*

⑯ Nikolaj Kirken (Nicholas Church). Though the green spire of the imposing church—named for the patron saint of seafarers—appears as old as the surrounding medieval streets, it is actually relatively young. The current building was finished in 1914; the previous structure, which dated from the 13th century, was destroyed by the 1728 fire. Today the church is an art gallery and exhibition center that often shows more experimental work. ⊠ *Nikolaj Pl.,* ☎ *33/93–16–26.* 🎟 *Varies according to special exhibitions.* ☉ *Daily noon—5.*

NEED A BREAK?   **Café Nikolaj** (⊠ Nikolajpl., ☎ 33/93–16–26), inside Nikolaj Kirken, is a reliable, inexpensive café with good Danish pastries and light meals. It's open noon to 3 for lunch and until 5 for cakes and drinks.

---

❶ Rådhus (City Hall). Completed in 1905, the mock-Renaissance building dominates **Rådhus Pladsen** (City Hall Square), the hub of Copenhagen's commercial district. Architect Martin Nyrop's creation was popular from the start, perhaps because he envisioned that it should give "gaiety to everyday life and spontaneous pleasure to all . . ."; accordingly, a statue of Copenhagen's 12th-century founder, Bishop Absalon, sits atop the main entrance.

Besides being an important ceremonial meeting place for Danish VIPs, the intricately decorated Rådhus contains the first **World Clock.** The multidialed, superaccurate astronomical timepiece has a 570,000-year calendar and took inventor Jens Olsen 27 years to complete before it was put into action in 1955. If you're feeling energetic, take a guided tour up the 350-ft bell tower for the panoramic, but not particularly inspiring, view.

The modern glass and gray-steel **bus terminal** flanking the square's northwest side has French granite floors, pear-tree-wood shelving, and underground marble bathrooms. The $2.8 million creation proved so architecturally contentious—more for its placement than for its design—that there was serious discussion of moving it.

Look up to see one of the city's most charming bronze sculptures, created by the Danish artist E. Utzon Frank in 1936. Diagonally across Rådhus Pladsen, atop a corner office building you'll see a **neon thermometer** and a **gilded barometer.** On sunny days there's a golden sculpture of a girl on a bicycle; come rain, a girl with an umbrella appears. ⊠ *Rådhus Pl.,* ☎ *33/66–25–82.* 🎟 *Tours Dkr 20, tower Dkr 10.* ☉ *Weekdays 9:30–4, Sat. 9:30–1. Tours in English weekdays at 3, Sat. at 10. Tower tours Mon.–Sat. at 3, also June–Sept. at 10 and 11. Call to confirm hrs.*

★ ❸ Strøget. Though it is referred to as one street, the city's pedestrian spine, pronounced *Stroy*-et, is actually a series of five streets: Frederiksberggade, Nygade, Vimmelskaftet, Amagertorv, and Østergade. By mid-morning, particularly on Saturday, it is congested with people, baby strollers, and street performers. Past swank and trendy, and sometimes flashy and trashy, boutiques of **Frederiksberggade** is the double square of **Gammeltorv** (Old Square) and **Nytorv** (New Square), in summer often crowded with street vendors selling cheap jewelry.

In 1728 and again in 1795, much of Strøget was heavily damaged by fire. When rebuilding, the city fathers straightened and widened the streets. Today, you can still see buildings from this reconstruction period, as well as a few that survived the fires.

In addition to shopping, you'll enjoy Strøget for strolling, as hundreds do. Outside the posh fur and porcelain shops and bustling cafés and restaurants, the sidewalks have a festive street-fair atmosphere.

⑧ Teatermuseum (Theater Museum). After you brush up on theater and ballet history, wander around the boxes, stage, and dressing rooms of the **Royal Court Theater** of 1767, which King Christian VII had built as the first court theater in Scandinavia. ⊠ *Christiansborg Ridebane 18,* ☎ *33/11–51–76.* ▣ *Dkr 20.* ◷ *Wed. 2–4, weekends noon–4.*

⑥ Thorvaldsen Museum. The 19th-century artist Bertel Thorvaldsen (1770–1844) is buried at the center of this museum in a simple, ivy-covered tomb. Greatly influenced by the statues and reliefs of classical antiquity, he is recognized as one of the world's greatest neoclassical artists and completed many commissions all over Europe. The museum, once a coachhouse to Christiansborg, now houses Thorvaldsen's interpretations of classical and mythological figures, and an extensive collection of paintings and drawings by other artists that Thorvaldsen assembled while living—for most of his life—in Rome. The outside frieze by Jørgen Sonne depicts the sculptor's triumphant return to Copenhagen after years abroad. ⊠ *Porthusg. 2, Slotsholmen,* ☎ *33/32–15–32.* ▣ *Dkr 20.* ◷ *Tues.–Sun. 10–5.*

⑩ Tøjhusmuseet (Royal Danish Arsenal Museum). This Renaissance structure—built by King Christian IV and one of central Copenhagen's oldest—contains impressive displays of uniforms, weapons, and armor in an arched hall 600 ft long. ⊠ *Tøjhusg. 3,* ☎ *33/11–60–37.* ▣ *Dkr 20.* ◷ *Tues.–Sun. noon–4.*

⑬ Vor Frelsers Kirken (The Church of Our Savior). Dominating the area around Christianshavn is the green-and-gold tower of this church, a Baroque structure built in 1696. Local legend has it that the staircase encircling it was built curling the wrong way around, and that when its architect reached the top and realized what he'd done, he jumped. At press time, a renovation was possible (but not yet scheduled) for 1999 or earlier. ⊠ *Skt. Annæg. 29,* ☎ *32/57–27–98.* ▣ *Tower Dkr 20.* ◷ *Mar.–Apr. and Nov., daily 11–2:30; May–Oct., daily 10–4:30; Dec.–Feb. 11–2. Tower closed in inclement weather.*

⑭ W. Ø. Larsens Tobakmuseet (W. O. Larsens Tobacco Museum). Looking like a storefront window from the outside, as this museum does contain an actual shop, the Tobacco Museum in fact has a full-fledged collection of pipes made in every conceivable shape from every possible material. Look for the tiny pipe that's no bigger than an embroidery needle. There are also paintings, drawings, and an amazing collection of smoking implements. ⊠ *Amagertorv 9,* ☎ *33/12–20–50.* ▣ *Free.* ◷ *Mon.–Thurs. 10–6, Fri. 10–7, Sat. 10–4.*

Around Amalienborg and Sites North

North of Kongens Nytorv, the city becomes a fidgety grid of parks and wider boulevards pointing northwest across the canal toward upscale Østerbro—wreathed by manors commissioned by wealthy merchants and bluebloods. In the mid-1700s, King Frederik V donated parcels of this land to anyone who agreed to build from the work of architect Niels Eigtved, who also designed the Kongelige Teater. The jewel of this crown remains Amalienborg and its Rococo mansions.

A Good Walk

At the end of Strøget, **Kongens Nytorv** ⑰ is flanked on its south side
by the **Kongelige Teater** ⑱, and backed by **Charlottenborg** ⑲, which
contains the Danish Academy of Fine Art (call to see if an exhibition
has opened the castle to the public). The street leading southeast from
Kongens Nytorv is **Nyhavn** ⑳, a onetime sailors' haunt and now a popular waterfront hub. From the south end of the harbor (north end of
Havnegade) depart high-speed craft to Malmö, Sweden; on the other
north side, Kvævthusbroen—at the end of Skt. Annæ Plads (☞ *below*)—
is the quay for boats to Oslo, Norway, and Bornholm, Denmark; farther north still, just before the perch of *The Little Mermaid,* depart
ships for Swinoujscie, Poland.

West of the harbor front is the grand square called Skt. Annæ Plads.
Perpendicular to the square is Amaliegade, its wooden colonnade bor-
dering the cobbled square of **Amalienborg** ㉑, the royal residence with
a pleasant garden on its harbor side. Steps west from the square is
Bredgade, where the Baroque **Marmorkirken** ㉒ flaunts its Norwegian
marble structure. Farther north on Bredgade is the Rococo **Kunstindustrimuseet** ㉓. Back on Bredgade (you can also take the more colorful, café-lined Store Kongensgade, just west), turn right onto
Esplanaden and you'll see the enormously informative **Frihedsmuseet** ㉔.
At the Churchillparken's entrance stands the English church, St. Albans. In the park's center, the **Kastellet** ㉕ serves as a reminder of the
city's grim military history. At its eastern perimeter is Langelinie, a waterfront promenade with a view of Denmark's best-known pinup, **Den
Lille Havfrued** ㉖. Wending your way back toward Esplanaden and the
town center, you'll pass the **Gefion Springvandet** ㉗.

TIMING

This walk amid parks, gardens, canals, and building exteriors should
take a full day. If it's nice, linger in the parks, especially along Kastellet and Amalienhaven, and plan on a long lunch at Nyhavn. The Kunstindustrimuseet merits about an hour, more if you plan on perusing
the design books in the museum's well-stocked library. The Frihedsmuseet may require more time: its evocative portrait of Danish life
during World War II intrigues even the most history-weary teens.
Avoid taking this tour Monday, when some sites are closed.

Sights to See

㉑ **Amalienborg** (Amalia's Castle). The four identical Rococo buildings
occupying this square have housed the royals since 1784. The Christian VIII palace across from the Queen's residence houses the **Amalienborg Museum,** which displays the second division of the Royal Collection
(the first is at Rosenborg Slot, ☞ *below*) and chronicles royal lifestyles
between 1863 and 1947. Here you can view the study of King Christian IX (1818–1906) and the drawing room of his wife, Queen Louise.
Rooms are packed with family gifts and regal baubles ranging from
tacky knickknacks to Fabergé treasures, including a nephrite and ruby
table clock, and a small costume collection.

In the square's center is a magnificent equestrian statue of King Frederik V by the French sculptor Jacques François Joseph Saly. It reput-
edly cost as much as all the buildings combined. Every day at noon,
the Royal Guard and band march from Rosenborg Slot through the
city for the changing of the guard. At noon on Queen Margrethe's birthday, April 16, crowds of Danes gather to cheer their monarch, who
stands and waves from her balcony. On Amalienborg's harbor side are
the trees, gardens, and fountains of **Amalienhaven.** ⊠ *Amalienborg Castle,* ☎ *33/12–21–86.* 🎫 *Dkr 35.* ☉ *Jan.–Apr. and mid-Oct.–mid-*

Dec., Tues.–Sun. 11–4; May, Sept.–mid-Oct. and mid-Dec.-end-Dec.,
daily 11–4; June–Aug. daily 10–4..

⑲ Charlottenborg (Charlotte's Castle). This Dutch Baroque–style castle
was built by Frederik III's half brother in 1670. Since 1754 the gar-
den-flanked property has housed the faculty and students of the Danish Academy of Fine Art. It is open only during exhibits, usually in winter.
⊠ *Nyhavn 2,* ☎ *33/13–40–22.* ⌹ *Dkr 20.* ⊙ *Closed to public, ex-*
cept for exhibitions. Exhibition hrs daily 10–5.

㉖ Den Lille Havfrue (*The Little Mermaid*). On the Langelinie promenade,
this somewhat overrated 1913 statue commemorates Hans Christian
Andersen's lovelorn creation, and is the subject of hundreds of travel
posters. Donated to the city by Carl Jacobsen, the son of the founder
of Carlsberg Breweries, the innocent waif has also been the subject of
some cruel practical jokes, including decapitation and the loss of an
arm, but she is currently in one piece. Especially on a sunny Sunday,
the Langelinie promenade is thronged with Danes and visitors making their pilgrimage to see the statue. On this occasion, you may want
to read the original Hans Christian Andersen tale; it's a heart-wrench-
ing story that's a far cry from the Disney cartoon.

★ **㉔ Frihedsmuseet** (Resistance Museum). Evocative, sometimes moving
displays commemorate the heroic Danish resistance movement, which
saved 7,000 Jews from the Nazis by hiding them and then smuggling
them to Sweden. The homemade tank outside was used to spread the
news of the Nazi surrender after World War II. ⊠ *Churchillparken,*
☎ *33/13–77–14.* ⌹ *Free.* ⊙ *May–Sept. 15, Tues.–Sat. 10–4, Sun. 10–*
5; Sept. 16–Apr., Tues.–Sat. 11–3, Sun. 11–4.

㉗ Gefion Springvandet (Gefion Fountain). Not far from *The Little Mer-*
maid yet another dramatic myth is illustrated. The goddess Gefion was
promised as much of Sweden as she could carve in a night. The story
goes that she changed her sons to oxen and created the island of Sjælland. ⊠ *East of Frihedsmuseet.*

㉕ Kastellet (Citadel). At Churchill Park's entrance stands the spired English church, **St. Albans.** From there, walk north on the main path and
you'll reach the Citadel. The structure's smooth, peaceful walking
paths, marina, and greenery belie its fierce past as a city fortification.
Built in the aftermath of the Swedish siege of the city on February 10,
1659, the double moats were among the improvements made to the
city's defense. The Citadel served as the city's main fortress into the
18th century; in a grim reversal during World War II, the Germans used
it as their headquarters during their occupation. ⊠ *Center of Churchill*
Park. ⌹ *Free.* ⊙ *Daily 6 AM–sunset.*

⑱ Kongelige Teater (Danish Royal Theater). The stoic, pillared and
gallery-fronted theater is the country's preeminent venue for music, opera,
ballet, and theater. The Danish Royal Ballet, its repertoire ranging from
classical to modern works, performs here.

The current building was opened in 1874, though the annex, known
as the **Nesting Box,** was not inaugurated until 1931. Statues of Danish poet Adam Oehlenschläger and author Ludvig Holberg—whose
works remain the core of Danish theater—flank the facade. Born in
Bergen, Norway, in 1684, Holberg came to Denmark as a student and
stayed. Often compared to Molière, he wrote 32 of his comedies in a
"poetic frenzy" between 1722 and 1728, and, legend has it, he com-
plained of interminable headaches the entire time. He published the
works himself, made an enormous fortune, and invested in real estate.

In the mid-'90s, the theater seemed to be taking his cue: an annex designed by Norwegian architect Sverre Fehn was planned for construction on the eastern side of the theater, but those plans—indeed the whole expansion—are now being reconsidered. ⊠ *Tordenskjoldsg. 3,* ☎ *33/69–69–69.* ⊙ *Guided tours, Sun. 11.*

★ ⓱ **Kongens Nytorv** (King's New Square). A mounted statue of Christian V dominates the square. Crafted in 1688 by the French sculptor Lamoureux, he is conspicuously depicted as a Roman emperor. Every year, at the end of June, graduating high school students arrive in horse-drawn carriages and dance beneath the furrowed brow of the sober statue.

NEED A
BREAK?

Dozens of restaurants and cafés line Nyhavn. Among the best is **Cap Horn** (⊠ Nyhavn 21, ☎ 33/12–85–04) for moderately priced, hearty, light, and completely organic Danish treats served in a cozy, art-filled dining room that looks like a ship's galley. Try the fried plaice, swimming in a sea of parsley butter with boiled potatoes. In the summertime, you'll have to keep a keen eye to grab a sidewalk table here, but enjoying an overstuffed focaccia sandwich and a Carlsberg, you'll be living life well.

⓭ **Kunstindustrimuseet** (Museum of Decorative Art). Originally built in the 18th century as a royal hospital, the fine Rococo-style museum houses a large selection of European and Asian crafts. You'll also find ceramics, silverware, tapestries, and special exhibitions usually focusing on contemporary design. The museum's excellent library is stocked with design books and magazines, and there's also a small café. ⊠ *Bredg. 68,* ☎ *33/14–94–52.* 🖃 *Dkr 35 (additional fee for some special exhibits).* ⊙ *Permanent collection, Tues.–Sun. 1–4; changing exhibits, Tues.–Sat. 10–4, Sun. 1–4.*

⓬ **Marmorkirken** (Marble Church). Officially the Frederikskirke, the ponderous Baroque sanctuary of precious Norwegian marble was begun in 1749 and lay unfinished from 1770 to 1874 due to budget restraints. It was finally completed and consecrated in 1894. Around the exterior are 16 statues of various religious leaders from Moses to Luther, and below them stand sculptures of outstanding Danish ministers and bishops. The hardy can scale 273 steps to the outdoor balcony. Walk past the exotic gilded onion domes of the **Russiske Ortodoks Kirke** (Russian Orthodox Church). ⊠ *Bredg.,* ☎ *33/15–37–63.* 🖃 *Free; balcony, Dkr 20.* ⊙ *Mon.–Tues. and Thurs.–Fri. 10:30–4:30; Weds. 10:30–6. Guided tours: Aug.–May, weekends 1; June–July, daily 1 and 3.*

Nyboder. Tour the neat, mustard-colored enclave of Nyboder, a perfectly laid-out compound of flat, long, former sailors' homes built by Christian IV. Like Nyhavn, this salty sailors' area was seedy and boisterous at the beginning of the 1970s, but today has become one of Copenhagen's more fashionable neighborhoods. Stroll by on your own or call Mr. Timler to make arrangements to visit one of the houses. ⊠ *West of Store Kongensg. and east of Rigensg.,* ☎ *33/32–10–05.*

★ ⓴ **Nyhavn** (New Harbor). This harbor-front neighborhood was built 300 years ago to attract traffic and commerce to the city center. Until 1970, the area was a favorite haunt of sailors. Though restaurants, boutiques, and antiques stores now outnumber tattoo parlors, many old buildings have been well preserved and have retained the harbor's authentic 18th-century maritime atmosphere; you can even see a fleet of old-time sailing ships from the quay. Hans Christian Andersen lived at various times in the Nyhavn houses at numbers 18, 20, and 67.

Down Vesterbrogade and Nørrebro

To the southwest of the city are the vibrant working-class and immigrant neighborhoods of Vesterbro, where you'll find a good selection of inexpensive ethnic restaurants and shops. You'll find more cafés, restaurants, clubs, and shops on Nørrebrogade and Skt. Hans Torv.

By the 1880s, many of the buildings that now line Vesterbro and Nørrebro were being hastily thrown up as housing for area laborers. Many of these flats—typically decorated with a row of pedimented windows and a portal entrance—have been renovated through a massive urban renewal program. But to this day, many share hall toilets, have no showers, and are heated only by kerosene ovens.

A Good Walk

Take the train from Østerport Station, off of Oslo Plads, to Nørreport Station on Nørrevoldgade and walk down Fiolstræde to **Vor Frue Kirken** ㉘, its very tall copper spire and four shorter ones crowning the area. Backtracking north on Fiolstræde you'll come to the main building of **Københavns Universitet** ㉙; on the corner of Krystalgade is the **Københavns Synagoge** ㉚.

Fiolstræde ends at the Nørreport train station. Perpendicular to Nørrevoldgade is Frederiksborggade, which leads northwest to the neighborhood of Nørrebro; to the south after the Kultorvet, or Coal Square, Frederiksborggade turns into the pedestrian street Købmagergade. From anywhere in the area, you can see the stout **Rundetårn** ㉛: it stands as one of Copenhagen's most beloved landmarks, with an observatory open fall and winter evenings. Straight down from the Rundetårn on Landemærket, Gothersgade gives way to **Rosenborg Slot** ㉜, its Dutch Renaissance design standing out against the vivid green of the well-tended Kongens Have. For a heavier dose of plants and living things, head across Øster Voldgade to the 25-acre **Botanisk Have** ㉝.

Leave the garden's north exit to reach the recently renovated and expanded **Statens Museum for Kunst** ㉞, notable for exceptional Matisse works. An adjacent building houses the **Hirschsprungske Samling** ㉟, with 19th-century Danish art.

Back at the Nørreport station, you can catch a train back to Copenhagen's main station, Hovedbanegården. When you exit on Vesterbrogade, take a right and you'll see the city's best-known attraction, **Tivoli** ㊱. At the southern end of the gardens, on Hans Christian Andersens Boulevard, the neoclassical **Ny Carlsberg Glyptotek** ㊲ contains one of the most impressive collections of antiquities and sculpture in northern Europe. Tucked between Sankt Jørgens Sø, or St. Jørgens Lake, and the main arteries of Vestersøgade and Gammel Kongevej is the **Tycho Brahe Planetarium** ㊳, with an Omnimax Theater.

Continue down Vesterbrogade into **Vesterbro** ㊴, Copenhagen's own Lower East Side of New York. Parallel to the south is Istedgade, Copenhagen's halfhearted red-light district.

Farther west down Vesterbrogade is **Københavns Bymuseum** ㊵, its entrance flanked by a miniature model of medieval Copenhagen. Beer enthusiasts and zymurgy fanatics can head south on Enghavevej and take a right on Ny Carlsbergvej for a tour of **Carlsberg Bryggeri** ㊶.

TIMING

All of the sites on this tour are relatively close together and can be seen in one day. Tivoli offers charms throughout the day; visit in the late afternoon, and stay until midnight, when colored electrical bulbs and fireworks illuminate the park. Note that some sites below close Monday or Tuesday; call ahead.

Sights to See

㉝ Botanisk Have (Botanical Garden). Trees, flowers, ponds, sculptures, and a spectacular 19th-century *Palmehuset* (Palm House) of tropical and subtropical plants blanket the garden's 25-plus acres. There's also an observatory and a geological museum. Take time to explore the gardens and watch the pensioners feed the birds. Some have been coming here so long that the birds actually alight on their fingers. ✉ *Gothersg. 128,* ☎ *35/32–22–40.* ✍ *Free.* ☉ *Gardens Jan.–Apr. and Oct.–Dec., daily 8:30–4; May–Sept., daily 8:30–6. Palm House daily 10–3.*

OFF THE
BEATEN PATH

ARBEJDERMUSEET – The vastly underrated Workers Museum chronicles the working class from 1870 to the present, with evocative life-size "day-in-the-life-of" exhibits, including reconstructions of a city street and tram and an original apartment once belonging to a brewery worker, his wife, and eight children. Changing exhibits focusing on Danish as well as international issues are often excellent. The museum also has a 19th-century-style restaurant serving old-fashioned Danish specialties and a '50s-style coffee shop. ✉ Rømersg. 22, ☎ 33/13–01–52. ✍ Dkr 30. ☉ July–Oct., daily 10–4; Nov.–June, Tues.–Sun. 10–4.

㊶ Carlsberg Bryggeri (Carlsberg Brewery). Four giant Bornholm granite elephants guard the entrance to this world-famous brewery; a tour of the draft horse stalls and **Carlsberg Museum** meets at this gate. At the end, you're rewarded with a few minutes to quaff a beer. ✉ *Ny Carlsbergvej 140,* ☎ *33/27–13–14.* ☉ *Tours weekdays at 11 and 2 or by arrangement for groups.*

㉟ Hirschsprungske Samling (Hirschsprung Collection). This recently renovated and reopened museum showcases paintings from the country's Golden Age—Denmark's mid-19th-century school of Naturalism—as well as a collection of paintings by the late-19th-century artists of the Skagen School. Their luminous works capture the play of light and water so characteristic of the Danish countryside. ✉ *Stockholmsg. 20,* ☎ *31/ 42–03–36.* ✍ *Dkr 25.* ☉ *Thurs.–Mon. 11–4, Wed. 11–9.*

Istedgade. In Copenhagen's halfhearted red-light district, mom-and-pop kiosks and ethnic restaurants stand side by side with seedy porn shops and shady outfits aiming to satisfy all proclivities. Though it is relatively safe, you may want to avoid the area for a late-night stroll. ✉ *Street south and parallel to Vesterbrogade, west of Tivoli.*

㊵ Københavns Bymuseum (Copenhagen City Museum). For a surprisingly evocative collection detailing Copenhagen's history, head to this 17th-century building in the heart of Vesterbro. Outside is a meticulously maintained model of medieval Copenhagen; inside there is also a memorial room for philosopher Søren Kierkegaard, the father of existentialism. ✉ *Vesterbrog. 59,* ☎ *33/21–07–72.* ✍ *Dkr 20.* ☉ *May–Sept., Tues.–Sun. 10–4; Oct.–Apr., Tues.–Sun. 1–4.*

㉚ Københavns Synagoge (Copenhagen Synagogue). This synagogue was designed by the contemporary architect Gustav Friedrich Hetsch, who borrowed from the Doric and Egyptian styles in creating the arklike structure. ✉ *Krystalg. 12.* ☉ *Daily services 4:15.*

㉙ Københavns Universitet (Copenhagen University). Denmark's leading school for higher learning was constructed in the 19th century on the site of the medieval bishops' palace. ✉ *Nørreg. 10,* ☎ *35/32–26–26.*

ALE AND ARTY

CARLSBERG. A BEER by any other name does not bring to mind the sculptures of Giacometti, archeological undertakings in Rome, or the music of Miles Davis. In Denmark, however, the company behind the world-famous beer supports much of everything that is a part of Danish culture. Call it the ale of art: perhaps the most altruistic beer in the world.

Carlsberg Breweries, which since 1970 has included the United Breweries/Tuborg, is owned by the Carlsberg Foundation. The umbrella organization annually pumps about 125 million DKr ($21 million) into Danish science, arts, and humanities—programs that touch nearly every aspect of Danish life. Under its own distinct statutes, the New Carlsberg Foundation, a branch of the mother foundation, kicks in 40 million DKr ($6.7 million) to the visual arts every year. While there is a strong tradition of corporate-backed foundations in Denmark, and many companies offer support to the arts and sciences, Carlsberg's scope and commitment to the culture of a single country is unique in the world.

Since its establishment in 1902, the New Carlsberg Foundation has helped build and support the Ny Carlsberg Glyptotek and its collection of antiquities. This Copenhagen museum boasts one of the world's finest collections of Etruscan art, and Europe's finest collection of Roman portraits. Among the other works are Oriental, Egyptian, and Roman masterpieces collected and donated by Carl Jacobsen, the son of Carlsberg-founder J. C. Jacobsen—an accomplished brewer in his own right. The museum's permanent collection also contains French sculpture, including works by Rodin and Degas, impressionist- and postimpressionist paintings by Manet, Cezanne, and Gauguin, and a Danish collection. Many Danish curators attribute the nation's grand state of the arts largely to the New Carlsberg Foundation. According to one, losing its sponsorship would "be a disaster." But what kind of beer company pours the bulk of its profits into high-falooting art? Herein lies what makes Carlsberg so unusual. The brewery does not own the foundation: The foundation owns a 51% majority stake in the brewery.

While the New Carlsberg Foundation technically handles endowments for the visual arts, the larger Carlsberg Foundation, which supports the sciences and humanities, overlaps into the area of fine art. Among the wide range of projects they have funded: major archeological excavations in the Roman Forum, studies of the ancient mosaics of the St. George Rotunda in Thessaloniki, Greece, and the complete and continued support of the Frederiksborg Museum north of Copenhagen. A royal residence that burned in 1859 was rebuilt and established as a museum of Danish history by J. C. Jacobsen; it now serves as the nation's portrait museum.

Between the larger foundation and the brewery itself are several smaller foundations, which further support music, industry, and society in general. The Carlsberg Brewery is also the owner of many businesses that deal in the decorative arts, including Holmegaard glass, Royal Copenhagen Porcelain, and Georg Jensen Silver, all of which exist under the umbrella company Royal Scandinavia. Of course, Carlsberg's associate concern, Tivoli Gardens, is considered by many a work of art in and of itself. Carlsberg also helps to fund annual events like the Copenhagen Jazz Festival and the Roskilde rock festival, as well as concerts and performances by international artists. Clearly, there is more to these noble suds than meets the lips. But just to make sure, order one and do your part to support the arts.

NEED A
BREAK? The nearby **Sømods Bolcher** (✉ Nørreg. 36, ☎ 33/12–60–46) is a must for children and candy lovers: its old-fashioned hard candy is pulled and cut by hand.

★ ③⑦ **Ny Carlsberg Glyptotek** (New Carlsberg Museum). Among Copenhagen's most important museums—thanks to its exquisite antiquities and Gauguins and Rodins—the neoclassical New Carlsberg Museum was donated in 1888 by Carl Jacobsen, son of the founder of the Carlsberg Brewery. Surrounding its lush indoor garden, a series of nooks and chambers houses works by Degas and other Impressionists, plus an extensive assemblage of Egyptian, Greek, Roman, and French sculpture, not to mention the best collection of Etruscan art outside Italy and Europe's finest collection of Roman portraits. A modern wing designed as a three-story treasure chest by the acclaimed Danish architect Henning Larsen houses an impressive pre-Impressionist collection including works from the Barbizon school; Impressionist paintings, including works by Monet, Sisley, and Pissaro; and a post-Impressionist section, with 50 Gauguin paintings plus 12 of his very rare sculpures. ✉ *Dantes Pl. 7,* ☎ *33/41–81–41.* 🖃 *Dkr 15, free Wed. and Sun.* ☉ *Tues.–Sun. 10–4.*

★ ③② **Rosenborg Slot** (Rosenborg Castle). This Dutch Renaissance castle contains ballrooms, halls, and reception chambers, but for all of its grandeur, there's an intimacy that makes you think the king might return any minute. Thousands of objects are displayed, including beer glasses, gilded clocks, golden swords, family portraits, a pearl-studded saddle, and gem-encrusted tables; an adjacent treasury contains the royal jewels. The castle's setting is equally welcoming: it's smack in the middle of the **Kongens Have** (King's Garden), amid lawns, park benches, and shady walking paths.

King Christian IV built the Rosenborg Castle as a summer residence but loved it so much that he ended up living and dying there. In 1849, when the absolute monarchy was abolished, the royal castles became state property, except for Rosenborg, which is still passed down from monarch to monarch. Once a year, during the fall holiday, the castle stays open until midnight, and visitors are invited to explore its darkened interior with bicycle lights. ✉ *Øster Voldg. 4A,* ☎ *33/15–32–86.* 🖃 *Dkr 45.* ☉ *Jan.–Apr. and Nov.–Dec. Sun. 11–2; May—Sept., daily 10–4; Oct., daily 11–3.*

★ ③① **Rundetårn** (Round Tower). Instead of climbing the stout Round Tower's stairs, visitors scale a smooth, 600-ft spiral ramp on which—legend has it—Peter the Great of Russia rode a horse alongside his wife, Catherine, who took a carriage. From its top, you enjoy a panoramic view of the twisted streets and crooked roofs of Copenhagen. The unusual building was constructed as an observatory in 1642 by Christian IV and is still maintained as the oldest such structure in Europe.

The art gallery features changing exhibits, and occasional concerts are held within its massive stone walls. An observatory and telescope are open to the public evenings mid-October through March, and an astronomer is on hand to answer questions. ✉ *Købmagerg. 52A,* ☎ *33/73–03–73.* 🖃 *Dkr 15.* ☉ *June–Aug., Mon.–Sat. 10–8, Sun. noon–8; Jan.–May and Oct.–Dec., Mon.–Sat. 10–5, Sun. noon–5; Sept., daily 10–5. Observatory and telescope mid-Oct.–Mar., Tues.–Wed. 7 PM–10 PM.*

③④ **Statens Museum for Kunst** (National Art Gallery). Old Master paintings—including works by Rubens, Rembrandt, Titian, El Greco, and Fragonard—as well as a comprehensive array of old and 20th-century Danish art comprise the gallery collection. Also very notable is the modern foreign art, which includes pieces by a very small but select group of artists, including Henri Matisse, Edvard Munch, Henri Laurens, Emil Nolde, and Georges Braque. Massively renovated and expanded in 1999, the space also includes a children's museum, an amphitheater, a documentation center and study room, a bookstore, and a restaurant. A sculpture garden filled with classical, modern, and whimsical pieces flanks the building. ⊠ *Sølvg. 48–50*, ☎ *33/74–84–94*. ⊡ *Dkr 40 (free Wed.)* ⏱ *Tues. and Thurs.–Sun. 10–5, Wed. 10–8*.

★ ☚ ㊱ **Tivoli.** Copenhagen's best-known attraction, conveniently next to its main train station, attracts an astounding number of visitors: 4 million people from May to September. Tivoli is more sophisticated than a mere funfair; among its attractions are a pantomime theater, open-air stage, elegant restaurants (24 in all), and frequent classical, jazz, and rock concerts. Fantastic flower exhibits color the lush gardens and float on the swan-filled ponds.

On Wednesday and weekend nights, elaborate fireworks are set off, and every day the Tivoli Guard, a youth version of the Queen's Royal Guard, performs. Try to see Tivoli at least once by night, when 100,000 colored lanterns illuminate the Chinese pagoda and the main fountain. The park was established in the 1840s, when Danish architect George Carstensen persuaded a worried King Christian VIII to let him build an amusement park on the edge of the city's fortifications, rationalizing that "when people amuse themselves, they forget politics." Call to double-check prices, which include family discounts at various times during the day. Tivoli is also open two weeks preceding Christmas. ⊠ *Vesterbrog. 3*, ☎ *33/15–10–01*. ⏱ *Dkr 45*.

☚ ㊳ **Tycho Brahe Planetarium.** This modern, cylindrical planetarium, which appears to be sliced at an angle, features astronomy exhibits. The **Omnimax Theater** takes you on visual odysseys as varied as journeys through space and sea, the stages of the Rolling Stones, or Kuwaiti fires from the Persian Gulf War. These films are not recommended for children under seven. ⊠ *Gammel Kongevej 10*, ☎ *33/12–12–24*. ⊡ *Dkr 68*. ⏱ *Show times vary. Open Mon., Wed., and Fri.–Sun. 10:30–9, Tues. and Thurs. 9:45–9*.

㊴ **Vesterbro.** Copenhagen's equivalent of New York's Lower East Side is populated by immigrants, students, and union workers. It's a great place to find ethnic groceries, discount shops, and cheap international restaurants. ⊠ *At the southern end of Vesterbrogade*.

㉘ **Vor Frue Kirken** (Church of Our Lady). Copenhagen's cathedral since 1924 occupies a site that has drawn worshipers since the 13th century, when Bishop Absalon built a chapel here. Today's church is actually a reconstruction: the original church was destroyed during the Napoleonic Wars. Five towers top the neoclassical structure. Inside you can see Thorvaldsen's marble sculptures depicting Christ and the 12 Apostles, and Moses and David, cast of bronze. ⊠ *Nørreg., Frue Pl.*, ☎ *33/15–10–78*. ⊡ *Free*. ⏱ *Call for hrs*.

....

OFF THE
BEATEN PATH

ZOOLOGISKE HAVE – Kids love the Zoological Gardens, home to more than 2,000 animals. In the small petting zoo and playground live cows, horses, rabbits, goats, and hens. The indoor rain forest is abuzz with butterflies, sloths, alligators, and other tropical creatures. Sea lions, lions, and elephants are fed in the early afternoon. Be warned: On sunny weekends, the line to enter runs far down Rosildevej; get here early. ⊠ *Roskildevej 32*, ☎ *36/30–20–01*. ⊡ *Dkr 65*. ⏱ *June–Aug., daily 9–6; Sept.–Oct. and Apr.–May, daily 9–5; Nov.–Mar., daily 9–4*.

....

DINING

In the more than 2,000 restaurants in Copenhagen, traditional Danish fare spans all price categories: you can order a light lunch of traditional smørrebrød, munch alfresco from a street-side *pølser* (sausage) cart, or dine out on Limfjord oysters and local plaice. Even the most upscale restaurants have moderate-price fixed menus. Though few Danish restaurants require reservations, it's best to call ahead to avoid a wait. The city's more affordable ethnic restaurants are concentrated in Vesterbro, Nørrebro, and the side streets off Strøget. And for less-expensive, savory noshes in stylish digs, consider lingering at a café (☞ Cafés *in* Nightlife and the Arts, *below*).

Rådhus Pladsen, Christiansborg Slot, and Strøget

$$$$ ✕ **Gyldne Fortun's Fiskekælldere.** Among the city's finest seafood restaurants, this "fish cellar" is brightly decorated with seashell-shaded halogen lamps and aquariums. Across the street from Christiansborg, it is popular with politicians as well as businesspeople. Try the fillets of Scandinavian sole poached in white wine, stuffed with salmon mousseline, glazed with hollandaise, and served with prawns. ⊠ *Ved Stranden 18,* ☎ *33/12–20–11. Reservations essential. AE, DC, MC, V. No lunch weekends.*

$$$$ ✕ **Kong Hans Kælder.** Five centuries ago this was a Nordic vineyard—
★   now it's one of Scandinavia's finest restaurants. Chef Thomas Rode Andersen's French-Danish-Asian–inspired dishes employ the freshest local ingredients and are served in a mysterious subterranean space with whitewashed walls and vaulted ceilings. Try the foie gras with raspberry-vinegar sauce or the warm oysters with salmon roe. Jackets are recommended. ⊠ *Vingårdstr. 6,* ☎ *33/11–68–68. AE, DC, MC, V. Closed Sun. and Mon. in June, July, and Aug.; the last two weeks in July, and Easter week. No lunch.*

$$$$ ✕ **Krogs.** This elegant canal-front restaurant has developed a loyal clien-
★   tele—both foreign and local—for its old-fashioned atmosphere and its innovative fish dishes. Pale-green walls are simply adorned with paintings of old Copenhagen to create an understated ambience. The menu includes such specialties as pan-grilled lobster flavored with vanilla oil and monkfish fillets in a beurre-blanc sauce flavored with arugula and tomato. Jackets are recommended. ⊠ *Gammel Strand 38,* ☎ *33/15–89–15. Reservations essential. AE, DC, MC, V. Closed Sun.*

$$$$ ✕ **Skt. Gertrudes Kloster.** The history of this medieval monastery goes back 700 years, and from the beginning its vaulted stone interiors have welcomed tradesmen and wayfarers. The dining room is bedecked with hundreds of icons, and the only light is provided by 2,000 candles. The French menu is extensive, with such specials as fresh fillet of halibut steamed in oyster sauce and l'Alsace duck breast in a sherry vinaigrette. A jacket and tie are recommended. ⊠ *32 Hauser Pl.,* ☎ *33/14–66–30. Reservations essential. AE, DC, MC, V. No lunch.*

$$ ✕ **Copenhagen Corner.** Diners here are treated to a superb view of the Rådhus Pladsen, as well as to terrific smørrebrød, both of which compensate for the uneven pace of the often-harried but hard-working staff. Specialties include fried veal with bouillon gravy and fried potatoes; entrecôte in garlic and bordelaise sauce paired with creamed potatoes; and a herring plate with three types of spiced marinated herring and boiled potatoes. ⊠ *H. C. Andersens Boulevard 1A,* ☎ *33/91–45–45. AE, DC, MC, V.*

$$ ✕ **El Meson.** At Copenhagen's best Spanish restaurant, you are seated at smoothly worn wooden tables in a dimly lit dining room hung with earthen crockery. The waitstaff is knowledgeable and serves generous

26

Dining
Copenhagen Corner, **27**
El Meson, **6**
Els, **11**
Flyvefisken, **21**
Gyldne Fortun's Fiskekældere, **26**
Ida Davidsen, **9**
Kashmir, **3**
Kommandanten, **17**
Kong Hans Kælder, **25**
Konrads, **18**
Krogs, **24**
L'Alsace, **19**
Peder Oxe, **20**
Pussy Galore's Flying Circus, **2**
Restaurant Le St. Jacques, **8**
Riz Raz, **22**
Sebastopol, **1**
Skt. Gertrudes Kloster, **5**
Victor, **15**
Wiinblad, **16**
Zeleste, **13**

Lodging
Ascot, **31**
Cab–Inn Scandinavia, **4**
Copenhagen Admiral, **14**
Copenhagen Danhostel, **32**
D'Angleterre, **16**
Kong Frederik, **23**
Missionhotellet Nebo, **30**
Neptun, **12**
Nyhavn 71, **26**
Phoenix, **10**
Plaza, **29**
Radisson SAS Scandinavia, **33**
Skovshoved, **7**
Triton, **28**

Copenhagen Dining and Lodging

Langeliniebr. **7** **8**

Dag Hammarskjölds Al.

Kristianiag.

Østbaneg.

Folke Bernadottes Al.

Østerport Station

Oslo Plads

St. Kongensg.

Grønningen

Churchill-parken

Forbindelsesv.

Langelinie

Yderhavn

Esplanaden

Stockholmsg.

Øster Anlæg

Rigensg.

Sølvg.

Fredericiag.

Bredgade

Amalieg.

Kongens Have

Kronprincessg.

Store Kongensg.

Dronningens Tværg. **9**

Adelg.

Borgerg.

Bredgade

10

Sankt Annæ Plads

Amalieg.

Amalieg.

Toldbodg.

Gothersg.

magerg. Gammelmønt

Ny Østerg. **17**

18 **15** Kongens

19 **16** Nytorv

Kr. Berning.

Bremerholm

11 **13** **12**

Nyhavn

Nyhavn Canal **14**

Inderhavn

HOLMEN

LMEN

rv

Østerg.

gertorv

Højbro

arstr.

24

mmel Strand

26

Heibergsg.

Holmenskanal

Holmenskanal

25

Holbergsg.

Havnegade

Christiansborg Slotsplads

Tøjhusgade

Børsg.

Chr. IV's Bro

Knippelsbro

CHRISTIANSHAVN

Sankt Annæ

Christians Brygge

hsholms
nal

Torveg.

Dronningensg.

Prinsessg.

Christianshavns Voldg.

Amagerbrog

Langebro

Langerbrog.

33
32 Amager Blvd

Stadsgraven

Vermlandsg.

portions of beef spiced with spearmint, lamb with honey sauce, and paella Valenciano—a mixture of rice, chicken, ham, shrimp, lobster, squid, green beans, and peas—for two. ⊠ *Hauser Pl. 12 (behind Kultorvet),* ☎ *33/11–91–31. AE, DC, MC, V. Closed Sun. No lunch.*

$$ ✕ **Peder Oxe.** On a 17th-century square, this lively, countrified bistro has rustic tables and 15th-century Portuguese tiles. All entrées—among them grilled steaks and fish and the best fancy burgers in town–come with an excellent self-service salad bar replete with whole tomatoes, feta cheese, and fresh greens. Damask-covered tables are set with heavy cutlery and opened bottles of hearty Pyrénées wine. A clever call-light for the waitress is above each table. In spring, when the high Northern sun is shining but the warmth still has not kicked in, you won't do badly sitting outside in the Gråbrødretorv (Grey Friars' Square) sipping drinks while wrapped in blankets left thoughtfully for patrons in wicker chairs. ⊠ *Gråbrødretorv 11,* ☎ *33/11–00–77. D, MC, V.*

$ ✕ **Flyvefisken.** Silvery stenciled fish swim along blue-and-yellow walls in this funky Thai eatery. Spicy concoctions include chicken with cashew nuts, and herring shark in basil sauce. The less-expensive health-food café Atlas Bar—in the basement—serves excellent food to a steady stream of students and hipsters. ⊠ *Lars Bjørnstr. 18,* ☎ *33/ 14–95–15. DC, MC, V. Closed Sun.*

$ ✕ **Riz Raz.** On a corner off Strøget, this Middle Eastern restaurant hops with young locals, families, couples, and anyone who appreciates good value and spicy fare. The inexpensive all-you-can-eat buffet is heaped with lentils, tomatoes, potatoes, olives, hummus, warm pita bread, *kufte* (Middle Eastern meatballs), yogurt and cucumbers, pickled vegetables, bean salads, and occasionally pizza. Don't be put off by the hordes— just join them, either in the restaurant's endless labyrinth of dining rooms or in the jam-packed summertime patio. ⊠ *Kompagnistr. 20,* ☎ *33/ 15–05–75. Reservations essential. DC, MC, V.*

Around Amalienborg and North

$$$ ✕ **Els.** When it opened in 1853, the intimate Els was the place to be seen before the theater, and the painted Muses on the walls still watch diners rush to make an eight o'clock curtain. Antique wooden columns complement the period furniture, including tables inlaid with Royal Copenhagen tile work. Chef Jens Larsen changes his nouvelle French-Danish four-course menu every two weeks, always incorporating game, fish, and market produce. Jackets are recommended. ⊠ *Store Strandestr. 3,* ☎ *33/14–13–41. AE, DC, MC, V. Closed Sun. lunch and July.*

$$$ ✕ **Kommandanten.** Fancifully decorated by master florist Tage Andersen
★   with brushed iron and copper furniture, down pillows, and foliage-flanked lights, this is among the city's most exclusive dinner spots, attracting well-heeled businesspeople and local celebrities—as well as two Michelin stars. The adventuresome international fare might include dishes like rabbit with bouillon-cooked lentils, herbs, and bacon, and marinated salmon with oysters and parsley. Jackets are recommended. ⊠ *Ny Adelg. 7,* ☎ *33/12–09–90. AE, DC, MC, V. Closed Sun. No lunch Sat.*

$$$ ✕ **Konrads.** Elegant and minimalist, this restaurant attracts young
★   people and stars, many of whom look like they just walked off a fashion runway. Considering its beige and linear decor, the restaurant seems as geared for people-watching as dining. The French-international menu is inventive without being off-the-wall, with offerings like potato tortellini filled with oysters and white cream sauce. Stick with the pasta and water and you might make it out of here without breaking the bank. *Pilestræde 12–14,* ☎ *33/93–29–29. Reservations essential. AE, DC, MC, V. Closed Sun.*

$$$ ✕ **L'Alsace.** Set in the cobbled courtyard of Pistolstræde and hung with
★ paintings by Danish surrealist Wilhelm Freddie, this restaurant is
peaceful and quiet, attracting such diverse diners as Queen Margrethe,
Elton John, and Pope Paul II. The hand-drawn menu lists oysters from
Brittany, terrine de foie gras, and *choucrôute à la Strasbourgeoise* (a
hearty mélange of cold cabbage, homemade sausage, and pork). Try
the superb fresh-fruit tarts and cakes for dessert, and ask to sit in the
patio overlooking the courtyard. ✉ *Ny Østerg. 9,* ☎ *33/14–57–43.
AE, DC, MC, V. Closed Sun.*

$$$ ✕ **Wiinblad.** This restaurant doubles as a gallery inspired by the work
of contemporary Danish artist Bjørn Wiinblad. Almost everything—
tiles, wall partitions, plaques, candlesticks, vases, and even some tables—has been made by the great Dane, and the effect is bright,
cheerful, and very elegant. The eatery offers an ample breakfast buffet, lunch, tea—fabulous and surprisingly affordable for a sweets' buffet and a cuppa, and grilled specialties for dinner. Try the pickled
herring with new potatoes and topped with sour cream, or the breast
of duck in cranberry cream sauce. It's in the D'Angleterre hotel (☞
Lodging, *below*). ✉ *D'Angleterre, Kongens Nytorv 34,* ☎ *33/12–80–
95. AE, DC, MC, V.*

$$ ✕ **Ida Davidsen.** Five generations old, this world-renowned lunch spot
is synonymous with smørrebrød. Dimly lit, with worn wooden tables
and news clippings of famous visitors, it's usually packed. Creative sand-
wiches include the H. C. Andersen, with liver pâté, bacon, and toma-
toes, and the airplane clipper—steak tartare shaped like a plane and
topped with caviar, smoked salmon, and egg yolk. You'll also enjoy a
terrific smoked duck that Ida's husband, Adam, smokes himself and
serves alongside a horseradish-spiked cabbage salad. ✉ *Store Kongensg.
70,* ☎ *33/91–36–55. Reservations essential. DC, MC, V. Closed week-
ends and July. No dinner.*

$$ ✕ **Restaurant Le St. Jacques.** This tiny restaurant barely accommodates
★ a dozen tables, but as soon as the sun shines, diners spill out of its icon-
filled dining room to sit at tables facing busy Østerbrogade. The chef
and owners come from some of the finest restaurants in town, but claim
they started this place to slow down the pace and enjoy the company
of their customers. The fare changes according to what is available at
the market, but expect fabulous concoctions—smoked salmon with
crushed eggplant, Canadian scallops with leeks and salmon roe in a
beurre blanc sauce, sole with basil sauce and reduced balsamic glaze,
and a savory *poussin* (young, small chicken) with sweetbreads scooped
into phyllo pastry atop a bed of polenta and lentils. Close tables and
chitchat with the owners give this a true café atmosphere. ✉ *Skt. Ja-
cobs Pl. 1,* ☎ *31/42–77–07. Reservations essential. DC, MC, V.*

$$ ✕ **Victor.** Excellent people-watching and good bistro fare are the call-
ing cards at this French-style corner café. It's best during weekend lunches,
when young and old gather for such specialties as rib roast, homemade
pâté, and smoked salmon and cheese platters. Come here for one of
the best brunches in town. Be warned, however, that the formal restau-
rant in the back of the space is quite expensive—order from the front
café side for a more inexpensive meal. ✉ *Ny Østerg. 8,* ☎ *33/13–36–
13. AE, DC, MC, V.*

$$ ✕ **Zeleste.** Zeleste is refreshingly proud to specialize in "con-fusion"
gastronomy. Outfitted with a short but well-worn bar, a covered and
heated atrium, and—upstairs—a u-shape dining room, it serves as a
soothing respite to Nyhavn's canal-front party. Although the food is
usually excellent, if you're ravenous, ask specifically about portions—
otherwise, you could end up with some tiny slivers of fried fois gras
or a few tortellini. For lunch, the famished will do well with either the
focaccia sandwich or the lobster salad served with toast and an excellent

roux dressing; if the latter is not at your table within five minutes, you get a free glass of champagne. ⊠ *Store Strandstræde 6,* ☎ *33/16–06–06. AE, DC, MC, V.*

Down Vesterbrogade and Nørrebro

$ ✕ **Kashmir.** This quiet, carpet-shrouded Indian restaurant is a favorite with locals, who come for the unusual vegetarian and fish menu. Specialties include tandoori-fried salmon, a hearty lentil soup, and the basic side dishes—such as *bhajis* (fried vegetables in tomato sauce), *raita* (yogurt and cucumbers), and nan, the thick round bread. ⊠ *Nørrebrog. 35,* ☎ *35/37–54–71. AE, MC, V.*

$ ✕ **Pussy Galore's Flying Circus.** Done up with a few Arne Jacobsen swan chairs, naive wall paintings, and tables smashed up against each other, this trendy gathering place is supposed to be as kitsch as its name. While the mix of decor is retro and does a good job of setting a '60s stage, the regulars who come here make it feel more like a low-key neighborhood bar. Frequented by both young families and black-clad poseurs, this place serves surprisingly down-to-earth and affordable fare, with eggs and bacon and other brunchy items along with hefty burgers and wok-fried delectables. *Skt. Hans Torv,* ☎ *35/24–53–00. AE, MC.*

$ ✕ **Sebastopol.** This laid-back eatery gets very crowded for brunch and weekend evenings, but, like its neighbor Pussy Galore, it's a good choice for visitors who want to get off the beaten tourist path. Populated by students and a local clientele, the menu is varied with lots of salads, warm sandwiches, and burgers—and just about the most American-style brunch in the city. When it's warm, tables are set outside on the square, where there's great people-watching. *Skt. Hans Torv,* ☎ *35/24–53–00. Reservations not accepted. MC, V.*

LODGING

Copenhagen is well served by a wide range of hotels, overall among Europe's most expensive. The hotels around the seedy red-light district of Istedgade—which looks more dangerous than it is—are the least expensive. In summer, reservations are recommended, but should you arrive without one, try the hotel booking desk in the tourist office. They can give you a same-day, last-minute price (if available) for about Dkr 300–Dkr 400 for a single hotel room. This service will also find rooms in private homes, with rates starting at about Dkr 200 for a single. Young travelers should head for **Huset** (⊠ Rådhusstr. 13, ☎ 33/15–65–18). Breakfast is included in the room rate and rooms have bath or shower at the following hotels unless otherwise noted.

Rådhus Pladsen, Christiansborg Slot, and Strøget

$$$$ ⌧ **Radisson SAS Scandinavia.** Near the airport, this is one of northern Europe's largest hotels, and Copenhagen's token skyscraper. An immense lobby, with cool, recessed lighting and streamlined furniture, gives access to the city's first (and only) casino. Guest rooms are large and somewhat institutional but offer every modern convenience, making this a good choice if you prefer convenience over character. Breakfast is not included in the rates. Last year, the hotel opened the Top of Town restaurant and wine bar, which overlooks the copper towers and skyline of Copenhagen. ⊠ *Amager Boulevarden 70, DK–2300 KBH S,* ☎ *33/96–50–00,* ⅨⅩ *33/96–55–00. 542 rooms, 52 suites. 4 restaurants, bar, room service, indoor pool, health club, casino, concierge, meeting rooms, free parking. AE, DC, MC, V.*

In case you want to see the world.

At American Express, we're here to make your journey a smooth one. So we have over 1,700 travel service locations in over 130 countries ready to help. What else would you expect from the world's largest travel agency?

do more

Travel

Call 1 800 AXP-3429 or visit
www.americanexpress.com/travel

In case you want to be welcomed there.

We're here to see that you're always welcomed at establishments everywhere. That's why millions of people carry the American Express® Card – for peace of mind, confidence, and security, around the world or just around the corner.

do more AMERICAN EXPRESS

Cards

In case you're running low.

We're here to help with more than 190,000 Express Cash locations around the world. In order to enroll, just call American Express at 1 800 CASH-NOW before you start your vacation.

do more AMERICAN EXPRESS®

Express Cash

And in case you'd rather be safe than sorry.

We're here with American Express® Travelers Cheques. They're the safe way to carry money on your vacation, because if they're ever lost or stolen you can get a refund, practically anywhere or anytime. To find the nearest place to buy Travelers Cheques, call 1 800 495-1153. Another way we help you do more.

do more

Travelers
Cheques

$$$ ⊞ **Kong Frederik.** North of Rådhus Pladsen and a two-minute walk from Strøget, this intimate hotel has the same British style as its sister hotel, the D'Angleterre (☞ *above*). The difference is the sun-drenched Queen's Restaurant, where a hearty morning buffet is served (not included in rates) in addition to lunch and dinner. The rooms are elegant, in English Colonial–style, with Asian vases, mauve carpets, and blue bedspreads. Ask for a top room for tower views. ⊠ *Vester Voldg. 25, DK–1552 KBH V,* ☎ *33/12–59–02,* FAX *33/93–59–01. 110 rooms, 13 suites. Restaurant, bar, room service, meeting rooms, free parking. AE, DC, MC, V.*

$$ ⊞ **Ascot.** This charming downtown hotel's two outstanding features are a wrought-iron staircase and an excellent breakfast buffet. The lobby is classic, with marble and columns, but the guest rooms and apartments are comfy, with modern furniture and bright colors; some have kitchenettes. If you're going to be staying a weekend, be aware that the nearby club, Pumpehuset, blasts music until the wee hours; at least make sure your room doesn't face it. ⊠ *Studiestr. 61, DK–1554 KBH V,* ☎ *33/12–60–00,* FAX *33/14–60–40. 155 rooms, 30 apartments. Restaurant, bar, exercise room, meeting rooms, free parking. AE, DC, MC, V.*

$ ⊞ **Copenhagen Danhostel.** This simple lodging is 4½ km (3 mi) outside of town, close to the airport. The hostel is spread over nine interconnecting buildings, all laid out on one floor. International Youth Hostel members—including student backpackers as well as families—use the communal kitchen, or buy breakfast and dinner from the restaurant. The hostel is also wheelchair-accessible. Before 5 PM on weekdays, take Bus 46 from the main station directly to the hostel. After 5, from Rådhus Pladsen or the main station, take Bus 10 to Mozartplads, and change to Bus 37. Ask the driver to signal your stop. ⊠ *Vejlands All 200, DK–2300 KBH S,* ☎ *32/52–29–08,* FAX *32/52–27–08. 64 rooms with 2 beds, 80 family rooms with 5 beds, 4 large communal bathrooms. Restaurant. No credit cards.*

Around Amalienborg and North

$$$$ ⊞ **D'Angleterre.** The grande dame of Copenhagen welcomes royalty
★   and rock stars—from Margaret Thatcher to Madonna—in palatial surroundings: an imposing New Georgian facade leads into an English-style sitting room. Standard guest rooms are furnished in pastels, with overstuffed chairs and modern and antique furniture. The spit-and-polish staff accommodates every wish. Breakfast is not included. ⊠ *Kongens Nytorv 34, DK–1050 KBH K,* ☎ *33/12–00–95,* FAX *33/12–11–18. 130 rooms, 28 suites. 2 restaurants, bar, room service, indoor pool, nightclub, concierge, meeting rooms, parking (fee). AE, DC, MC, V.*

$$$$ ⊞ **Nyhavn 71.** In a 200-year-old warehouse, this quiet, soothing, and
★   freshly renovated hotel is a good choice for privacy-seekers. It overlooks the old ships of Nyhavn, and its nautical interiors have been preserved with their original thick plaster walls and exposed brick. The rooms are tiny but cozy, with warm woolen spreads, dark woods, soft leather furniture, and crisscrossing timbers. Breakfast is not included. ⊠ *Nyhavn 71, DK–1051 KBH K,* ☎ *33/11–85–85,* FAX *33/93–15–85. 84 rooms, 6 suites. Restaurant, bar, room service, concierge, meeting rooms, free parking. AE, DC, MC, V.*

$$$ ⊞ **Neptun.** This elegant, central hotel was bought years ago with the intention of making it the bohemian gathering place of Copenhagen, but these days it is more practical than artsy and welcomes business guests, tourists, and even large tour groups. The lobby and lounge are light, with classical furnishings and pale tones, and guest rooms have

a tasteful modern decor. Many rooms face an interior covered courtyard. Next door is a regional Danish restaurant. ⊠ *Skt. Annæ Pl. 14–
20, DK–1250 KBH K,* ☎ *33/13–89–00,* ℻ *33/14–12–50. (In the U.S.,
call Best Western, 800/528–1234.) 133 rooms, 13 suites. Restaurant,
room service, meeting rooms, free parking. AE, DC, MC, V.*

$$$ 🏨 **Phoenix.** This luxury hotel has automatic glass doors, crystal chan-
deliers, and gilt touches everywhere. The staff is multilingual and adept
at accommodating both a business and tourist clientele. The suites and
business-class rooms are adorned with faux antiques and 18-carat
gold-plate bathroom fixtures, whereas the standard rooms are very small,
measuring barely 9 by 15 ft. It's so convenient to central-city attrac-
tions that the hotel gets a certain amount of street noise; light sleep-
ers should ask for rooms above the second floor. ⊠ *Bredg. 37, DK–
1260 KBH K,* ☎ *33/95–95–00,* ℻ *33/33–98–33. 212 rooms, 7 suites.
Restaurant, pub (closed Sun.), meeting room. AE, DC, MC, V.*

$$$ 🏨 **Skovshoved.** This delightful, art-filled inn is 8 km (5 mi) north of
town, near a few old fishing cottages beside the yacht harbor. Licensed
since 1660, it has retained its provincial charm. Its larger rooms overlook the sea, smaller ones rim the courtyard; all have both modern and
antique furnishings. ⊠ *Strandvejen 267, DK–2920 Charlottelund,* ☎
39/64–00–28, ℻ *39/64–06–72. 20 rooms. Restaurant, bar, meeting
room. AE, DC, MC, V.*

$$ 🏨 **Copenhagen Admiral.** A five-minute stroll from Nyhavn, over-
looking old Copenhagen and Amalienborg, the monolithic Admiral was
once a grain warehouse but now affords travelers no-nonsense ac-
commodations. With massive stone walls—broken by rows of tiny win-
dows—it's one of the less expensive top hotels, cutting frills and prices.
Its guest rooms are spare, with jutting beams and modern prints. ⊠
Toldbodg. 24–28, DK–1253 KBH K, ☎ *33/11–82–82,* ℻ *33/32–55–
42. 366 rooms, 52 suites. Restaurant, bar, sauna, nightclub, meeting
rooms, free parking. AE, DC, MC, V.*

Down Vesterbrogade and Nørrebro

$$$ 🏨 **Plaza.** With its convenient location and plush homey atmosphere,
this hotel attracts the likes of Tina Turner and Keith Richards. Close
to Tivoli and the main station, the building opens with a stately lobby
and the adjacent Russian restaurant, Alexander Nevski, with one of
the best vodka selections in town. The older rooms are scattered with
antiques; newer ones are furnished in a more modern style. The Library
Bar is an elegantly cozy and atmospheric place for a drink, but the prices
can be staggering. ⊠ *Bernstorffsg. 4, DK–1577 KBH V,* ☎ *33/14–92–
62,* ℻ *33/93–93–62. 93 rooms, 6 suites. Restaurant, bar, room service,
concierge, meeting rooms, parking (fee). AE, DC, MC, V.*

$$ 🏨 **Triton.** Despite seedy surroundings, this streamlined hotel attracts a
cosmopolitan clientele thanks to a central location in Vesterbro. The large
rooms, in blond wood and warm tones, all include modern bathrooms
and state-of-the-art fixtures. The buffet breakfast is exceptionally gen-
erous, the staff friendly. There are also family rooms, with a bedroom
and a dining-sitting area with a foldout couch. ⊠ *Helgolandsg. 7–11,
DK–1653 KBH V,* ☎ *33/31–32–66,* ℻ *33/31–69–70. 123 rooms, 2
suites, 4 family rooms. Bar, meeting room. AE, DC, MC, V.*

$ 🏨 **Cab–Inn Scandinavia.** This bright hotel is just west of the lakes and
Vesterport Station. Its impeccably maintained rooms are distinctly
small, but designed with superefficiency to include ample showers, stow-
away and bunk beds, and even electric water kettles. The hotel is pop-
ular with business travelers in winter and kroner-pinching backpackers
and families in summer. Its sister hotel, the **Cab–Inn Copenhagen** (☎
33/21–04–00, ℻ *33/21–74–09)* is just around the corner, at Danasvej

32–34, but it's only open between April and September. ✉ *Vodroffsvej 55–57, DK–1900 Frederiksberg C,* ☎ *35/36–11–11,* FAX *35/36–11–14. 201 rooms. Breakfast room, snack bar, exercise room, meeting rooms. AE, DC, MC, V.*

$ 🖭 **Missionhotellet Nebo.** Though it's between the main train station and Istedgade's seediest porn shops, this budget hotel is still prim, comfortable, and well maintained by a friendly staff. Its dormlike guest rooms, of which fewer than half have a bathrom, are furnished with industrial carpeting, polished pine furniture, and plain duvet covers. Baths, showers, and toilets are at the center of each hallway, and downstairs there's a sunny breakfast restaurant with a tiny courtyard. ✉ *Istedg. 6, DK–1650 KBH V,* ☎ *33/21–12–17,* FAX *33/23–47–74. 96 rooms, 40 with bath. AE, DC, MC, V.*

NIGHTLIFE AND THE ARTS

Nightlife

Most nightlife is concentrated in the area in and around Strøget, though there are student and "leftist" cafés and bars in Nørrebro and more upscale spots in Østerbro. Many restaurants, cafés, bars, and clubs stay open after midnight, a few until 5 AM. Copenhagen used to be famous for jazz, but unfortunately that has changed in recent years, with many of the best clubs closing down. However, you'll find nightspots catering to almost all musical tastes, from bop to ballroom music—and for the younger crowd, house, rap, and techno—in trendy clubs soundtracked by local DJs. The area around Nikolaj Kirken has the highest concentration of trendy discos and dance spots.

Bars and Lounges

Peder Oxe's basement (✉ Gråbrødretorv 11, ☎ 33/11–11–93) is casual and young, though nearly impossible to squeeze into on weekends. The **Library,** in the Plaza (✉ 4 Bernstorffsg., ☎ 33/14–92–62), is an elegant spot for a quiet but pricey drink. The more than 270-year-old **Hviids Vinstue** (✉ Kongens Nytorv 19, ☎ 33/15–10–64) attracts all kinds, young and old, single and coupled, for a glass of wine or cognac. **Bang og Jensen**(✉ Istegade 130, ☎ 33/25–53–18) in the spotty-but-becoming-gentrified Vesterbro neighborhood, is a regular café during the day. From 9 PM till 2 AM, however, it turns into a cocktail bar jamming with loud music and a disco ambience.

Cafés

Café life appeared in Copenhagen in the '70s and quickly became a compulsory part of its urban existence. The cheapest sit-down eateries in town, where a cappuccino and sandwich often cost less than Dkr 60, cafés are lively and relaxed at night, the crowd always interesting. **Café Sommersko** (✉ Kronprinsensg. 6, ☎ 33/14–81–89) is the granddaddy, with a surprisingly varied menu (try the delicious french fries with pesto or the wok specialties) and an eclectic crowd. **Krasnapolsky** (✉ Vesterg. 10, ☎ 33/32–88–00) packs a young, hip, and painfully well-dressed audience at night, a more mixed group for its quiet afternoons. **Café Dan Turrell** (✉ Skt. Regneg. 3, ☎ 33/14–10–47), another old café, as of late has become terribly chic with good food and candlelight. **Victors Café** (✉ Ny Østerg. 8, ☎ 33/13–36–13) is all brass and dark wood, lovely for a light lunch. At the chic **Europa** (✉ Amagertorv 1, ☎ 33/14–28–09), people-watching and coffee naturally go together. The juncture of Købmagergade and Strøget marks the Art Nouveau–style **Café Norden** (✉ Østerg. 61, ☎ 33/11–77–91), where substantial portions make up for minimal table space. **Bjørg's** (✉ Vester Voldgade 19, ☎ 33/14–53–20) is a newcomer to the scene, but it's also one of the best, with a zinc bar, red seating, and lots of large windows where guests slouch over huge burgers, club sandwiches, and excellent coffees. **Juice & Java** (⊠ Kronprinsensgade 11, ☎ 33/16–21–23) is a fresh place to either pick up or sit down and enjoy fresh-pressed juices mixed with yogurt, bagels, sandwiches, and excellent homemade cakes. **Amokko Kaffehus** (⊠ Dag Hammarsjolds Allé 38-40, ☎ 35/25–35–36), about a ten-minute walk from the Østerport train station, is a coffee-lover's dream café, with specialty java served alongside inventive sandwiches and salads. On Nørrebro's main square, Skt. Hans Torv, the all-in-one rock club-restaurant-café **Rust** (⊠ Guldbergsg. 8, ☎ 35/24–52–00) is packed all the time. Hearty, fresh dishes are served inside, and there's grill food served outside on the terrace. Come evening, **Sebastopol** (⊠ Skt. Hans Torv 2, ☎ 35/36–30–02) is packed with gussied-up locals; sample the ample weekend brunch.

Casino

The **Casino Copenhagen** at the SAS Scandinavia (⊠ Amager Boulevarden 70, ☎ 33/11–51–15) has American and French roulette, blackjack, baccarat, and slot machines. Admission is Dkr 80 (you must be 18 years old and show a photo ID), and a dress code (jackets required and no sportswear or jeans) is enforced. The casino is open 2 PM to 4 AM.

Discos and Dancing

Most discos open at 11 PM, have cover charges of about Dkr 40, and pile on steep drink prices. Among the most enduring clubs is **Woodstock** (⊠ Vesterg. 12, ☎ 33/11–20–71), where a mixed audience grooves to '50s to '80s music. The very popular English-style **Rosie McGees** (⊠ Vesterbrog. 2A, ☎ 33/32–19–23) pub serves American and Mexican eats and dancing. At the fashionable **Park Café** (⊠ Østerbrog. 79, ☎ 35/26–63–42), there's an old-world café with live music downstairs, a disco upstairs, and a movie theater next door. The lively **Club Absalon** (⊠ Frederiksbergg. 38, ☎ 33/16–16–98), popular with folks in uniforms (policemen, soldiers, and nurses among them), has live music on the ground floor and a disco above. **Søpavillionen** (⊠ Gyldenløvesg. 24, ☎ 33/15–12–24), between St. Jørgen's and Peblinge lakes, glows white on the outside; within there's pop and disco on Friday and Saturday night for an older crowd. At the **Røde Pimpernel** (⊠ Kattesundet 4, ☎ 33/12–20–32), an adult audience gathers for dancing to live orchestras, trios, and old-time music. **Sabor Latino** (⊠ Løngestræde 39, ☎ 33/11–97–66) is the United Nations of discos, with an international crowd dancing to salsa and other Latin rhythms.

Gay Bars

Women and men pack **Pan Club**'s (⊠ Knabrostr. 3, off Strøget, ☎ 33/11–37–84) with three floors of coffee and cocktail bars; the disco's open Wednesday through Saturday night (Dkr 40 cover). The **Amigo Bar** (⊠ Schønbergsg. 4, ☎ 33/21–49–15) serves light meals and is popular with men of all ages. Much larger is the mammoth **Club Amigo** (⊠ Studiestr. 31A, ☎ 33/15–33–32), which includes an indoor pool and sauna, as well as a disco, GeO2. The dark, casual **Cosy Bar** (⊠ Studiestr. 24, ☎ 33/12–74–27) is the place to go in the wee hours (it usually stays open until 8 AM). **Sebastian Bar Café** (⊠ Hyskenstr. 10, ☎ 33/32–22–79) is relaxed for a drink or coffee, and is among the best cafés in town, with art exhibits upstairs and a bulletin board downstairs.

The small **Central Hjørnen** (⊠ Kattesundet 18, ☎ 33/11–85–49) has been around for about 70 years. **Masken** (⊠ Studiestr. 33, ☎ 33/91–09–37) is a relaxed bar welcoming both men and women. The cozy lesbian café **Babooshka** (⊠ Turesensg. 9, ☎ 33/15–05–36) also welcomes men. **Hotel Windsor** (⊠ Frederiksborgg. 30, ☎ 33/11–08–30,

FAX 33/11–63–87) is a gay-friendly hotel that doubles as a great breakfast greasy spoon. The men-only **Men's Bar** (✉ Teglgaardstraede 3, ☎
33/12–73–03) is dark and casual, with a leather and rubber dress
code. It's easy to meet mostly men at **Can Can** (✉ Mikkel Bryggesg.
11, ☎ 33/11–50–10), a small place with a friendly bartender.

For more information, call or visit the **Landsforeningen for Bøsser og
Lesbiske** (Gay and Lesbian Association, ✉ Teglgaardstr. 13, Boks
1023, 1007 KBH K, ☎ 33/13–19–48), which has a library and more
than 45 years of experience. Check out the free paper *Panbladet* for
listings of nightlife events and clubs.

Jazz Clubs

Hard times have thinned Copenhagen's once-thriving jazz scene.
Among the clubs still open, most headline local talents, but European
and international artists also perform, especially in July, when the
Copenhagen Jazz Festival spills over into the clubs. **La Fontaine** (✉ Kompagnistr. 11, ☎ 33/11–60–98) is Copenhagen's quintessential jazz
dive, with sagging curtains, impenetrable smoke, and lounge lizards.
Copenhagen Jazz House (✉ Niels Hemmingsensg. 10, ☎ 33/15–26–
00) is infinitely more upscale, attracting European and some international names to its chic, modern, barlike ambience. **Tivoli Jazzhouse
Mantra** (✉ Vesterbrog. 3, ☎ 33/11–11–13) is Tivoli's jazz club, attracting
big names but also offering up ambient and techno nights.

Rock Clubs

Copenhagen has a good selection of rock clubs, most of which cost
less than Dkr 50. Almost all are filled with young, fashionable crowds.
They tend to open and go out of business with some frequency, but
you can get free entertainment newspapers and flyers advertising gigs
at almost any café. **Vega** (✉ Engavevej 40, ☎ 33/25–70–11) plays live
techno, house, and rock and is one of the most enduring spots in
town. **Base Camp** (✉ Halvtolv 12, ☎ 70/23–23–18) is a cavernous
restaurant located in a former military hangar; after dinner, it mutates
into a nightclub with live music. The **Pumpehuset** (✉ Studiestr. 52, ☎
33/93–19–60) is the place for soul and rock. For good old-fashioned
rock and roll, head to **Lades Kælder** (✉ Kattesundet 6, ☎ 33/14–00–
67), a local hangout just off Strøget.

The Arts

The most complete English calendar of events is listed in the tourist
magazine *Copenhagen This Week,* and includes musical and theatri-
cal events as well as films and exhibitions. Copenhagen's main theater
and concert season runs from September through May, and tickets can
be obtained either directly from theaters and concert halls or from ticket
agencies. **Billetnet** (✉ Main post office, Tietgensg. 37, ☎ 70/15–65–
65), a box-office service available at all post offices, has tickets for most
major events. The main phone line is sometimes difficult to get through
to: for information go in person to the post office on Købmagergade,
just off Strøget, or check in at any post office. Keep in mind that same-
day purchases at the box office at **Tivoli** (✉ Vesterbrog. 3, ☎ 33/15–
10–12), are half-price if you pick them up after noon; the half-price
tickets are for shows all over town, but the ticket center, naturally, also
has regular tickets for the park's own performances.

Film

Films open in Copenhagen a few months to a year after their U.S. premieres. Nonetheless, the Danes are avid viewers, willing to pay Dkr
65 per ticket, wait in lines for premieres, and read subtitles. Call the
theater for reservations, and pick up tickets (which include a seat num-

ber) an hour before the movie. Most theaters have a café. Among the city's alternative venues for second-run films is **Vester Vov Vov** (⊠ Absalonsg. 5, ☎ 33/24–42–00) in Vesterbro. The **Grand** (⊠ Mikkel Bryggersg. 8, ☎ 33/15–16–11) shows new foreign and artsy films, and is just next door to its sister café.

Opera, Ballet, and Theater

Tickets at the **Kongelige Teater** (Danish Royal Theater; ⊠ Tordenskjoldsg. 3, ☎ 33/14–10–02; ☞ Exploring Copenhagen, *above*) are reasonably priced at Dkr 70–Dkr 400 but, especially for prime seats, can sometimes be hard to get; the season runs October to May. It is home to the Royal Danish Ballet, one of the premier companies in the world. Not as famous, but also accomplished, are the **Royal Danish Opera** and the **Royal Danish Orchestra,** the latter of which performs in all productions. Plays are exclusively in Danish. For information and reservations, call the theater. Beginning at the end of July, you can order tickets for the next season by writing to the theater (⊠ Danish Royal Theater, Attn. Ticket Office, Box 2185, DK–1017 KBH). For English-language theater, especially comedy, call the professional **London Toast Theater**(☎ 33/22–86–86).

OUTDOOR ACTIVITIES AND SPORTS

Beaches

North of Copenhagen along the old beach road, **Strandvejen,** you'll find a string of lovely old seaside towns and beaches. **Bellevue Beach** (⊠ Across the street from Klampenborg Station) is packed with locals and has cafés, kiosks, and surfboard rentals. **Charlottelund Fort** (⊠ Bus 6 from Rådhuspl.) is a bit more private, but you'll have to pay (about Dkr 10) to swim off the pier. The beaches along the tony town of **Vedbæk,** 18 km (11 mi) north of Copenhagen, are not very crowded.

Biking

Bike rentals (Dkr 100–Dkr 300 deposit and Dkr 35–Dkr 70 per day) are available throughout the city, and most roads have bike lanes. You might also be lucky and find an advertisement-flanked "city bike," parked at busy points around the city including Kongens Nytorv and the Nørreport train station. Deposit Dkr 20 and pedal away; your money is returned when you return the bike. Follow all traffic signs and signals; bicycle lights and reflectors must be used at night. For more information, contact the **Dansk Cyclist Forbund** (Danish Cyclist Federation, ⊠ Rømersg. 7, ☎ 33/32–31–21).

Golf

Some clubs do not accept reservations; call for details. Virtually all clubs in Denmark require your being a member of another club for admittance. Handicap requirements vary widely.

One of Denmark's best courses, often the host of international tournaments, is the 18-hole **Rungsted Golf Klub** (⊠ Vestre Stationsvej 16, ☎ 45/86–34–44). A 30 handicap for all players is required on weekdays; on weekends and holidays there's a 24 handicap for men and a 29 handicap for women. The 18-hole **Københavns Golf Klub** (⊠ Dyrehaven 2, ☎ 39/63–04–83) is said to be Scandinavia's oldest. Greens fees range from Dkr 180 to Dkr 240.

Health and Fitness Clubs

A day pass for weights and aerobics at the **Fitness Club** (⊠ Vesterbrog. 2E at Scala, across the street from Tivoli, ☎ 33/32–10–02) is Dkr 75. **Form og Figur** (Form and Figure) offers one-day aerobics passes for Dkr 75 at the SAS Globetrotter Hotel (⊠ Engvej 171, ☎ 32/55–00–70) in Amager, and a pool, weights, treadmill, and stationary bikes for Dkr 75 at the SAS Scandinavia Hotel (⊠ Amager Boulevarden 70, ☎ 32/54–28–88) and weights, aerobics, and stationary bikes in Østerbro (⊠ Øster Alle42, ☎ 35/55–00–71).

Horseback Riding

You can ride at the Dyrehavebakken (Deer Forest Hills) in Lyngby at the **Fortunens Ponyudlejning** (⊠ Ved Fortunen 33, ☎ 45/87–60–58). A one-hour session, in which both experienced and inexperienced riders go out with a guide, costs about Dkr 95.

Running

The 6-km (4-mi) loop around the three lakes just west of city center—St. Jorgens, Peblinge, and Sortedams—is a runner's nirvana. There are also paths at the Rosenborg Have; the Frederiksberg Garden (near Frederiksberg Station, corner of Frederiksberg Allé and Pile Allé); and the Dyrehaven, north of the city near Klampenborg.

Soccer

Danish soccer fans call themselves *Rolegans*—which loosely translates as well-behaved fans—as opposed to hooligans, and idolize the national team's soccer players as superstars. When the rivalry is most intense (especially against Sweden and Norway), fans don face paint, wear head-to-toe red and white, incessantly wave the *Dannebrog* (Danish flag), and have a good time whether or not they win. The biggest stadium in town for national and international games is **Parken** (⊠ Øster Allé 50, ☎ 35/43–31–31). Tickets (Dkr 140 for slightly obstructed views, Dkr 220–Dkr 320 for unobstructed; local matches are less expensive than international ones) can be bought through Billetnet (☎ 38/88–70–22).

Swimming

Swimming is very popular here, and pools are crowded but well maintained. Separate bath tickets can also be purchased. Admission to local pools (Dkr 20–Dkr 50) includes a locker key, but you'll have to bring your own towel. Most pools are 25 m long. The beautiful **Frederiksberg Svømmehal** (⊠ Helgesvej 29, ☎ 38/14–04–04) still maintains its old art deco decor with sculptures and decorative tiles. In the modern concrete **Vesterbro Svømmehal** (⊠ Angelg. 4, ☎ 33/22–05–00), many enjoy swimming next to the large glass windows. The 50-m **Lyngby Svømmehal** (⊠ Lundoftevej 53, ☎ 45/87–44–56) is one of metropolitan Copenhagen's newest pools, with a separate diving pool.

Tennis

Courts fees for guests are very high, often including court rental (around Dkr 85 per person) and a separate nonmembers' user fee (as high as Dkr 140). If you must volley, courts are available to guests at some sports centers before 1 PM only. **Københavns Boldklub** (⊠ PeterBangs Vej 147, ☎ 38/71–41–50) is in Frederiksberg, a neighborhood just west of central Copenhagen. **Hellerup Idræts Klub** (⊠ Hartmannsvej 37, ☎ 39/62–14–28) is about 5 km (3 mi) north of town. **Skovshoved Idræts Forening** (⊠ Krørsvej 5A, ☎ 39/64–23–83) is along the old beach road about 10 km (6 mi) north of town.

SHOPPING

A showcase for world-famous Danish design and craftsmanship, Copenhagen seems to have been designed with shoppers in mind. The best buys are such luxury items as crystal, porcelain, silver, and furs. Look for offers and sales (*tilbud* or *udsalg* in Danish) and check antiques and secondhand shops for classics at cut-rate prices.

Although prices are inflated by a hefty 25% Value-Added Tax (Danes call it MOMS), non–European Union citizens can receive about an 18% refund. For more details and a list of all tax-free shops, ask at the tourist board for a copy of the *Tax-Free Shopping Guide* and *see* Taxes *in* Smart Travel Tips A to Z.

Department Stores

Illum (⊠ Østerg. 52, ☎ 33/14–40–02), not to be confused with Illums Bolighus (☞ Design, *below*), is well stocked, with a lovely rooftop café and excellent basement grocery. **Magasin** (⊠ Kongens Nytorv 13, ☎ 33/11–44–33), Scandinavia's largest, also has a top-quality basement marketplace. **Hennes and Mauritz** (⊠ Amagertorv 11, ☎ 33/32–60–09) actually has stores all over town and offers reasonably priced clothing and accessories for men, women, and children; best of all are the to-die-for baby clothes.

Shopping Districts, Streets, and Malls

The pedestrian-only **Strøget** and adjacent **Købmagergade** are *the* shopping streets, but wander down the smaller streets for lower-priced, offbeat stores. You'll find the most exclusive shops at the end of Strøget, around Kongens Nytorv, and on Ny Adelgade, Grønnegade, and Pistolstræde. **Scala,** the city's glittering café- and boutique-studded mall, is across the street from Tivoli and has a trendy selection of clothing stores and a main-floor food court for the famished. Farther south in the city, on **Vesterbrogade,** you'll find discount stores—especially leather and clothing shops.

Specialty Stores

Antiques

For silver, porcelain, and crystal, the well-stocked shops on **Bredgade** are upscale and expensive. On Strøget, **Royal Copenhagen Porcelain** (⊠ Amagertorv 6, ☎ 33/13–71–81) carries old and new china, porcelain patterns, and figurines, as well as seconds. **Kaabers Antikvariat** (⊠ Skinderg. 34, ☎ 33/15–41–77) is an emporium for old and rare books, prints, and maps. For silver, Christmas plates, or porcelain, head to **H. Danielsens** (⊠ Læderstr. 11, ☎ 33/13–02–74). **Danborg Gold and Silver** (⊠ Holbergsg. 17, ☎ 33/32–93–94) is one of the best places for estate jewelry and silver flatware. For furniture, the dozens of **Ravnsborggade** stores carry traditional pine, oak, and mahogany furniture, and smaller items as lamps and tableware. (Some of them sell tax-free items and can arrange shipping.)

Audio Equipment

For high-tech design and acoustics, **Bang & Olufsen** (⊠ Østerg. 3, ☎ 33/15–04–22) is so renowned that its products are in the permanent design collection of New York's Museum of Modern Art. (Check prices at home first to make sure you are getting a deal.) You'll find B&O and other international names at **Fredgaard** (⊠ Nørre Voldg. 17, ☎ 33/13–82–45), near Nørreport Station.

Clothing

Petitgas Chapeaux (⊠ Købmagerg. 5, ☎ 33/13–62–70) is a venerable shop for old-fashioned men's hats. The **Company Store** (⊠ Frederiksbergg. 24, ☎ 33/11–35–55) is for trendy, youthful styles, typified by the Danish Matinique label. If you are interested in the newest Danish designs, keep your eyes open for cooperatives and designer-owned stores. Among the most inventive handmade women's clothing shops is **Met Mari** (⊠ Vesterg. 11, ☎ 33/15–87–25). Thick, traditional, patterned, and solid Scandinavian sweaters are available at the **Sweater Market** (⊠ Frederiksbergg. 15, ☎ 33/15–27–73). **Artium** (⊠ Vesterbrog. 1, ☎ 33/12–34–88) offers an array of colorful, Scandinavian-designed sweaters and clothes alongside useful and artful household gifts.

Crystal and Porcelain

Minus the V.A.T., such Danish classics as Holmegaard crystal and Royal Copenhagen porcelain are less expensive than they are back home. Signed art glass is always more expensive, but be on the lookout for seconds as well as secondhand and unsigned pieces. **Rosenthal Studio-Haus** (⊠ Frederiksberg. 21 on Strøget, ☎ 33/14–21–02) offers the lead-crystal wildlife reliefs of Mats Johansson as well as the very modern functional and decorative works of many other Italian and Scandinavian artisans. **Bodum Hus** (⊠ Østergade 10 on Strøget, ☎ 33/36–40–80) shows off a wide variety of reasonably priced Danish-designed functional, and especially kitchen-oriented, accoutrements; the milk foamers are indispensable for cappuccino lovers. **Skandinavisk Glas** (⊠ Ny Østerg. 4, ☎ 33/13–80–95) has a large selection of Danish and international glass and a helpful, informative staff.

The **Royal Copenhagen** shop (⊠ Amagertorv 6, ☎ 33/13–71–81) has firsts and seconds. For a look at the goods at their source, try the **Royal Scandinavia Factory** (⊠ Smalleg. 45, ☎ 33/86–48–48). Holmegaards Glass can be purchased at either the Royal Copenhagen store on Amagertorv or at the Royal Scandinavia factory on Smallegade (for seconds); alternatively, you can travel to their dedicated factory (☎ 55/54–50–00), 97 km (60 mi) south of Copenhagen near the town of Næstved.

Design

Part gallery, part department store, **Illums Bolighus** (⊠ Amagertorv 6, ☎ 33/14–19–41) shows off cutting-edge Danish and international design—art glass, porcelain, silverware, carpets, and loads of grown-up toys. **Lysberg, Hansen and Therp** (⊠ Bredg. 75, ☎ 33/14–47–87), one of the most prestigious interior-design firms in Denmark, has sumptuous showrooms done up in traditional and modern styles. **Gubi Design** (⊠ Grønnegade 10, ☎ 33/32–63–68) is where to go for the super-clean *Wallpaper* look; the chic kitchens are amazing and amazingly priced, but if you can't afford to move one back home, you can at least gain inspiration before the renovation. Wizard florist **Tage Andersen** (⊠ Ny Adelg. 12, ☎ 33/93–09–13) has a fantasy-infused gallery-shop filled with one-of-a-kind gifts and arrangements; browsers (who generally don't purchase the pricey items) are charged a Dkr 40 admission.

Fur

Denmark, the world's biggest producer of ranched minks, is the place to go for quality furs. Furs are ranked into four grades: Saga Royal,

Saga, Quality 1, and Quality 2. Copenhagen's finest furrier, dealing only in Saga Royal quality, and purveyor to the royal family is **Birger Christensen** (⊠ Østerg. 38, ☎ 33/11–55–55), which presents a new collection yearly from its in-house design team. Expect to spend about 20% less than in the United States for same-quality furs ($5,000–$10,000 for mink, $3,000 for a fur-lined coat), but as in all things related to shopping, do your homework before you leave home. Birger Christensen is also among the preeminent fashion houses in town, carrying Donna Karan, Chanel, Prada, Kenzo, Jil Sander, and Yves Saint Laurent. **A. C. Bang** (⊠ Vesterbrogade 1, ☎ 33/15–17–26), close to Tivoli, carries less expensive furs, but has an Old-World, old-money aura and very high quality.

Silver

Check the silver standard of a piece by its stamp. Three towers and "925S" (which means 925 parts out of 1,000) mark sterling. Two towers are used for silver plate. The "826S" stamp (also denoting sterling, but less pure) was used until the 1920s. Even with shipping charges, you can expect to save 50% versus American prices when buying Danish silver (especially used) at the source. For one of the most recognized names in international silver, visit **Georg Jensen** (⊠ Amagertorv 4, ☎ 33/11–40–80), an elegant, austere shop aglitter with velvet-cushioned sterling. **Peter Krog** (⊠ 4 Bredg., ☎ 33/12–45–55) stocks collectors' items in silver, primarily Georg Jensen place settings, compotes, and jewelry. **Era Hartogsohn** (⊠ Palæg. 8, ☎ 33/15–53–98) carries all sorts of silver knickknacks and settings. The **English Silver House** (⊠ Pilestr. 4, ☎ 33/14–83–81) is an emporium of used estate silver. The city's largest (and brightest) silver store is **Sølvkælderen** (⊠ Kompagnistr. 1, ☎ 33/13–36–34), with an endless selection of tea services, place settings, and jewelry.

Street Markets

Check with the tourist board or the tourist magazine *Copenhagen This Week* for flea markets. Bargaining is expected. For a good overview of antiques and junk, visit the flea market at **Israels Plads** (⊠ Near Nørreport Station), open May–October, Saturday 8–2. It is run by more than 100 professional dealers, and prices are steep, but there are loads of classic Danish porcelain, silver, jewelry, and crystal, plus books, prints, postcards, and more. Slightly smaller than the Israels Plads market, and with lower prices and more junk, is the market behind **Frederiksberg Rådhus** (summer Saturday mornings). The junk and flea market that takes place Saturday in summer and stretches from Nørrebros Rundel down the road along the Assistens Kirkegårn (cemetery) claims to be one of the longest in the world.

SIDE TRIPS FROM COPENHAGEN

Experimentarium

8 km (5 mi) north of Copenhagen.

In the beachside town of Hellerup is the user-friendly **Experimentarium,** where more than 300 exhibitions are clustered in various Discovery Islands, each exploring a different facet of science, technology, and natural phenomena. A dozen body- and hands-on exhibits allow you to take skeleton-revealing bike rides, measure your lung capacity, stir up magnetic goop, play ball on a jet stream, and gyrate to gyroscopes. Once a bottling plant for the Tuborg Brewery, this center organizes one or two special exhibits a year; past installations have included interactive exhibits of the brain and tongue-wagging, life-size dinosaurs. Take Bus 6 or 650S from Rådhus Plads or the S-train to Hellerup; transfer to bus 21 or 650S. Alternatively, take the S-train to Svanemøllen station, then walk ten minutes north. ⊠ *Tuborg Havnevej 7*, ☎ 39/27–33–33. ▣ *Dkr 75; combined admission for a child and parent, Dkr 108.* ☉ *Mid-Aug.–mid-June, Mon., Wed.–Fri. 9–5, Tues. 9–9, weekends 11– 5; mid-June–mid.–Aug., daily 10–5.*

Dragør

22 km (14 mi) east of Copenhagen (take Bus 30 or 33 from Rådhus Pladsen).

On the island of Amager, less than a half hour from Copenhagen, the quaint fishing town of Dragør (pronounced *drah*-wer) feels far away in distance and time. The town's history is apart from the rest of Copenhagen's because it was settled by Dutch farmers in the 16th century. King Christian II ordered the community to provide fresh produce and flowers for the royal court. Today, neat rows of white, terra-cotta-roofed houses trimmed with wandering ivy, roses, and the occasional waddling goose characterize the still meticulously maintained community. According to local legend, the former town hall's chimney was built with a twist so that meetings couldn't be overheard.

The **Dragør Museum** (⊠ Strandlinien 4, ☎ 32/53–41–06), in one of the oldest houses in town, contains a collection of furniture, costumes, drawings, and model ships. Admission is Dkr 20. A ticket to the Dragør Museum also affords entrance to the nearby **Mølsted Museum** (⊠ Dr. Dichs Pl. 4, ☎ 32/53–41–06), displaying paintings by the famous local artist Christian Mølsted. If you're still energetic, swing by the **Amager Museum** (⊠ Hovedg. 4 and 12, ☎ 32/53–02–50), which details the Dutch colony. Admission is Dkr 20. All three museums are small and have varying hours, so call first.

Frilandsmuseet

16 km (10 mi) north of Copenhagen.

Just north of Copenhagen is Lyngby, its main draw the **Frilandsmuseet,** an open-air museum. About 50 farmhouses and cottages representing various periods of Danish history have been painstakingly dismantled, moved, reconstructed, and filled with period furniture and tools. The museum is surrounded by trees and gardens; bring lunch and plan to spend the day. To get here, take the S-train to the Sorgenfri Station, then walk right and follow the signs. ⊠ *Frilandsmuseet, 100 Kongevejen, Lyngby,* ☎ *45/85–02–92.* ▣ *Dkr 40; free Wednesdays.* ☉ *Easter– Sept., Tues.–Sun. 10–5; Oct., daily 10–4; call to confirm Oct. hrs.*

Museet for Moderne Kunst, Arken

20 km (12 mi) south of Copenhagen (take the S-train in the direction of either Hundige, Solrød Strand, or Køge to Ishøj Station, then pick up bus 128 to the museum).

Architect Søren Robert Lund was just 25 when awarded the commission for this forward-looking museum, which he designed in metal and white concrete set against the flat coast south of Copenhagen. The museum, also known as the **Arken,** opened in March 1996 to great acclaim, both for its architecture and its collection. Unfortunately, for about two years following its opening, it was plagued with a string of stranger-than-fiction occurrences, including a director with an allegedly bogus resume. The situation has greatly improved and today its massive sculpture room exhibits both modern Danish and international art, as well as experimental works. Dance, theater, film, and multimedia exhibits are additional attractions. ⊠ *Skovvej 42,* ☎ *43/42–02–22.* ☑ *Dkr 40.* ☉ *Tues., Thurs.–Sun., 10–5, Wed. 10–9.*

COPENHAGEN A TO Z

Arriving and Departing

By Car

The E–20 highway, via bridges, connects Fredericia (on Jylland) with Middelfart (on Fyn), a distance of 16 km (10 mi), and goes on to Copenhagen, another 180 km (120 mi) east. Farther north, from Århus (in Jylland), you can get direct auto-catamaran service to Kalundborg (on Sjælland). From there, Route 23 leads to Roskilde, about 72 km (45 mi) east. Take Route 21 east and follow the signs to Copenhagen, another 40 km (25 mi). Make reservations for the ferry in advance through the Danish State Railways (DSB, ⊠ Hovedbanegården, DK–1570 KBH K, ☎ 70/13–14–15). In June 2000, Copenhagen will be linked to Malmø, Sweden, via the Øresund bridge and tunnel for both cars and trains.

By Ferry

Frequent ferries connect Copenhagen with Sweden, including several daily ships from Malmö, Limhamn, Landskrona, and Helsingborg. There is also a high-speed craft from Malmö.

By Plane

Copenhagen Airport, 10 km (6 mi) southeast of downtown in Kastrup, is the gateway to Scandinavia. International and domestic flights are served by **SAS** (☎ 32/32–00–00). Among the other airlines that serve Copenhagen Airport are **British Airways** (☎ 80/20–80–22) and **Icelandair** (☎ 33/12–33–88).

Between the Airport and Downtown: Although the 10-km (6-mi) drive from the airport to downtown is quick and easy, public transportation is excellent and much cheaper. The airport's sleek new subterranean train system takes less than 10 minutes to zip passengers into Copenhagen's main train station. Buy a ticket upstairs (Dkr 16.50); there are three trains an hour into Copenhagen, while a fourth travels farther to Roskilde. **SAS coach buses** leave the international arrivals terminal every 15 minutes, from about 5:42 AM to about 9:45 PM, cost Dkr 40, and take 25 minutes to reach Copenhagen's main train station on Vesterbrogade. Another SAS coach from Christiansborg, on Slotsholmsgade, to the airport runs every 15 minutes between 8:30 AM and noon, and every halfhour from noon to 6 PM. **HT** city buses depart from the international arrivals terminal every 15 minutes, from 4:30 AM (Sunday 5:30) to 11:52 PM, but take a long, circuitous route. Take Bus 250S for the Rådhus Pladsen and transfer. Tickets (one way) cost about Dkr 20.

The 20-minute **taxi** ride downtown costs from Dkr 100 to Dkr 160 and up. Lines form at the international arrivals terminal. In the unlikely event there is no taxi available, call ☎ 35/35–35–35.

By Train

Copenhagen's **Hovedbanegården** (Central Station, ⊠ Vesterbrog.) is the hub of the DSB network and is connected to most major cities in Europe. Intercity trains leave every hour, usually on the hour, from 6 AM to 10 PM for principal towns in Fyn and Jylland. Find out more from **DSB** (☎ 70/13–14–15). You can make reservations at the central station, at most other stations, and through travel agents.

Getting Around

Copenhagen is small, with most sights within its one-square-mi center. Wear comfortable shoes and explore it on foot. Or follow the example of the Danes and rent a bike. For those with aching feet, an efficient transit system is available.

By Bicycle

Bikes are delightfully well suited to Copenhagen's flat terrain and are popular among Danes as well as visitors. Bike rental costs Dkr 35–Dkr 70 a day, with a deposit of Dkr 100–Dkr 300. You may also be lucky enough to find a free city bike chained up at bike racks in various spots throughout the city, including Nørreport and Nyhavn. Insert a Dkr 20 coin, which will be returned to you when you return the bike.

Rentals: Københavns Cycler (⊠ Reventlowsg. 11, ☎ 33/33–86–13). **Østerport Cykler** (⊠ Oslo Plads, ☎ 33/33–85–13). **Urania Cykler** (⊠ Gammel Kongevej 1, ☎ 33/21–80–88).

By Bus and Train

The **Copenhagen Card** offers unlimited travel on buses and suburban trains (S-trains), admission to more than 60 museums and sites around Sjælland, and a reduction on the ferry crossing to Sweden. You can buy the card, which costs Dkr 155 (24 hours), Dkr 255 (48 hours), or Dkr 320 (72 hours) and is half-price for children, at tourist offices and hotels and from travel agents.

Trains and buses operate from 5 AM (Sunday 6 AM) to midnight. After that, night buses run every half hour from 1 AM to 4:30 AM from the main bus station at Rådhus Pladsen to most areas of the city and surroundings. Trains and buses operate on the same ticket system and divide Copenhagen and surrounding areas into three zones. Tickets are validated on a time basis: on the basic ticket, which costs about Dkr 11 per hour, you can travel anywhere in the zone in which you started. A discount *klip kort* (clip card), good for 10 rides, costs Dkr 75 and must be stamped in the automatic ticket machines on buses or at stations. Get zone details for S-trains by their information line (☎ 33/14–17–01). The buses have an automatic answering menu that is barely helpful in Danish, but try pressing one on your phone and wait for a human to pick up. You might do better by asking a bus driver.

By Car

If you are planning on seeing the sites of central Copenhagen, a car is not convenient. Parking spaces are at a premium and, when available, are expensive. A maze of one-way streets, relatively aggressive drivers, and bicycle lanes make it even more complicated. If you are going to drive, choose a small car that's easy to parallel park, bring a lot of small change to feed the meters, and be very aware of the cyclists on your right-hand side: they always have the right-of-way.

By Taxi

The shiny computer-metered Mercedes and Volvo cabs are not cheap. The base charge is Dkr 15, plus Dkr 8–Dkr 10 per km. A cab is available when it displays the sign FRI (free); it can be hailed or picked up in front of the main train station or at taxi stands, or by calling ☎ 35/35–35–35. Outside of the central city, always call for a cab, as your attempts will be in vain. Surcharges apply if you order a cab and at night.

Contacts and Resources

Car Rentals

All major international car rental agencies are represented in Copenhagen; most are located near the Vesterport Station. Try **Europcar** (⊠

Copenhagen Airport, ☎ 32/50–30–90). Also try **Budget-Pitzner** (⊠ Copenhagen Airport, ☎ 32/50–90–65).

Currency Exchange

Almost all banks exchange money. Most hotels cash traveler's checks and exchange major foreign currencies, but they charge a substantial fee and give a lower rate. The exception to the rule—if you travel with cash—are the several locations of **Forex.** For up to $500, Forex charges only Dkr 20 for the entire transaction. Keep your receipt and they'll even change it back to dollars for free. For traveler's checks, they charge Dkr 10 per check. Den Danske Bank exchange is open during and after normal banking hours at the **main railway station,** daily June to August 7 AM–10 PM, and daily September to May, 7 AM–9 PM. **American Express, Nyman and Schultz** (⊠ Nørregade 7A, 3rd Floor, ☎ 33/12–23–01) is open weekdays 9–5 and Saturday 9–noon. In Copenhagen center are the several locations of **The Change Group** including (⊠ Vesterbrog. 9A; Østerg. 61; Vimmelskaftet 47; Frederiksbergg. 5; ☎ 33/93–04–15), open April to October, daily 10–8, November to March, daily 10–6. **Tivoli** (⊠ Vesterbrog. 3., ☎ 33/15–10–01) also exchanges money; it is open May to September, daily noon–11 PM.

You can use **ATM**s to get cash with credit cards; you will find machines in all of Denmark's cities and many larger towns. ATMs typically accept Visa, MasterCard, and Cirrus cards, and Jyske Bank machines accept PLUS cards.

Doctors and Dentists

Emergency dentists (⊠ 14 Oslo Pl.), near Østerport Station, are available weekdays 8 PM–9:30 PM and weekends and holidays 10 AM–noon. Cash is the only accepted payment.

Look in the phone book under *læge.* After normal business hours, **emergency doctors** (☎ 38/88–60–41) make house calls in the central city. Fees are payable in cash only; night fees are approximately Dkr 300–Dkr 400.

Embassies

U.S. (⊠ Dag Hammarskjölds Allé 24, ☎ 35/55–31–44). **Canada** (⊠ Kristen Bernikows G. 1, ☎ 33/12–22–99). **U.K.** (⊠ Kastesvej 40, ☎ 35/44–52–00).

Emergencies

Police, fire, and ambulance (☎ 112). **Auto Rescue/Falck** (☎ 70/10–20–30). **Rigshospitalet** (⊠ Blegdamsvej 9, ☎ 35/45–35–45). **Frederiksberg Hospital** (⊠ Nordre Fasanvej 57, ☎ 38/34–77–11).

English-Language Bookstores

Boghallen (⊠ Rådhus Pl. 37, ☎ 33/11–85–11, ext. 309), the bookstore of the Politiken publishing house, offers a good selection of English-language books. **Arnold Busck** (⊠ Kobmagerg. 49, ☎ 33/12–24–53), has an excellent selection, and also textbooks, CDs, and comic books.

Guided Tours

The Copenhagen Tourist Board monitors all tours and has brochures and information. Most tours run through the summer until September. Only the Grand Tour of Copenhagen, which covers the exteriors of the major sites, and the Open Top Tour, which covers less ground but more quickly, are year-round. It's always a good idea to call first to confirm availability. **The Grand Tour of Copenhagen** (2½ hours) includes Tivoli, the New Carlsberg Museum, Christiansborg Castle, Stock Exchange, Danish Royal Theater, Nyhavn, Amalienborg Castle, Gefion Fountain, Grundtvig Church, and Rosenborg Castle. The

City Tour (1½ hours) is more general, passing the New Carlsberg Museum, Christiansborg Castle, Thorvaldsen Museum, National Museum, Stock Exchange, Danish Royal Theater, Rosenborg Castle, National Art Gallery, Botanical Gardens, Amalienborg Castle, Gefion Fountain, and *The Little Mermaid*. **The Open Top Tours** (about 1 hour), which are given on London-style double-decker buses, include stops at Amalienborg, Stock Exchange, Christiansborg, *The Little Mermaid*, Louis Tussaud's Wax Museum, the National Museum, Ny Carlsberg Glyptotek, Nyhavn, Thorvaldsen Museum, and Tivoli, and give attendees the option to disembark and embark on a later bus. For tour information call **Copenhagen Excursions** (☎ 32/54–06–06).

Biking Tours (Self-Guided): BikeDenmark (✉ Åboulevarden 1, ☎ 35/36–41–00) offers two different self-guided city cycling tours. Choose between the 3- to 4-hour **Copenhagen Tour**, which includes the exteriors of the "musts" of the city, including *The Little Mermaid* and Amalienborg. The second is the 8- to 9-hour **Dragør Tour**, during which you leave the city and bike to the old-fashioned fishing hamlet near Copenhagen. There, you can swim at the beach and explore the ancient heart of the former Dutch colony. The tour package includes maps and a detailed route description. The rental price of the bike, which is available from **Københavns Cycle** (✉ Reventlowsg. 11, ☎ 33/33–86–13) is an additional Dkr 50 per bike.

Boat Tours: The **Harbor and Canal Tour** (1 hour) leaves from Gammel Strand and the east side of Kongens Nytorv from May to mid-September. Contact **Canal Tours** (☎ 33/13–31–05) or the tourist board (☞ Visitor Information, *below*). The **City and Harbor Tour** (2½ hours) includes a short bus trip through town and sails from the Fish Market on Holmens Canal through several more waterways, ending near Strøget. Just south of the embarkation point for the City and Harbor Tour, you'll find the equally charming **Netto Boats** (☎ 32/54–41–02), which also offers hour-long tours for about half the price of their competitors.

Commercial Tours: Tours of the **Carlsberg Bryggeri** (✉ Ny Carlsbergvej 140, ☎ 33/27–13–14; ☞ Exploring Copenhagen, *above*), which include a look into the draft horse stalls, meet at the Elephant Gate weekdays at 11 and 2. **The Royal Porcelain Factory** (✉ Smalleg. 45, ☎ 38/86–48–59) conducts tours that end at its shop on weekdays at 9, 10, and 11 from mid-September through April, and weekdays at 9, 10, 11, 1, and 2 from May through mid-September.

Walking Tours: Walking tours begin in front of the **Tourist Information Office** (✉ Bernstorffsg. 1, ☎ 33/11-13-25) at 10:30 Monday–Saturday between May and September, and take approximately two hours (call 32/97–14–40 to confirm). There are three different routes: Uptown on Monday and Thursday, Crosstown on Tuesday and Friday, and Downtown on Saturday. American Richard Karpen, who has been living in Denmark for 14 years, offers information on both the interiors and exteriors of buildings and gives insight into the lifestyles, society, and politics of the Danes. A tour of Rosenborg Castle, including the treasury, is at 1:30 Monday–Thursdays between May and September.

Late-Night Pharmacies
Steno Apotek (✉ Vesterbrog. 6C, ☎ 33/14–82–66) is open 24 hours a day. **Sønderbro Apotek** (✉ Amangerbrog. 158, ☎ 32/58–01–40) is also open around the clock.

Travel Agencies
American Express, Nyman and Schultz (✉ Nørregade 7A, ☎ 33/12–23–01). **Carlson Wagonslit** (✉ Bredgade 65, ☎ 33/63–77–77). **DSB Travel Bureau** (✉ Copenhagen Main Train Station, ☎ 33/14–11–26).

For student and budget travel, try **Kilroy Travels Denmark** (⊠ Skinderg. 28, ☎ 33/11–00–44). For charter packages, stick with **Spies** (⊠ Nyropsg. 41, ☎ 70/10–42–00). **Star Tours** (⊠ H. C. Andersens Boulevard 12, ☎ 33/11–88–88) also handles packages.

Visitor Information

Wonderful Copenhagen Tourist Information (⊠ Bernstorffsg. 1, DK–1577 Copenhagen V, ☎ 33/11–13–25) is open May through the first two weeks of September, daily 9–9; the rest of September through April, Monday through Friday 9–4:30 and Saturday 9–1:30. Youth information in Copenhagen is available from **Ungdoms Information** (⊠ Rådhusstr. 13, ☎ 33/73–06–50).

3 SJÆLLAND AND ITS ISLANDS

THE GODDESS GEFION is said to have carved Sjælland (Zealand) from Sweden. If she did, she must have sliced the north deep with a fjord, while she chopped the south to pieces and left the sides bowing west. Though the coasts are deeply serrated, Gefion's myth is more dramatic than the flat, fertile land of rich meadows and beech stands.

Slightly larger than the state of Delaware, Sjælland is the largest of the Danish islands. From Copenhagen, almost any point on it can be reached in an hour and a half, making it the most traveled portion of the country—and it is especially easy to explore thanks to the road network. To the north of the capital, ritzy beach towns line up between Hellerup and Humlebæk. Helsingør's Kronborg, which Shakespeare immortalized in *Hamlet,* and Hillerød's stronghold of Frederiksborg, considered one of the most magnificent Renaissance castles in Europe, also lie to the north. To the west of Copenhagen is Roskilde, medieval Denmark's most important town, with an eclectic cathedral that served as northern Europe's spiritual center 1,000 years ago.

West and south, rural towns and farms edge up to seaside communities and fine white beaches, often encompassed by forests. Beaches with summer cottages, white dunes, and calm waters surround Gilleleje and the neighboring town of Hornbæk. The beach in Tisvildeleje, farther west, is quieter and close to woods. Even more unspoiled are the lilliputian islands around southern Sjælland, virtually unchanged over the past century. Most of Sjælland can be explored in day trips from Copenhagen. The exceptions are the northwestern beaches around the Sejerø Bugt (Sejerø Bay) and those south of Møn, all of which require at least a night's stay and a day's loll.

Biking
Sjælland's flat landscape allows easy biking. Most roads have cycle lanes, and tourist boards stock with maps detailing local routes.

Canoeing
About 15 km (10 mi) north of Copenhagen, especially in the Lyngby area, several calm lakes and rivers are perfect for canoeing: the Mølleå (Mølle River) and the Bagsværd, Lyngby, and Furesø (Bagsværd, Lyngby, and Fur lakes). **Frederiksdal Kanoudlejning** (⌂ Nybrovej 520, at the Hotel Hvidehus, Lyngby, ☎ 45/85–67–70) offers hourly and daily rentals and package canoe tours throughout the region.

Fishing
Sjælland's lakes, rivers, and coastline teem with plaice, flounder, cod, and catfish. Buy the Dkr 100 license, required to fish along Sjælland's coast, at any post office. Elsewhere, check with the local tourist office for license requirements. It is illegal to fish within 1,650 ft of the mouth of a stream.

Shopping
Shopping here can be considerably cheaper than in Copenhagen. Pedestrian streets run through the center of most towns, and flea markets are usually held Saturday morning.

Rungsted

㊷ *21 km (13 mi) north of Copenhagen.*

Between Copenhagen and Helsingør is **Rungstedlund,** the elegant, airy former manor of Baroness Karen Blixen. The author of *Out of Africa* and several accounts of aristocratic Danish life wrote under the pen

Sjælland and Its Islands

KEY
— Rail Lines
‑ ‑ Ferry

Kattegat

N

TO GRENA
TO GRENA
TO EBELTOFT

SWEDEN

Gilleleje **47**
Tisvildeleje
Hornbæk
Helsingborg
Frederiksværk
Lisleje
Esrum So.
44
Helsingør
Havnebyen
Hundested
Fredensborg
45
43
Humlebæk
Sjællands Odde
Rørvig
46
Hillerød
Rungsted
Nykøbing
Højby
Roskilde Fjo.
42
Ven
Sejerø
Vig
Isefjord
Øresund
Bug
Frederikssund
Vedbæk
Sejerø
Odsherred
Ølstykke
Furesø
Klampenborg
TO ÅRHUS
Hørve
Fårevejle
53
Stenløse
Lyngby
Kalundborg
Holbæk
Roskilde Fjord
TO MALMÖ
23
1 – 41
Kastrup
Ubby
Undløse
23
Såby
48
København (Copenhagen)
Dragør
Jammerland Bugt
225
Kirke Hvalsø
49
Lejre
Roskilde
22
Ruds Vedby
Sjælland
Køge Bugt
Gørlev
Høng
E66
Sorø
E66
50
Køge
TO RØNNE
Musholm Bugt
Slaglese
Ringsted
Trælleborg
Fugelbjerg
Haslev
Hårlev
Stevns Klint
Halsskov
53
22
Slæd
Store Heddinge
TO NYBORG
Korsør
54
E4
151
Rødvig
Højerup
Skælskør
Næsted
Fakse
Lohals
265
Fakse Ladeplads
Karrebæksminde
Langeland
Karrebæksminde Bu
22
265
Præstø
Nyord
Fakse Bugt
Smålandsfarvandet
Vordingborg
Mern
Stege
287
51
Møn
TO SPODSBJERG
Femø
Stor Strømmen
59
Farø
Hjelm Bugt
Tårs
Fejø
289
Askø
Nørre Alslev
Bogø
287
9
E4
Nakskov
Saskøbing
Falster
Stubbekøbing
Lolland
52
Maribo
Nykøbing
283
Marielyst
SWEDEN
Femer Bælt
Nysted
Guldborg Sund
DENMARK
Rødbyhavn
Gedser
E66
GERMANY

0   10 miles
0   15 km

TO PUTTGARDEN
TO TRAVEMÜNDE
TO WARNEMÜNDE

name Isak Dinesen. The manor house, where she lived as a child and to which she returned in 1931, is open as a museum and displays manuscripts, photographs, and memorabilia documenting her years in Africa and Denmark. Leave time to wander around the gardens. ⊠ *Rungstedlund*, ☎ 42/57–10–57. ☎ *Dkr 30 (for combined train and admission tickets, call DSB (☞ Arriving and Departing in Sjælland and Its Islands A to Z, below).* ☉ *May–Sept., daily 10–5; Oct.–Apr., Wed.–Fri. 1–4, weekends 11–4.*

Dining

$$ × **Strandmollekroen.** Stop for a meal at this 200-year-old beachfront
★   inn in Klampenborg as you drive north from Copenhagen to Rungsted. It's burnished with deep-green walls and filled with antiques and hunting trophies, but the best views are of the Øresund from the back dining room. Elegantly served seafood and steaks are the mainstays, and for a bit of everything, try the seafood platter, with lobster, crab claws, and Greenland shrimp. ⊠ *Strandvejen 808*, ☎ 39/63–01–04. *AE, DC, MC, V.*

Humlebæk

43   *10 km (6 mi) north of Rungsted, 30 km (19 mi) north of Copenhagen.*

★ ☺   This elegant seaside town is home of the must-see **Louisiana,** a modern art museum famed for its stunning location and architecture as much as for its collection. Even if you can't tell a Monet from a Duchamp, you should make the 30-minute trip to see its elegant rambling structure, surrounded by a large park. Housed in a pearly 19th-century villa surrounded by dramatic views of the Øresund waters, the permanent collection includes modern American paintings and Danish paintings from the COBRA (a trend in northern European painting that took its name from its active locations, Copenhagen, Brussels, and Amsterdam) and Deconstructionism movements. Be sure to see the haunting collection of Giacomettis backdropped by picture windows overlooking the sound. The children's wing has pyramid-shape chalkboards, kid-proof computers, and weekend activities under the guidance of an artist or museum coordinator. This makes for a good side trip from Copenhagen; walk north from the station about 10 minutes. ⊠ *Gammel Strandvej 13*, ☎ 49/19–07–19. ☎ *Dkr 48 (for combined train and admission tickets, call DSB; ☞ Arriving and Departing in Sjælland and Its Islands A to Z, below).* ☉ *Daily 10–5, Wed. until 10.*

Helsingør

44   *19 km (12 mi) north of Humlebæk, 47 km (29 mi) north of Copenhagen.*

★   At the northeastern tip of the island is Helsingør, the departure point for ferries to the Swedish town of Helsingborg, and the site of **Kronborg Slot** (Kronborg Castle). William Shakespeare based *Hamlet* on Danish mythology's Amleth, and used this castle as the setting even though he had never seen it. Built in the late 16th century, it's 600 years younger than the Elsinore we imagine from the tragedy. It was built as a Renaissance tollbooth: From its cannon-studded bastions, forces collected Erik of Pomerania's much-hated Sound Dues, a tariff charged to all ships crossing the sliver of water between Denmark and Sweden. Well worth seeing are the 200-ft-long dining hall and the dungeons, where there is a brooding statue of Holger Danske. According to legend, the Viking chief sleeps, but will awaken to defend Denmark when it is in danger. (The largest Danish resistance group during World War II called itself Holger Danske after its fearless forefather.) ⊠ *Helsingør,*

☏ 49/21–30–78. ⧉ *Dkr 30.* ☉ *May–Sept., daily 10:30–5; Oct. and Apr., Tues.–Sun. 11–4; Nov.–Mar., Tues.–Sun. 11–3.*

Thanks to the hefty tolls collected by Erik of Pomerania, Helsingør prospered. Stroll past the carefully restored medieval merchants' and ferrymen's houses in the middle of town. On the corner of Stengade and Skt. Annæ Gade near the harbor you'll find **Skt. Olai's Kirke,** the country's largest parish church and worth a peek for its elaborately carved wooden altar. ⊠ *St. Olai G. 51,* ☏ *49/21–00–98 between 9 and noon only.* ⧉ *Free.* ☉ *May 15–Sept. 14, daily noon–3, tours at 2; Sept. 15–May 14, daily noon–2.*

Next door to Skt. Olai's Kirke is the 15th-century **Carmelite Kloster** (Carmelite Convent), one of the best-preserved examples of medieval architecture in Scandinavia. After the Reformation it was used as a hospital, and by 1630 it had become a poorhouse. ⊠ *Skt. Annæ G. 38,* ☏ *49/21–17–74.* ⧉ *Dkr 10.* ☉ *Tour daily at 2; call ahead.*

If you want to know more about Helsingør, head to the modest **By Museum** (Town Museum), which has exhibits of 19th-century handicrafts, dolls, and a model of the town. ⊠ *Skt. Annæ G. 36,* ☏ *49/21–00–98.* ⧉ *Dkr 10.* ☉ *Daily noon–4.*

OFF THE BEATEN PATH

MARIENLYST SLOT – One kilometer (½ mile) north of Helsingør is the Louis XVI–style Marienlyst Castle. Built in 1587, it provided King Frederik II with a garden, as well as a delicate change of scenery from the militant Kronborg. Today the gardens have been replanted, and inside are paintings by north Sjælland artists and a gallery with changing arts and crafts exhibitions. ⊠ *Marienlyst Allé,* ☏ *49/28–37–91.* ⧉ *Dkr 20.* ☉ *Daily noon–5.*

Dining and Lodging

$$$ ✕⊡ **Hotel Hamlet.** A few minutes from the harbor, this overly renovated hotel has lost some of its charm but makes an attempt at character with raw timbers and deep-green walls. The rooms are furnished in rose schemes and dark wood, and all are comfortable, if nondescript. Downstairs, the Ophelia Restaurant serves traditional Danish seafood, steaks, and open-face sandwiches. ⊠ *Bramstrstrædet 5, DK–3000,* ☏ *49/21–28–02,* FAX *49/26–01–30. 36 rooms. Restaurant, bar, meeting room. AE, DC, MC, V.*

Outdoor Activities and Sports

GOLF

The **Helsingør Golf Klub** (⊠ Gamle Hellebækvej, Helsingør, ☏ 49/21–29–70) has 18 holes on a beautiful, parklike course, with trees and, on clear days, views across the sound to Sweden. A weekday handicap of 36 for men and women, and a weekend handicap of 24 for men and 36 for women, is expected.

Nightlife and the Arts

Some summers, **Kronborg Castle** (☞ *above*) is the site of outdoor performances of *Hamlet* by internationally renowned theater groups. The schedule varies from year to year, so check with the tourist board.

Fredensborg

❹❺ *15 km (9 mi) southwest of Helsingør, 33 km (20 mi) northwest of Copenhagen.*

Commanding this town is the **Fredensborg Slot** (Castle of Peace), built by Frederik IV to commemorate the 1720 peace treaty with Sweden. The castle, with a towering domed hall in the center, was originally inspired by French and Italian castles, but 18th-century reconstructions, concealing the original design, instead serve as a review of domestic architecture. The castle became a favorite of Frederik V, who lined the gardens with marble sculptures of ordinary people. It is now the summer residence of the royal family, and interiors are closed except in July. The lovely Baroque Gardens include a series of wide, horizontal waterfalls, called Cascades. The neatly trimmed park around the palace, connecting with Lake Esrum, is lovely for a stroll. ☎ 42/28–00–25. ☼ *Palace July, daily 1–5; Baroque Gardens, May–Aug., daily 10–9; Sept., daily 10–7; Mar., Apr., and Oct., daily 10–5; Nov.–Feb., daily 10–4.*

Dining and Lodging

$$$$ ✕⊞ **Hotel Store Kro.** Built by King Frederik IV, this magnificent Re-
★ naissance annex to Fredensborg Castle is the archetypal stately inn. In-
side it's appointed with European antiques and paintings; outside,
glass gazebos and classical statues overlook a lovely garden. The rooms
are equally sumptuous, with delicately patterned wallpapers and an-
tiques. The romantic restaurant, specializing in French fare, has a fire-
place and a grand piano. ⊠ *Slotsg. 6, DK–3480,* ☎ *42/28–00–47,* FAX
*42/28–45–61. 49 rooms. Restaurant, bar, room service, sauna, meet-
ing rooms. AE, DC, MC, V.*

$$$$ ⊞ **Marienlyst.** This hotel is full of flashy neon, bolts of drapery, and
★ glass. A large casino and endless lounges provide weekend entertain-
ment, but when guests tire of gambling, there's a huge second-floor
"Swinging Pool," with a water slide, swim-up bar, and sauna. The rooms
are all plush and pastel, with every convenience. ⊠ *Nordre Strandvej
2, DK–3000,* ☎ *49/21–40–00,* FAX *49/21–49–00. 220 rooms, 11 suites.
2 restaurants, 2 bars, room service, indoor pool, sauna, casino, night-
club, meeting rooms. AE, DC, MC, V.*

Hillerød

❹❻ *10 km (6 mi) southwest of Fredensborg, 41 km (26 mi) northwest of
Copenhagen.*

Hillerød's **Frederiksborg Slot** was acquired and rebuilt by Frederik II,
but the fortress was demolished by his son, king-cum-architect Chris-
tian IV, who rebuilt it as one of Scandinavia's most magnificent cas-
tles. With three wings and a low entrance portal, the moated
Dutch-Renaissance structure covers three islets and is peaked with dozens
of gables, spires, and turrets. The two-story marble gallery known as
the **Great Hall,** audaciously festooned with drapery, paintings, and re-
liefs, sits on top of the vaulted chapel, where monarchs were crowned
for 200 years. Devastated by a fire in 1859, the castle was reconstructed
with the support of the Carlsberg Foundation, and it now includes the
National Portrait Gallery. ☎ 48/26–04–39. ▣ *Dkr 30.* ☼ *Apr.–Oct.,
daily 10–5; Nov.–Mar., daily 11–3.*

Dining

$ ✕ **Slotsherrenskro.** Under the shadow of the Frederiksborg Castle, this
family restaurant bustles in what used to be the castle stables. Antique
on the outside, it's bright orange inside, with prints and paintings of
royalty and the castle. Popular with visitors to the castle, the Danish
menu ranges from quick open-face sandwiches to savory stews, soups,
and steaks. ⊠ *Slotherrens Kro,* ☎ *48/26–75–16. DC, MC, V. Closed
Dec.–Apr. No dinner Thurs.*

Gilleleje

❹❼ *25 km (16 mi) north of Hillerød, 55 km (35 mi) northwest of Copen-
hagen.*

Gilleleje is at the very top of Sjælland. Once a small fishing community, it experiences a population explosion every summer, when northern Europeans take to its woods and fine, sandy beaches. It was a favorite getaway of philosopher Søren Kierkegaard, who wrote: "I often stood there and reflected over my past life. The force of the sea and the struggle of the elements made me realize how unimportant I was." The less existential will go for a swim and visit the philosopher's monument on a nearby hill. The old part of town, with its thatched and colorfully painted houses, is good for a walk.

Odsherred

34 km (21 mi) southwest of Gilleleje, 80 km (50 mi) northwest of Copenhagen (via Roskilde).

This hammer-shape peninsula is curved by the Sejerø Bugt (Sejerø Bay) and dotted with hundreds of **burial mounds.** Getting here involves driving to Hundested, then taking the 25-minute ferry ride to Rørvig.

If you are a devotee of ecclesiastical art, make a pilgrimage to explore the frescoes of the Romanesque-Gothic-Renaissance **Højby Kirke** (Højby Church) in the town of Højby, near Nykøbing Sjælland. In the town of Fårevejle is the Gothic **Fårevejle kirke,** with the earl of Bothwell's chapel. **Sjællands Odde** (Zealand's Tongue), the tiny strip of land north of the Sejerø Bay, offers slightly marshy but private beach strands. Inside the bay, the beaches are once again smooth and blond.

Roskilde

48 *101 km (63 mi) southeast of Odsherred, 32 km (20 mi) west of Copenhagen (on Rte. 156).*

Roskilde is Sjælland's second-largest town and one of its oldest, celebrating its 1,000-year anniversary in 1998 (☞ Nightlife and the Arts, *below*). For a weekend in the end of June, it's filled with the rock music of the **Roskilde Festival,** said to be the largest outdoor concert in northern Europe, attracting some 75,000 people.

Roskilde was the royal residence in the 10th century and became the spiritual capital of Denmark and northern Europe in 1170, when Bishop Absalon built the **Roskilde Domkirke** (Roskilde Cathedral) on the site of a church erected 200 years earlier by Harald Bluetooth. Overwhelming the center of town, the current structure took more than 300 years to complete and thus provides a one-stop crash course in Danish architecture. Inside are an ornate Dutch altarpiece and the sarcophagi—ranging from opulent to modest—of 38 Danish monarchs. Predictably, Christian IV is interred in a magnificent chapel with a massive painting of himself in combat and a bronze sculpture by Thorvaldsen. In modest contrast is the newest addition, the simple brick chapel of King Frederik IX, who died in 1972, outside the church. On the interior south wall above the entrance is a 16th-century clock showing St. George charging a dragon, which hisses and howls, echoing throughout the church and causing Peter Døver, "the Deafener," to sound the hour. A squeamish Kirsten Kiemer, "the Chimer," shakes her head in fright but manages to strike the quarters. ⊠ *Domkirkestr. 10,* ☎ *46/35–27–00.* � *Dkr 10.* ☉ *Hours vary; call ahead.*

Less than a kilometer (½ mi) north of the cathedral, on the fjord, is the modern **Vikingeskibshallen** (Viking Ship Museum), containing five Viking ships sunk in the fjord 1,000 years ago. Submerged to block the passage of enemy ships, they were discovered in 1957. The painstaking recovery involved building a watertight dam and then draining the water from that section of the fjord. The splinters of wreckage were then preserved and reassembled. A deep-sea trader, warship, ferry, merchant ship, and fierce 92½-ft man-of-war attest to the Vikings' sophisticated and aesthetic boat-making skills. ✉ *Strandengen,* ☎ *46/32–21–15.* ☞ *Dkr 50.* ☉ *Apr.–Oct., daily 9–5; Nov.–Mar., daily 10–4.*

Dining and Lodging

$$ ✕ **Club 42.** This popular Danish restaurant spills out into the walking
★ street with a few tables in the summertime, while inside the roof opens over the dining room. The fare is typically Danish, including smørrebrød and spareribs, simply prepared and served with potato salad. The rest of the menu includes lots of meat and potatoes, as well as fish. ✉ *Skomagerg. 42,* ☎ *46/35–17–64. DC, MC, V.*

$$ 🏨 **Hotel Prindsen.** Central in downtown Roskilde, this convenient hotel, built 100 years ago, is popular with business guests. The elegant dark-wood lobby leads to nondescript rooms that are, nonetheless, homey and comfortable. Downstairs, the restaurant La Bøf serves up grill and fish fare, and next door there's a cozy bar. ✉ *Alg. 13, DK–4000,* ☎ *46/35–80–10,* ꜰᴀх *46/35–81–10. 38 rooms. Restaurant, bar, meeting room. AE, DC, MC, V.*

$ 🏨 **Roskilde Vandrehjem Hørgården.** In front of a grassy yard, this youth hostel is perfect for families and budget travelers. In a former schoolhouse 2 km (1 mi) east of the Roskilde Domkirke, it looks straight out of third grade, and the rooms, with bunks, look like camp. You can have use of the kitchen. ✉ *Hørhusene 61, DK–4000,* ☎ *46/35–21–84,* ꜰᴀх *46/32–66–90. 21 rooms with 4 beds each, 8 showers. No credit cards. Closed Oct.–Apr.*

Nightlife and the Arts

To celebrate the town's 1,000th birthday in 1998, concerts, performances, and exhibits will run all year, and on September 5th, a cultural blowout will keep shops, cinemas, museums, and libraries open late into the night. Call the Roskilde Tourist Board (☞ Visitor Information *in* Sjælland and Its Islands A to Z, *below*) for a schedule of events.

The young head to **Gimle** (✉ Ringstedg. 30, ☎ 46/35–12–13) for live rock on the weekends. At **Bryggergården** (✉ Alg. 15, ☎ 46/35–01–03), or "The Draft Horse," adults have a late supper and beer in cozy surroundings. During the summer, **Mullerudi** (✉ Djalma Lunds Gord 7, ☎ 46/37–03–25) is an arty spot with indoor and outdoor seating and live jazz.

Outdoor Activities and Sports

GOLF

Roskilde has an 18-hole **golf course** (✉ Kongemarken 34, ☎ 46/37–01–80) with views of the twin-peaked Roskilde Cathedral and an encircling forest.

Shopping

CRAFTS

Between Roskilde and Holbæk is **Kirke Sonnerup Kunst-håndværk** (Art Handicrafts, ✉ Englerupvej 62, Såby, ☎ 46/49–25–77), with a good selection of pottery, glass, clothing, and woodwork produced by more than 50 Danish artists.

Lejre

🔵 *10 km (6 mi) west of Roskilde, 40 km (25 mi) west of Copenhagen.*

🅒 The 50-acre **Lejre Forsøgscenter** (Lejre Archaeological Research Center) compound contains a reconstructed village dating from the Iron Age and two 19th-century farmhouses. In summer a handful of hardy

Danish families live here and are under the observation of researchers; they go about their daily routine—grinding grain, herding goats, eating with their hands, and wearing furs and skins—providing a clearer picture of ancient ways of life. In Bodalen (Fire Valley), visitors (especially children) can grind corn, file an ax, and sail in a dugout canoe. ⊠ *Slangæleen 2,* ☎ *46/48–08–78.* ⊞ *Dkr 50.* ☉ *May–Sept., daily 10–5.*

Køge

50 *20 km (13 mi) southeast of Lejre, 40 km (25 mi) southwest of Copenhagen.*

The well-preserved medieval town of Køge is known for its historic witch hunts. In the centrally located **Køge Museum,** a 17th-century merchant's house, you will see souvenirs from Hans Christian Andersen, costumes, local artifacts, an executioner's sword, and a 13th-century stone font. The story goes that the font had to be removed from the town church after a crippled woman committed an unsavory act into it, hoping her bizarre behavior would cure her. Also on exhibit are 16th-century silver coins from a buried treasure of more than 2,000 coins found in the courtyard of Langkildes Gård. ⊠ *Nørreg. 4,* ☎ *56/63–42–42.* ⊞ *Dkr 20.* ☉ *June–Aug., daily 10–5; Sept.–May, weekdays 2–5, weekends 1–5.*

The old part of Køge is filled with 300 half-timber houses, all protected by the National Trust; it's a lovely area for a stroll. At the end of Kirkestræde, the 15th-century **Skt. Nikolai Kirke** (St. Nicholas Church) was once a lighthouse; its floor is covered with more than 100 tombs of Køge VIPs. Carved angels line the church's walls, but most have had their noses struck off—a favorite pastime of drunken Swedish soldiers in the 1700s. ⊠ *Kirkestr.,* ☎ *56/65–13–59.* ⊞ *Free.* ☉ *June–Aug., weekdays 10–4; Sept.–May, weekdays 10–noon. Tower tours late July–mid-Aug., weekdays at 11, noon, and 1.*

If you have time, visit the **Kunstmuseet Køge Skitsesamling** (Art Museum Køge Sketches Collection) for its changing exhibitions and an extensive permanent collection of sketches, sculpture, and other modern Danish art. ⊠ *Nørreg. 29,* ☎ *56/63–34–14.* ⊞ *Dkr 15. Free with admission ticket from the Køge Museum (☞ above).* ☉ *Tues.–Sun. 11–5.*

En Route   Twenty-four kilometers (15 miles) south of Køge near Rødvig, you should stop at the chalk cliffs called Stevns Klint to see the 13th-century **Højerup Kirke** built above them. As the cliffs eroded, first the cemetery, then the choir toppled into the sea. In recent years the church has been restored and the cliffs below bolstered by masonry to prevent further damage. ⊠ *Højerup Church, Stevns Klin.* ⊞ *Dkr 5.* ☉ *Apr.–Sept., daily 11–5.*

Møn

51 *85 km (52 mi) south of Stevns Klint, 130 km (81 mi) south of Copenhagen.*

The whole island of Møn is pocked with nearly 100 Neolithic burial mounds, but it is most famous for its dramatic chalk cliffs, the northern **Møns Klint,** three times as large as Stevns Klint (☞ En Route, *above*). Rimmed by a beech forest, the milky-white 75-million-year-old bluffs plunge 400 ft to a small, craggy beach—accessible by a path and more than 500 steps. Wear good walking shoes, and take care; though a park ranger checks the area for loose rocks, the cliffs crumble suddenly. Once there, Danish families usually hunt for blanched fossils of cuttlefish, sea urchins, and other sea life. The cliffs are an important navigational marker for ships, defining south Sjælland's otherwise flat topography.

You can walk to a delightful folly of the 18th century, **Liselund Slot** (not to be confused with a hotel of the same name), 4 km (2½ mi) north of the cliffs. Antoine de la Calmette, the island's sheriff and a royal chamberlain, took his inspiration from Marie Antoinette's *Hameau* (*Hamlet*) at Versailles and built the structure in 1792 for his beloved wife. The thatched palace, complete with English gardens, combines a Norwegian country facade with elegant Pompeian interiors. In this lovely setting, Hans Christian Andersen wrote his fairy tale *The Tinder Box*. The palace has been open to the public since 1938. ☎ 55/81–21–78. ☞ *Dkr 20.* ☉ *Tours (Danish and German only) May–Oct., Tues.–Fri. 10:30, 11, 1:30, and 2; weekends also 2, 4, and 4:30.*

Møn's capital, **Stege,** received its town charter in 1268. Take time to explore its medieval churches, including Elmelunde, Keldby, and Fanefjord, all famous for their naive frescoes. Thought to have been completed by a collaborative group of artisans, the whimsical paintings include pedagogic and biblical doodlings.

Lodging

$$ 🏰 **Liselund Ny Slot.** Set in a grand old manor on an isolated estate,
★   this modern hotel offers refined accommodations minus stodginess. The square staircase and painted ceilings have been preserved. The rooms are fresh and simple, with wicker and pastel schemes, half of them overlooking a swan-filled pond and the forest. The downstairs restaurant serves Danish cuisine. ☒ *Liselund Ny Slot, DK–4791 Børre,* ☎ 55/81–20–81, FAX *55/81–21–91. 25 rooms, 1 suite. Restaurant, meeting rooms. AE, DC, MC, V.*

Falster

3 km (2 mi) south of Bogø, 24 km (15 mi) south of Møn, 99 km (62 mi) south of Copenhagen.

Accessible by way of the striking Farø Bridge or the parallel Storstrømsbroen (Big Current Bridge) from Vordingborg, Falster is shaped like a tiny South America and has excellent blond beaches to rival those of its tropical twin. Among the best are the southeastern Marielyst and southernmost Gedser. Almost everywhere on the island you'll find cafés, facilities, and water-sports rentals. Falster is also one of the country's major producers of sugar beets.

☜ The **Middelaldercentret** (Center for the Middle Ages), a reconstructed medieval village, invites school classes to dress up in period costumes and experience life a millennium ago. Day guests can participate in activities that change weekly—from cooking to medieval knife-making to animal herding and, on weekends, folk dances and other cultural happenings. ☒ *Nykøbing Falster,* ☎ 54/86–19–34. ☞ *Dkr 45.* ☉ *May–Sept., daily 10–4.*

Dining and Lodging

$$$ ✕ **Czarens Hus.** This stylish old inn dates back more than 200 years, when it was a guest house and supply store for area farmers and merchants. Deep-green walls, gold trim, and chandeliers provide a background for antique furnishings. The specialty of the house is Continental Danish cuisine, which translates as creative beef and fish dishes, often served with cream sauces. Try the *Zar Beuf* (calf tenderloin in a mushroom-and-onion cream sauce). ☒ *Langg. 2, Nykøbing Falster,* ☎ 54/85–28–29. AE, DC, MC, V.

$$ ✕ **Brasserie Kælder and Køkken.** Done up in bright colors with a modern decor, this central and very popular café-restaurant is touted as one of the best in the area. The menu varies, with basics like steaks, sand-

wiches, and nachos, as well as the slightly more experimental, including ham with pineapple sauce, grilled ostrich steaks, and beef slices with Gorgonzola. ⊠ *Torvet 19, Nykøbing Falster,* ☎ *54/85–82–82. DC, MC, V. Closed Dec. 24–Jan. 2.*

$$ 🏨 **Hotel Falster.** This sleek and efficient hotel accommodates conference guests as well as vacationers with a comfortable and businesslike ambience. Rustic brick walls and Danish antiques mix with sleek Danish-design lamps and sculpture. Rooms are comfortably done with dark wood and modular furniture. ⊠ *Skovalleen, Nykøbing Falster, DK–4800,* ☎ *54/85–93–93,* FAX *54/82–21–99. 70 rooms. Restaurant, bar, meeting room. AE, DC, MC, V.*

Outdoor Activities and Sports

GOLF

The 18-hole **Sydsjælland Golf Klub** (⊠ Præstolandevej 39, Mogenstrup, ☎ 53/76–15–55) is more than 25 years old, and the park course is lined with a number of small lakes.

Lolland

🔁 *19 km (12 mi) west of Nykøbing Falster.*

The history of Lolland dates back more than 1,000 years, to a man named Saxe, who sat at the mouth of the fjord and collected a toll. He later cleared the surrounding land and leased it. It became known as Saxtorp and eventually Sakskøbing, the island's capital. Though most people head straight for the beaches, the area has a few sights, including a water tower with a smiling face and an excellent car museum near the central 13th-century **Ålholm Slot** (closed to the public). The **Ålholm Automobile Museum** is northern Europe's largest, with more than 200 vehicles. The town is accessible by bridge from Nykøbing Falster. ⊠ *Ålholm Parkvej, Nysted,* ☎ *54/87–19–11.* 🎫 *Dkr 60.* 🕐 *Sept. and Oct., Thurs. and Sun. 11–4.*

🐾 The **Knuthenborg Safari Park,** just 8 km (5 mi) west of Sakskøbing and also on Lolland, has a drive-through range where you can rubberneck at tigers, zebras, rhinoceroses, and giraffes, and pet camels, goats, and ponies. Besides seeing 20 species of animals, children can also play in Miniworld's jungle gym, minitrain, and other rides. ⊠ *Knuthenborg Safaripark, DK–4930 Maribo,* ☎ *54/78–80–88.* 🎫 *Dkr 78.* 🕐 *Late Apr.– late Sept., daily 9–5; late Sept.–late-Oct., weekends 9–5.*

Lodging

$$ 🏨 **Lalandia.** This massive water-park hotel has an indoor pool, beachside view, and lots of happy families. On the southern coast of Lolland, about 27 km (16 mi) southwest of Sakskøbing, the modern white apartments, with full kitchen and bath, accommodate up to eight people. There are three family-style restaurants—a steak house, Italian buffet, and pizzeria. ⊠ *Rødbyhavn, DK–4970 Rødby,* ☎ *54/60–42–00,* FAX *54/60–41–44. 636 apartments. 3 restaurants, bar, indoor pool, sauna, 9-hole golf course, 5 tennis courts, health club, playground, meeting rooms. AE, DC, MC, V.*

$ 🏨 **Hotel Saxkjøbing.** Behind its yellow half-timber facade, this comfortable hotel is short on character and frills, but the rooms are bright, sunny, and modern, if very simply furnished. In town center, the hotel is convenient to everything. Its family-style restaurant serves pizzas, steaks, and salads. ⊠ *Torvet 9, Sakskjøbing, DK–4990,* ☎ *54/70–40– 39,* FAX *54/89–53–50. 30 rooms, 20 with bath. Restaurant, bar, meeting room. AE, DC, MC, V.*

En Route   Kids adore and flock to **BonBon Land,** in the tiny southern Sjælland town of Holme Olstrup between Rønnede and Næstved. Filled with rides and friendly costumed grown-ups, the park is an old-fashioned playland, with a few eating and drinking establishments thrown in for adults. ☎ *53/76–26–00.* 💰 *Dkr 115, Dkr 99 off-season.* ☉ *Mid-May–mid-June and mid-Aug.–mid-Sept., weekdays 10–6 and weekends 9:30–8; mid-June–mid-Aug., daily 9:30–8; mid-Sept.–mid-Oct., weekends 9:30–5.*

Halsskov

 95 km (60 mi) northwest of Falster, 110 km (69 mi) southwest of Copenhagen.

Europe's second-longest tunnel-bridge, Storebæltsbro—the entire fixed-link length of which will be 18 km (11 mi)—links Halsskov, on west Sjælland, to Nyborg, on east Fyn. Rail traffic traverses the west bridge and tunnel while auto traffic passes on the east and west bridge. The **Storebæltsbro Udstillings Center** (Great Belt Exhibition Center), which details the tunnel-bridge construction process, includes videos and models and makes for an informative stop. ⊠ *Halsskov Odde,* ☎ *58/35–01–00.* 💰 *Dkr 35.* ☉ *May–Sept., daily 9–9; Oct.–Apr., Tues.–Sun. 10–5.*

Outdoor Activities and Sports

CANOEING

Just 15 km (10 mi) east of Slagelse and 30 km (19 mi) east of Halsskov is the Susâ (Sus River), where you can arrange hour-, day-, and week-long trips. Call **Susåen Kanoudlejning** regarding canoe rentals (☎ *57/64–61–44*).

GOLF

The 18-hole **Korsør Course** (⊠ Ørnumvej 8, Korsør, ☎ 58/37–18–36) is in Korsør, less than 3 km (2 mi) south of Halsskov.

Shopping

In Næstved, 49 km (31 mi) southeast of Halsskov, the **Holmegaards Glassværker** (Glass Workshop, ⊠ Glassværksvej 52, Fensmark, ☎ 55/54–62–00) sells seconds of glasses, lamps, and occasionally art glass, with savings of up to 50% off wholesale costs.

OFF THE
BEATEN PATH

TRÆLLEBORG – Viking enthusiasts will want to head 18 km (11 mi) north-east from Halsskov to Slagelse to see its excavated Viking encampment with a reconstructed army shelter. No longer content to rely on farmer warriors, the Viking hierarchy designed the geometrically exact camp within a circular, moated rampart, thought to be of Asian inspiration. The 16 barracks, of which there is one model, could accommodate 1,300 men. ⊠ Trælleborg Allé, ☎ 58/54–95–06. 💰 Dkr 40. ☉ Mid-Mar.–Oct., daily 10–5; Nov.–mid-Mar., daily noon–4.

Sjælland and Its Islands A to Z

Arriving and Departing

BY CAR

There are several **DSB** car ferries from Germany. They connect Kiel to Bagenkop, on the island of Langeland (from there, drive north to Spodsbjerg and take another ferry to Lolland, which is connected to Falster and Sjælland by bridges); Puttgarden to Rødbyhavn on Lolland; and Travemünde and Warnemünde to Gedser on Falster. Sjælland is connected to Fyn, which is connected to Jylland, by bridges and frequent ferries. If you are driving from Sweden, take a car ferry from either Helsingborg to Helsingør or Limhamn to Dragør. Or sail directly to Copenhagen (☞ Arriving and Departing *in* Copenhagen A to Z *in* Chapter 2). In Denmark, call DSB (international, ☎ 70/13–14–16; domestic, ☎ 70/13–14–15); in Sweden, call DSB Sweden (☎ 46/31–80–57–00).

BY PLANE
Copenhagen Airport is Sjælland's only airport (☞ Arriving and Departing *in* Copenhagen A to Z *in* Chapter 2).

BY TRAIN
Most train routes to Sjælland, whether international or domestic, are directed to Copenhagen. Routes to north and south Sjælland almost always require a transfer at Copenhagen's main station. For timetables, call **DSB** (☎ international, ☎ 70/13–14–16; domestic, ☎ 70/13–14–15).

Getting Around

BY CAR
Highways and country roads throughout Sjælland are excellent, and traffic—even around Copenhagen—is manageable most of the time. As elsewhere in Denmark, take care to give right-of-way to the bikes driving to the right of the traffic.

BY PUBLIC TRANSPORTATION
The **Copenhagen Card,** which affords free train and bus transport, as well as admission to museums and sites, is valid within the HT-bus and rail system, which extends north to Helsingør, west to Roskilde, and south to Køge (☞ Getting Around *in* Copenhagen A to Z *in* Chapter 2). Every town in Sjælland has a central train station, usually within walking distance of hotels and sights. (For long distances, buses are not convenient.) The only part of the island not connected to the DSB network is the sliver of northwestern peninsula known as Sjællands Odde. Trains leave from Holbæk to Højby, where you can bus to the tip of the point. For information, call the private railway company **Odsherrede** (☎ 53/41–00–03). Two vintage trains dating from the 1880s run from Helsingør and Hillerød to Gilleleje; call for info (☎ 48/30–00–30 or 42/12–00–98).

Contacts and Resources

EMERGENCIES
Police, Fire, or Ambulance: (☎ 112).

Hospitals: Helsingør (✉ Esrumvej 145, ☎ 48/29–29–29). **Roskilde** (✉ Roskilde Amtssygehus, Køgevej 7, ☎ 46/32–32–00).

Pharmacies: Helsingør (✉ Axeltorvs, Groskenstr. 2A, ☎ 49/21–12–23). **Stengades** (✉ Steng. 46, ☎ 49/21–86–00). **Roskilde** (✉ Dom Apoteket, Alg. 52, ☎ 46/32–32–77). **Svane** (✉ Skomagerg. 12, ☎ 42/32–23–00).

GUIDED TOURS
Check with the local tourism boards for general sightseeing tours in the larger towns or for self-guided walking tours. Most tours of Sjælland begin in Copenhagen. For information, call **Copenhagen Excursion** (☎ 32/54–06–06).

Boat Tour: The turn-of-the-century *Saga Fjord* (☎ 46/75–64–60) gives tours of the waters of the Roskildefjord from April through September; meals are served on board. Schedules vary; call ahead.

Castle Tours: The **Afternoon Hamlet Tour** (5 hours) includes Frederiksborg Castle and the exterior of Fredensborg Palace and Kronborg Castle. The seven-hour **Castle Tour of North Zealand** visits Frederiksborg Castle and the outside of Fredensborg Palace, and stops at Kronborg Castle.

Walking Tours: The six-hour Roskilde **Vikingland Tour** includes the market and cathedral, Christian IV's Chapel, and the Viking Ship Museum.

VISITOR INFORMATION

Helsingør (✉ Havnepl. 3, ☎ 49/21–13–33). **Hillerød**(✉ Slangerupgade 2, ☎ 48/24–26–26). **Køge** (✉ Vesterg. 1, ☎ 53/65–58–00). **Lolland** (✉ Østergårdg. 7, Nykøbing Falster, ☎ 54/85–13–03). **Roskilde** (✉ Gullandsstræde 15, ☎ 46/35–27–00). **Sakskøbing** (✉ Torveg. 4, ☎ 54/70–56–30 summer; ☎ 53/89–45–72 winter). **Stege and Møn** (✉ Storeg. 2, Stege, ☎ 55/81–44–11).

4 FYN AND THE CENTRAL ISLANDS

CHRISTENED THE GARDEN of Denmark by its most famous son, Hans Christian Andersen, Fyn (Funen)
is the smaller of the country's two major islands. A
patchwork of vegetable fields and flower gardens, the flat-as-a-board
countryside is relieved by beech glades and swan ponds. Manor houses
and castles pop up from the countryside like magnificent mirages.
Some of northern Europe's best-preserved castles are here: the 12th-
century Nyborg Slot, travel pinup Egeskov Slot, and the lavish Valdemars Slot. The fairy-tale cliché often attached to Denmark really does
spring from this provincial isle, where the only faint pulse emanates
from Odense, its capital. Trimmed with thatched houses and green parks,
the city makes the most of the Andersen legacy but surprises with a
rich arts community at the Brandts Klædefabrik, a former textile factory turned museum compound.

Towns in Fyn are best explored by car. It's even quick and easy to reach
the smaller islands of Langeland and Tåsinge—both are connected to
Fyn by bridges. Slightly more isolated is Ærø, where the town of
Ærøskøbing, with its painted half-timber houses and winding streets,
seems caught in a delightful time warp.

Biking

Flat and smooth, Fyn is perfect for biking. Packages with bike rental,
hotel accommodations, and half-board (breakfast and one meal) for
the entire region are available from **Hotel Svendborg** (✉ Centrumpl.,
5700 Svendborg, ☎ 62/21–17–00).

Markets

Wednesday and Saturday are market days in towns across Fyn throughout the summer. Often held in the central square, these morning markets offer fresh produce, flowers, and cheeses.

Nightlife and the Arts

Castle concerts are held throughout the summer at Egeskov, Nyborg,
and Valdemar castles and the rarely opened Krengerup manor house
near Assens.

Nyborg

54 *136 km (85 mi) southwest of Copenhagen, including the bridge across
the Great Belt, 30 km (19 mi) southeast of Odense.*

Like most visitors, you should begin your tour of Fyn in Nyborg, a
13th-century town that was Denmark's capital during the Middle
Ages. The city's major landmark, the moated 12th-century **Nyborg Slot**
(Nyborg Castle), was the seat of the Danehof, the Danish parliament
from 1200 to 1413. It was here that King Erik Klipping signed the country's first constitution, the Great Charter, in 1282. In addition to ge-
ometric wall murals and an armory collection, the castle houses
changing art exhibits. ✉ *Slotspl.,* ☎ *65/31–02–07.* ⌷ *Dkr 10.* ☉ *June–
Aug., daily 10–5; Mar.–May and Sept.–Oct., Tues.–Sun. 10–3.*

Cross Gammel Torv and walk down the street to the **Nyborg Museum,**
housed in a half-timber merchant's house from 1601, for a picture of
17th-century life. Aside from furnished rooms, there's a small brewery. ✉ *Slotspl. 11,* ☎ *65/31–02–07.* ⌷ *Dkr 10.* ☉ *June–Aug., daily
10–5; Mar.–May and Sept.–Oct., Tues.–Sun. 10–3.*

Finally, a travel companion that doesn't snore on the plane or eat all your peanuts.

123 456 7891 2345
J.D. SMITH

When traveling, your MCI WorldCom Card is the best way to keep in touch. Our operators speak your language, so they'll be able to connect you back home—no matter where your travels take you. Plus, your MCI WorldCom Card is easy to use, and even earns you frequent flyer miles every time you use it. When you add in our great rates, you get something even more valuable: peace-of-mind. So go ahead. Travel the world. MCI WorldCom just brought it a whole lot closer.

You can even sign up today at www.mci.com/worldphone or ask your operator to make a collect call to 1-410-314-2938.

EASY TO CALL WORLDWIDE

1. **Just dial the WorldPhone access number of the country you're calling from.**
2. **Dial or give the operator your MCI WorldCom Card number.**
3. **Dial or give the number you're calling.**

Australia ◆	
To call using OPTUS	1-800-551-111
To call using TELSTRA	1-800-881-100
Bahamas/Bermuda	1-800-888-8000
British Virgin Islands	1-800-888-8000
Costa Rica ◆	0-800-012-2222
Denmark	8001-0022
Norway ◆	800 -19912
India	000-127
For collect access	000-126
United States/Canada	1-800-888-8000

For your complete WorldPhone calling guide, dial the WorldPhone access number for the country you're in and ask the operator for Customer Service. In the U.S. call 1-800-431-5402.

◆ Public phones may require deposit of coin or phone card for dial tone.

EARN FREQUENT FLYER MILES

AmericanAirlines®
AAdvantage®

Continental Airlines
OnePass

▲**Delta Air Lines**
SkyMiles

▰ **MILEAGE PLUS.**
United Airlines

U·S AIRWAYS
DIVIDEND MILES

MCI WorldCom, its logo and the names of the products referred to herein are proprietary marks of MCI WorldCom, Inc. All airline names and logos are proprietary marks of the respective airlines. All airline program rules and conditions apply.

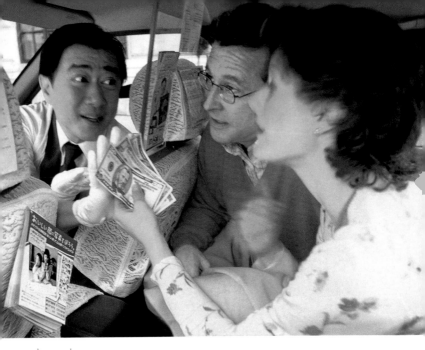

The first thing you need overseas is the one thing you forget to pack.

FOREIGN CURRENCY DELIVERED OVERNIGHT

Chase Currency To Go® delivers foreign currency to your home by the next business day*

It's easy—before you travel, call 1-888-CHASE84 for delivery of any of 75 currencies

Delivery is free with orders of $500 or more

Competitive rates— without exchange fees

You don't have to be a Chase customer—you can pay by Visa® or MasterCard®

 CHASE

THE RIGHT RELATIONSHIP IS EVERYTHING.®

1•888•CHASE84
www.chase.com

Fyn and the Central Islands

KEY
— Rail Lines
--- Ferry

Dining and Lodging

$$ ✕ **Danehofkroen.** Outside Nyborg Slot, this family-run restaurant does a brisk lunch business, serving traditional Danish meals to tourists who enjoy a view of the castle and its tree-lined moat. The menu is basic meat and potatoes, with such dishes as *flæskesteg* (sliced pork served with the crisp rind). ⊠ *Slotspl.,* ☎ 65/31–02–02. *Reservations essential. No credit cards. Closed Mon.*

$$$$ ▣ **Hesselet.** A modern brick slab outside, this hotel is a refined Anglo-Asian sanctuary on the inside. Guest rooms have cushy, modern furniture, most with a splendid view of the Storebæltsbro. ⊠ *Christianslundsvej 119, DK–5800 Nyborg,* ☎ 65/31–30–29, ⊠ 65/31–29–58. *43 rooms, 3 suites. Restaurant, bar, room service, indoor pool, sauna, tennis courts, meeting rooms. AE, DC, MC, V.*

Shopping

ANTIQUES

Many of Fyn's manor houses and castles now double as antiques emporiums. The largest is at **Hindemae** (⊠ Near Rte. 315, 12 km/7 mi west of Nyborg, exit 46 or 47 in Ullerslev, ☎ 65/35–22–05). A modest selection of antiques is for sale at **Hønnerup Hovgård** (⊠ Hovgårdsvej 6, Hønnerup, 40 km/25 mi northwest of Nyborg, ☎ 64/49–13–00); take exit 55 to Route 161 toward Middelfart; follow the signs to Hønnerup.

Kerteminde

⑤⑤ *21 km (13 mi) north of Nyborg, 20 km (13 mi) northeast of Odense.*

Kerteminde is an important fishing village and picturesque summer resort. On Langegade, walk past the neat half-timber houses to Møllebakken and the museum of the Danish painter **Johannes Larsen** (1867–1961). Across from a crimson strawberry patch and a 100-year-old windmill, the artist built a large country villa that has been perfectly preserved, right down to the teacups. In front, you'll see a sculpture of a woman by Kai Nielsen. Local legend has it that one night, after a particularly wild party in Copenhagen, its legs were broken off. An ambulance was called, and once it arrived, the enraged driver demanded that the artists pay a fine. A chagrined Larsen paid, and in return kept the wounded sculpture. ⊠ *Møllebakken,* ☎ *65/32–37–27.* 🖾 *Dkr 40.* ☉ *June–Aug., daily 10–5; Mar.–May and Sept.–Oct., Tues.–Sun. 10–4; Nov.–Feb., Tues.–Sun. 11–4.*

Dining

$$$$ ✕ **Rudolf Mathis.** This busy harborside restaurant is topped by two chimneys venting open grills that broil popular fish dishes. Favorites are catfish with butter, fennel, and Pernod sauce, and grilled turbot in green-pepper-and-lime sauce. ⊠ *Dosseringen 13,* ☎ *65/32–32–33. AE, DC, MC, V. Closed Mon. Jan.–Mar. and Sun. Oct. and Dec.*

Shopping

CERAMICS

Just a few miles west of Kerteminde is **Bjørnholt Keramik** (⊠ Risingevej 12, Munkebo, ☎ 65/97–40–90), where you can watch ceramics in the making.

Ladby

56 *4 km (2½ mi) south of Kerteminde, 16 km (10 mi) east of Odense.*

The village of Ladby is best known as the home of the 1,100-year-old remains of the **Ladbyskibet.** This Viking chieftain's ship burial is complete with hunting dogs and horses for his trip to Valhalla—the afterlife. ⊠ *Vikingevej 12,* ☎ *65/32–16–67.* 🖾 *Dkr 25.* ☉ *Mid-May–mid-Sept., daily 10–6; Mar.–mid-May and mid-Sept.–Oct., daily 10–4; Nov.–Feb., weekends 11–3.*

Odense

57 *20 km (12 mi) southwest of Ladby on Route 165, 144 km (90 mi) west of Copenhagen.*

It's no coincidence that Odense, the capital of Fyn and third largest city in Denmark, is reminiscent of a storybook village—much of its charm is built upon the legend of its most famous son, author Hans Christian Andersen. First see the flourishing **Kongens Have** (King's Garden) and 18th-century **Odense Castle,** now a government building. Walking east on Stationsvej to Thomas B. Thriges Gade and Hans Jensens stræde, you'll come to the **Hans Christian Andersen Hus** (Hans Christian Andersen House) amid half-timber houses and cobbled streets. Inside, the storyteller's life is chronicled through his photographs, drawings, letters, and personal belongings. The library has Andersen's works in more than 100 languages, and you can listen to fairy tales on tape. ⊠ *Hans Jensensstr. 37–45,* ☎ *66/14–88–14 ext. 4611.* 🖾 *Dkr 30.* ☉ *June–Aug., Tues.–Sun. 9–7; Sept.–May, Tues.–Sun. 10–4.*

The sleek **Carl Nielsen Museum** creates multimedia exhibits of the life and work of Denmark's most famous composer (1865–1931) and of his wife, the sculptor Anne Marie Carl-Nielsen (yes, that's the way she took his name). ⊠ *Claus-Bergs G. 11,* ☎ *66/14–88–14, ext. 4671.* 🖾 *Dkr 15.* ☉ *Nov.–Mar., Thurs.–Fri. 4–8, weekends noon–4; Apr.–May, and Sept.–Oct., Thurs.–Sun. noon to 4; June–Aug., Tues.–Sun., noon–4.*

Møntergården, Odense's museum of urban history, occupies four 17th-century row houses in a shady, cobbled courtyard. Exhibits range from interiors of the Middle Ages to Denmark's Nazi occupation to an impressive coin collection. ⊠ *Overg. 48–50,* ☎ *66/14–88–14, ext. 4611.* 🎫 *Dkr 15.* ⊙ *Daily Tues.–Sun. 10–4.*

The stately **St. Knuds Kirke,** built from the 13th to the 15th century, is the only purely Gothic cathedral in Denmark. The intricate wooden altar covered with gold leaf was carved by German sculptor Claus Berg. Beneath the sepulchre are the bones of St. (King) Knud, killed during a farmers' uprising in 1086, and his brother. ⊠ *Toward the pedestrian zone of St. Knuds Kirkestræde, in front of Andersen Park.*

In the diminutive **H. C. Andersens Barndomshjem** (H. C. Andersen's Childhood Home), the young boy and his parents lived in a room barely 5 ft by 6 ft. ⊠ *Munkemøllestr. 3–5,* ☎ *66/14–88–14, ext. 4611.* ⊙ *Jun.–Aug., daily 10–4; Sept.–May, Tues.–Sun. 11–3.*

For something completely different—relatively speaking—head to the **Superbowl Odense,** just west of the center of town. An indoor entertainment center with bowling alleys, amusement arcades, restaurants, and a go-cart track, its crowning attraction is the **Elvis Presley Museum,** which, according to its organizers, is the only one outside of the United States. It includes photographs, jumpsuits, big belts, and a mini Graceland diorama. ⊠ *Grønløkken 3,* ☎ *66/19–16–40.* 🎫 *Dkr 35.* ⊙ *Daily 10–5.*

Filosofgangen is the embarkation point for the **Odense River Cruises** (☎ *65/95–79–96*). Here you can catch a boat (May–mid-Aug., daily on the hour 10–5, returning 35 minutes later) downriver to the Fruens Bøge (Lady's Beech Forest) and then walk down Erik Bøghs Sti (Erik Bøgh's Footpath) to **Den Fynske Landsby** (the Fyn Village). Among the country's largest open-air museums, it includes 25 farm buildings and workshops, a vicarage, a water mill, and a theater, which in summer stages adaptations of Andersen's tales. Afterward, cruise back to town center or catch Bus 21 or 22, and walk down the boutique- and café-lined pedestrian street Vestergade (Kongensgade running perpendicular to the town hall), which in summer is abuzz with street performers, musicians, and brass bands. ⊠ *Sejerskovvej 20,* ☎ *66/14–88–14, ext. 4642.* 🎫 *Dkr 30.* ⊙ *June–Aug., daily 9:30–7; Apr.–May and Sept.–Oct., Tues.–Sun. 10–5; Nov.–Mar., Sun. 11–5.*

★ Occupying a former textile factory, the four-story artist compound **Brandts Klædefabrik** now houses the **Museet for Fotokunst** (Museum of Photographic Art), **Danmarks Grafiske Museum** (Danish Graphics Museum), **Dansk Presse Museum** (Danish Press Museum), and **Kunsthallen** (Art Gallery). National and international exhibits vary widely, but the photography museum and the art gallery show especially experimental work. ⊠ *North of the river and parallel to Kongensgade, Brandts Passage 37,* ☎ *66/13–78–97.* 🎫 *Combined ticket Dkr 50; photography museum DKr 25; graphics museum Dkr 20; press museum Dkr 20; art gallery Dkr 30; combined graphics and press museum Dkr 25.* ⊙ *July and Aug., daily 10–5; Sept.–June, Tues.–Sun. 10–5.*

OFF THE BEATEN PATH

HOLLUFGÅRD – This 16th-century manor now houses the city's archaeological department. Although the house itself remains closed, its grounds contain a completely renovated old barn and adjacent buildings showing special exhibits, including the archaeological find of the month and an ecology display. Nearby are a sculpture center, where you can see an artist at work, and a sculpture garden. Take Bus 61 from the railway station on Østre Stationsvej 10 km (6 mi) south of Odense. ⊠ *Hestehaven 201,* ☎ *66/14–88–14, ext. 4638* 🎫 *Dkr 25.* ⊙ *Apr.–Oct., Tues.–Sun. 10–5.; Nov.–Apr., Sun. 11–4.*

Dining and Lodging

$$$$ ✕ **Marie Louise.** Near the pedestrian street, this elegant whitewashed dining room glitters with crystal and silver. The daily French-Danish menu typically offers such specialties as salmon scallop with bordelaise sauce and grilled veal with lobster-cream sauce. Business and holiday diners are sometimes treated to gratis extras—such as quail's egg appetizers or after-dinner drinks. ⊠ *Lottrups Gaard, Vesterg. 70–72,* ☎ *66/17–92–95. AE, DC, MC, V. Closed Sun. and July.*

$$$ ✕ **La Petite Cuisine Française.** This romantic little restaurant, tucked in the Brandts Passage, can accommodate about 40 guests, all of whom must make reservations at least a few days in advance. The southern French specialties change every day according to what can be purchased fresh at the market. Typical dishes include Asian-inspired marinated duck breast, grilled skewered salmon or catfish with vegetables, and white mocha parfait for dessert. Dishes can be combined in three- to five-course menus. ⊠ *Brandts Passage 13,* ☎ *66/14–11–00. Reservations essential. DC, MC, V.*

$$ ✕ **Den Gamle Kro.** Built within the courtyards of several 17th-century homes, this popular restaurant has walls of ancient stone sliced by a sliding glass roof. The French-Danish menu includes fillet of sole stuffed with salmon mousse and chateaubriand with garlic potatoes, but there's also inexpensive smørrebrød. ⊠ *Overg. 23,* ☎ *66/12–14–33. DC, MC, V.*

$$ ✕ **Le Provence.** A few minutes from the pedestrian street, this intimate restaurant with a bright yellow and orange dining room puts a modern twist on Provençal cuisine. Dishes might be venison in blackberry sauce and tender duck breast cooked in sherry. ⊠ *Pogestræde 31,* ☎ *66/12–12–96. DC, MC, V.*

$ ✕ **Den Grimme Ælling.** The name of this chain restaurant means the
★ Ugly Duckling, but inside it's simply homey, with pine furnishings and family-style interiors. It's also extremely popular with tourists and locals alike, thanks to an all-you-can-eat buffet heaped with cold and warm dishes. ⊠ *Hans Jensensstr. 1,* ☎ *65/91–70–30. DC, MC.*

$ ✕ **Målet.** A lively crowd calls this sports club its neighborhood bar. After the steaming plates of schnitzel served in a dozen ways, soccer is the chief delight of the house. ⊠ *Jernbaneg. 17,* ☎ *66/17–82–41. Reservations not accepted. No credit cards.*

$$$ ☷ **First Hotel Grand Odense.** A century old, with renovated fin-de-siècle charm, this imposing four-story, brick-front hotel greets guests with old-fashioned luxury. The original stone floors and chandeliers lead to a wide staircase and upstairs guest rooms that are modern, with plush furnishings and sleek marble bathrooms. ⊠ *Jernabaneg. 18, DK–5000 Odense C,* ☎ *66/11–71–71,* ⟨FAX⟩ *66/14–11–71. 134 rooms, 13 suites. Room service, sauna. AE, DC, MC, V.*

$ ☷ **Hotel Ydes.** Constantly under undisturbing renovation, this well-kept, bright, and colorful hotel is a good bet for students and budget-conscious travelers tired of barracks-type accommodations. The plain hospital-style rooms are spotless and comfortable. ⊠ *Hans Tausensg. 11, DK–5000 Odense C,* ☎ *66/12–11–31. 30 rooms, 24 with bath. Café. MC, V.*

Nightlife and the Arts

CAFÉS AND BARS

Odense's central Arcade is an entertainment mall, with bars, restaurants, and live music ranging from corny sing-alongs to hard rock. For a quiet evening, stop by **Café Biografen** (⊠ Brandts Passage, ☎ 66/13–16–16) for an espresso or beer, light snack, and the atmosphere of an old movie house. Or settle in to see one of the wide variety of films screened here.

The **Air Pub** (⊠ Kongsg. 41, ☎ 66/14–66–08) is a Danish pub that caters to a slightly older crowd—thirty- and forty-something—with meals and a small dance floor. **Klos Ands** (⊠ Vineg. 76, ☎ 66/13–56–00) used to be just for grown-ups, but its specialty, malt whiskey, is now drawing a younger crowd, too. At the **All Night Boogie Dance Café** (⊠ Nørreg. 21, ☎ 66/14–00–39), a laid-back crowd grooves to pop, disco, and '60s music.

CASINO

Fyn's sole casino is in the slick glass atrium of the **SAS Hans Christian Andersen Hotel** (⊠ Claus Bergs G. 7, Odense, ☎ 66/14–78–00), where you can gamble at blackjack, roulette, and baccarat.

JAZZ CLUBS

Grøntorvet Café and Bar (⊠ Sortebrødre Torv 9, ☎ 66/14–34–37) presents live jazz at 5 PM Thursday and 2 PM Saturday. **Dexter's** (⊠ Vinderg. 65, ☎ 66/13–68–88) has all kinds of jazz—from Dixieland to fusion—Friday and Saturday nights.

THEATER

In summer the young members of the **Hans Christian Andersen Parade** present a pastiche of the Bard's fairy tales in a couple of different languages at Lotzes Have, an herb garden behind the Hans Christian Andersen Museum. **Den Fynske Landsby** (☞ *above*) stages Andersen plays from mid-July to mid-August.

Outdoor Activities and Sports

GOLF

The **Odense Eventyr Golfklub** (☎ 66/17–11–44) is 4 km (2½ mi) southwest of Odense, and was built in 1993. The 27-hole **Odense Golf Klub** (☎ 65/95–90–00), 6 km (4 mi) southeast of Odense, was built in 1980 and is relatively flat, with some trees and woods. The nine-hole driving range and putting greens in **Blommenlyst** (☎ 65/96–80–08) are 12 km (7 mi) from Odense, west toward Middelfart.

Shopping

Flensted Uromageren Hus (⊠ Ramsherred 4, ☎ 66/12–70–44), famous for its paper mobiles, is just across from the Hans Christian Andersen Hus. Inside, handmade mobiles range from simple paper hangings to intricate ceramic balloons.

Assens

⑤⑧ *38 km (24 mi) southwest of Odense.*

★ Near the quiet town of Assens is one of the most extraordinary private gardens in Denmark: Tove Sylvest's sprawling **Seven Gardens.** A privately owned botanical United Nations, the gardens represent the flora of seven European countries, including many plants rare to Denmark. ⊠ *Å Strandvej 62, Ebberup,* ☎ *64/74–12–85.* ▭ *Dkr 25.* ☉ *Mid-Mar.–Oct., daily 10–5.*

Very close by on the same street is the **Hviids Have,** a 4,000-square-meter Japanese garden complete with elegant ponds traversed upon by rough-plank walkways, as well as stone settings and just enough greenery. ⊠ *Å Strandvej 33, Ebberup,* ☎ *64/74–11–02.* ▭ *Dkr 25.* ☉ *June–Aug., daily 10–6.*

☾ Children will appreciate a detour 18 km (11 mi) northeast to Fyn's **Terrarium,** where they can examine all kinds of slippery and slithery creatures, including snakes, iguanas, alligators, and the nearly extinct blue frog. ⊠ *Kirkehelle 5, Vissenbjerg,* ☎ *64/47–18–50.* ▭ *Dkr 40.* ☉ *May–Aug., daily 10–6; Sept.–Apr., daily 10–4.*

Fåborg

59 *30 km (18 mi) south of Odense (via Rte. 43).*

The surrounding beaches of this lovely 12th-century town are invaded by sun-seeking Germans and Danes in summer. Four times a day you can hear the dulcet chiming of a carillon, the island's largest. In town center is the controversial *Ymerbrønden* sculpture by Kai Nielsen, depicting a naked man drinking from an emaciated cow while it licks a baby. The 18th-century **Den Gamle Gård** (Old Merchant's House), of 1725, chronicles the local history of Fåborg through furnished interiors and exhibits of glass and textiles. ⊠ *Holkeg. 1,* ☎ *62/61–33–38.* ⊡ *Dkr 20.* ☉ *Mid-May–Sept., daily 10: 30–4:30.*

The **Fåborg Museum for Fynsk Malerkunst** (Fyn Painting Museum) has a good collection of turn-of-the-century paintings and sculpture by the Fyn Painters, a school of artists whose work captures the dusky light of the Scandinavian sun. ⊠ *Grønneg. 75,* ☎ *62/61–06–45.* ⊡ *Dkr 25.* ☉ *June–Aug., daily 10–5; Apr.–May and Sept.–Oct., daily 10–4; Nov.–Mar., daily 11–3.*

Dining and Lodging

$ ✕ **Vester Skerninge Kro.** Midway between Fåborg and Svendborg, this traditional inn is cluttered and comfortable. Pine tables are polished from years of serving hot stews and homemade *medister pølse* (mild grilled sausage) and *æggekage* (fluffy omelet made with cream, smoked bacon, chives, and tomatoes). ⊠ *Krovej 9, Vester Skerninge,* ☎ *62/24–10–04. No credit cards. Closed Tues.*

$$$$ ✕▥ **Falsled Kro.** Once a smuggler's hideaway, the 500-year-old Fal-
★   sled Kro is now one of Denmark's most elegant inns. A favorite among well-heeled Europeans, it has appointed its cottages sumptuously with European antiques and stone fireplaces. The restaurant combines French and Danish cuisines, using ingredients from its garden and markets in Lyon. ⊠ *Assensvej 513, DK–5642 Millinge,* ☎ *62/68–11–11* ᵮᴬˣ *62/68–11–62. 14 rooms, 3 apartments. Restaurant, room service, 3-hole golf course, horseback riding, boating. AE, DC, MC, V. Closed Jan. and Feb.*

$$$ ✕▥ **Steensgaard Herregårdspension.** A long avenue of beeches leads to this 700-year-old moated manor house, 7 km (4½ mi) northwest of Fåborg. The rooms are elegant, with antiques, four-poster beds, and yards of silk damask. The fine restaurant serves wild game from the manor's own reserve. ⊠ *Steensgaard 4, DK–5642 Millinge,* ☎ *62/61–94–90,* ᵮᴬˣ *62/61–78–61. 15 rooms, 13 with bath. Restaurant, tennis court, horseback riding. AE, DC, MC, V. Closed Jan.*

Svendborg

60 *25 km (15 mi) east of Fåborg (via Rte. 44 east), 44 km (28 mi) south of Odense.*

Svendborg is Fyn's second-largest town, and one of the country's most important—not to mention happy—cruise harbors. It celebrates its eight-century-old maritime traditions every July, when old Danish wooden ships congregate in the harbor for the circular Fyn *rundt,* or regatta. Play your cards right, and you might hitch aboard and shuttle between towns. Contact the tourist board or any agreeable captain. With many charter-boat options and good marinas, Svendborg is an excellent base from which to explore the hundreds of islands of the South Fyn archipelago.

In Svendborg center is Torvet—the town's market square. To the left on Fruestræde is the black-and-yellow **Anne Hvides Gård,** the oldest secular structure in Svendborg and one of the four branches of **Svend-borgs Omegns Museum** (Svendborg County Museum). This evocative exhibit includes 18th- and 19th-century interiors and glass and silver collections. ⊠ *Fruestr. 3,* ☎ *62/21–02–61.* ☜ *Dkr 15.* ☉ *Late May–mid-June, daily 10–4; mid-June–late Oct., daily 10–5.*

Bagergade (Baker's Street) is lined with some of Svendborg's oldest half-timber houses. At the corner of Grubbemøllevej and Svinget is the **Viebæl-tegård,** the headquarters of the Svendborg County Museum, a former poorhouse. You can wander through dining halls, washrooms, and the "tipsy clink," where, as recently as 1974, inebriated citizens were left to sober up. ⊠ *Grubbemøllevej 13,* ☎ *62/21–02–61.* ☜ *Dkr 20. Combined admission to Anne Hvides and Svendborgs Omegns museums Dkr 30.* ☉ *May–mid-June, daily 10–4; mid-June–Oct., daily 10–5; Nov., Dec., Mar., and Apr., daily 1–4; Jan. and Feb., weekdays 1–4.*

Dining and Lodging

$ ✕ **Ærø.** A dim hodgepodge of ship parts and nautical doodads, this restaurant looks like it's always been there, just as is. It's peopled by brusque waitresses and serious local trenchermen who exchange orders from a menu that is staunchly old-fashioned, featuring *frikadeller* (fried meatballs), fried *rødspætte* (plaice) with hollandaise sauce, and dozens of smørrebrød options. ⊠ *Brøg. 1 ved, Ærøfærgen,* ☎ *62/21–07–60. DC, MC, V. Closed Sun.*

$$ 🏨 **Margrethesminde.** The Fyn equivalent of a bed-and-breakfast, this manor house is 16 km (10 mi) west of Svendborg. Owners Marlene Philip and Henrik Nielsen furnished the sunny house with bright colors and modern furnishings, and serve their guests a generous breakfast, ranging from Danish pastries or dark bread and cheese to bacon and eggs. Two of the six rooms are singles. ⊠ *Fåborgvej 154, DK–5762 Vester Skerninge,* ☎ *62/24–10–44,* 📠 *62/24–10–62. 6 rooms, 1 with bath. Bicycles. MC.*

Nightlife and the Arts

A diverse crowd congregates at **Bortløbne Banje** (⊠ Klosterpl. 7, ☎ 62/22–31–21) to hear live rock and blues. **Chess** (⊠ Vesterg. 7, ☎ 62/22–17–16) is popular with a young crowd that comes for the live bands. **Crazy Daizy** (⊠ Frederiksg. 6, ☎ 62/21–67–60) attracts a casual, over-21 crowd to dance to oldies and rock on Saturday nights, and a younger crowd on Fridays. The restaurant **Orangi** (⊠ Jessens Mole, ☎ 62/22–82–92), an old sailing ship moored in the harbor, hires live jazz in summer.

Kværndrup

🔞 *15 km (9 mi) north of Svendborg, 28 km (18 mi) south of Odense.*

★ Over this town presides the moated Renaissance **Egeskov Slot,** one of the best-preserved island-castles in Europe. Peaked with copper spires and surrounded by Renaissance, Baroque, English, and peasant gardens, the castle has an antique-vehicle museum and the world's largest maze, designed by the Danish scientist-turned-poet Piet Hein. The castle is still a private home, though visitors can see a few of the rooms, including the great hall, the hunting room, and the Riborg Room, where the daughter of the house was locked up from 1599 to 1604 after giving birth to a son out of wedlock. ⊠ *Kværndrup,* ☎ *62/27–10–16.* ☜ *Castle and museum Dkr 110.* ☉ *Castle May–June and Aug.–Sept., daily 10–5; July, daily 10–8. Museum June and Aug., daily 9–6; July, daily 9–8; May and Sept., daily 10–5.*

Troense

⑫ *3 km (2 mi) south of Svendborg (via the Svendborg Sound Bridge), 43 km (27 mi) south of Odense.*

Tåsinge island is known for its local 19th-century drama involving Elvira Madigan (recall the movie?) and her married Swedish lover, Sixten Sparre. Preferring heavenly union to earthly separation, they shot themselves and are now buried in the island's central Landet churchyard. Brides throw their bouquets on the lovers' grave.

★ Troense is Tåsinge's main town, and one of the country's best-preserved maritime villages, with half-timber buildings opening through hand-carved doors. South of town is **Valdemars Slot** (Valdemars Castle), dating from 1610, one of Denmark's oldest privately owned castles. You can wander through almost all the sumptuously furnished rooms, libraries, and the candle-lit church. There's also an X-rated 19th-century cigar box not to be missed. ⊠ *Slotsalleen 100, Troense,* ☎ *62/22–61–06 or 62/22–50–04.* ☐ *Dkr 45.* ☉ *June–Aug., daily 10–6; May and Sept.–Oct., daily 10–5.*

Dining

$$$ ✕ **Restaurant Valdemars Slot.** Beneath the castle, this domed restaurant is ankle-deep in pink carpet and aglow with candlelight. Fresh French and German ingredients and wild game from the castle's preserve are the menu staples. Venison with cream sauce and duck breast *à l'orange* are typical of the French-inspired cuisine. A less expensive annex, Den Grå Dame, serves traditional Danish food. The third eatery, Æblehaven, serves inexpensive sausages and upscale fast-food. ⊠ *Slotsalleen 100, Troense,* ☎ *62/22–59–00. AE, DC. Closed Mon.*

Shopping

For delicate hand-blown glass, visit **Glasmagerne** (⊠ Vemmenæsvej 10, Tåsinge, ☎ 62/54–14–94).

Langeland

⑬ *16 km (10 mi) southeast of Troense, 64 km (40 mi) southwest of Odense.*

Reached by a causeway bridge from Tåsinge Langeland is the largest island of the southern archipelago, rich in relics, with smooth, tawny beaches. Bird-watching is excellent on the southern half of the island, where migratory flocks roost before setting off on their cross-Baltic journey. To the south are Ristinge and Bagenkop, two towns with good beaches; at Bagenkop you can catch the ferry to Kiel, Germany.

Outdoor Activities and Sports

FISHING

Langeland has particularly rich waters for fishing, with cod, salmon, flounder, and gar. For package tours, contact **Ole Dehn** (⊠ Sønderg. 22, Lohals, DK–5953 Tranekær, ☎ 62/55–17–00).

Ærøskøbing

★ ⑭ *30 km (19 mi) south of Svendborg, 74 km (46 mi) south of Odense, plus a one-hour ferry ride, either from Svendborg or Langeland.*

The island of Ærø, where country roads wend through fertile fields, is aptly called the Jewel of the Archipelago. About 27 km (16 mi) southeast of Søby on the island's north coast, the storybook town of Ærøskøbing is the port for ferries from Svendborg. Established as a market town in the 13th century, it did not flourish until it became a sailing center during the 1700s. At night when the streetlights illuminate the cobbled streets, it is as though time has stood still.

Ferries provide the only access to Ærø. The ferry from Svendborg to Ærøskøbing takes 1 hour, 15 minutes. In addition, there's a one-hour ferry from Fåborg to Søby, a town on the northwest end of the island; and a shorter one from Rudkøbing—on the island of Langeland—to Marstal, on the eastern end of Ærø.

Down the main central road in Ærøskøbing, take a left onto Smedgade to visit one of Denmark's most arresting shrines to obsession. History is recorded in miniature at the **Flaskeskibssamlingen** (Bottle Ship Collection), thanks to a former ship's cook known as Peter Bottle, who painstakingly built nearly 2,000 bottle ships in his day. The combination of his life's work and the enthusiastic letters he received from fans and disciples around the world make for a surprisingly moving collection. ⊠ Smedg. 22, Ærøskøbing, ☎ 62/52–29–51. ⊑ Dkr 20. ☉ May–Oct., daily 10–5; Nov.–Apr., Tues.–Thurs. 1–3, Sat., 10–2, Sun. 10–1.

Lodging

$$ ⊡ **Ærøhus.** A half-timber building with a steep red roof, the Ærøhus looks like a rustic cottage on the outside, an old, but overly renovated, aunt's house on the inside. Hanging pots and slanted walls characterize the public areas, and pine furniture and cheerful duvets keep the guest rooms simple and bright. The garden's five cottages have small terraces. ⊠ Vesterg. 38, DK–5970, ☎ 62/52–10–03, ℻ 62/52–21–23. 30 rooms, 17 with bath; 5 cottages. Restaurant. AE, V.

Fyn and the Central Islands A to Z

Arriving and Departing

BY CAR

From Copenhagen, take the E20 west to Halsskov, near Korsør, and drive onto the Great Belt Bridge, which costs about Dkr 210 per car. You'll arrive near Nyborg, which is 30 minutes from either Odense or Svendborg.

BY TRAIN

Direct trains from Copenhagen's main station depart for the 90-minute trip to Odense's train station hourly, every day. You can also book a first-class train seat to Odense direct from Copenhagen Airport; a second-class seat requires a transfer at either the main station or the Høje Taastrup station. Stations in both towns are central, close to hotels and sites. The one-way fare is about Dkr 175 second-class, Dkr 263 first-class. A reservation, which is required during rush hour, costs an additional Dkr 15 (☎ 70/13–14–15).

Getting Around

BY BICYCLE

With their level terrain and short distances, Fyn and the Central Islands are perfect for cycling. You can rent bikes at **City Cykler** (⊠ Vesterbro 27, Odense, ☎ 66/13–97–83). **Fåborg Sportshandel** (⊠ Havneg. 40, Fåborg, ☎ 62/61–28–22) also lets bikes.

BY BUS AND TRAIN

Large towns are served by intercity trains. The Nyborg–Odense–Middelfart and the Odense–Svendborg routes are among the two most important. The other public transportation option is by bus. Timetables are posted at all bus stops and central stations. Passengers buy tickets on board and pay according to the distance traveled (☎ 66/11–71–11). For central Odense, the **Odense Eventyrpas** (Adventure Pass), available at the tourism office, affords admission to sites and museums and free city bus and train transport. The cost for a 48-hour pass is Dkr 90; for a 24-hour pass, Dkr 50.

BY CAR

The highways of Fyn are excellent, and small roads meander beautifully on two lanes through the countryside. Traffic is light, except during the height of summer in highly populated beach areas.

Contacts and Resources

EMERGENCIES

Police, fire, or ambulance (☎ 112). **Odense University Hospital,** (✉ J. B. Winsløws Vej, ☎ 66/11–33–33). **Doctor** (☎ 65/90–60–10 between 4 PM and 7 AM). **Other Emergencies** (Falck, ☎ 66/11–22–22). **Ørnen Apoteket** (✉ Vesterg. 80, Odense, ☎ 66/12–29–70).

GUIDED TOURS

Few towns offer organized tours, but check the local tourist offices for step-by-step walking brochures.

Hans Christian Andersen Tours: Full-day tours to Odense depart from Copenhagen's Rådhus Pladsen mid-May to mid-September, Sunday at 9 AM, and cost about Dkr 500. (Six of 11 hours are spent in transit.) Call ☎ 32/54–06–06 for reservations.

Walking Tours: The two-hour Odense tour departs from the tourist office during July and August at 11 AM every Tuesday, Wednesday, and Thursday and costs Dkr 30. It includes the exteriors of the Hans Christian Andersen sites and the cathedral.

VISITOR INFORMATION

Odense (✉ City Hall, ☎ 66/12–75–20). **Kerteminde** (✉ Strandg. 1, ☎ 65/32–11–21). **South Fyn Tourist Board** (✉ Centrumpl., Svendborg, ☎ 62/21–09–80). **Nyborg** (✉ Torvet 9, ☎ 65/31–02–80). **Ærøskøbing** (✉ Torvet, ☎ 62/52–13–00).

5   JYLLAND

JYLLAND (JUTLAND), Denmark's western peninsula, is the only part of the country naturally connected to mainland Europe; its southern boundary is the frontier with Germany. In contrast to the smooth, postcard-perfect land of Fyn and Sjælland, this Ice Age–chiseled peninsula is bisected at the north by the craggy Limfjord and spiked below by the Danish "mountains." Himmelbjerget, the zenith of this modest range, peaks at 438 ft. Farther south, the Yding Skovhøj plateau rises 568 ft—modest hills just about anywhere else.

The windswept landscapes filmed in *Babette's Feast,* the movie version of the Karen Blixen (Isak Dinesen) novel, trace the west coast northward to Skagen, a luminous, dune-covered point (geographically similar to the Outer Banks of North Carolina). To the east, facing Fyn, Jylland is cut by deep fjords rimmed with forests. The center is dotted with castles, parklands, and the famed Legoland. Ribe, Denmark's oldest town, lies to the south and west; Århus and Aalborg, respectively Denmark's second- and fourth-largest cities, face east and have nightlife and sights to rival Copenhagen's.

Nearly three times the size of the rest of Denmark, with long distances between towns, the peninsula of Jylland can easily take at least several days, even weeks, to explore. If you are pressed for time, concentrate on a single tour or a couple of cities. Delightful as they are, the islands are suitable only for those with plenty of time, as many require an overnight stay. The following tour focuses on chunks of the peninsula and is organized as you would explore them with a car.

Canoeing
Canoe rentals (about Dkr 220 per day) are available in the lake district, Limfjord, and almost all lakes and rivers. One- to three-day package tours are available throughout the region, with either camping or hostel accommodations. For more information, contact the local tourist boards.

Fishing
The lake district is a great place for fishing and angling. License requirements vary and package tours are also available; contact any local tourist office for details.

Kolding

⑥⑤ *71 km (44 mi) northwest of Odense (via the Little Belt Bridge), 190 km (119 mi) west of Copenhagen.*

The well-preserved **Koldinghus,** a massive stonework structure that was once a fortress, then a royal residence in the Middle Ages, is today a historical museum. In the winter of 1808, during the Napoleonic Wars, Spanish soldiers set fire to most of it while trying to stay warm. ⊠ *Rådhusstr.,* ☎ *75/50–15–00, ext. 5400.* ⊡ *Dkr 45.* ⊘ *Daily 10–5.*

Dining and Lodging
$$$ ✕▥ **Hotel Koldingfjord.** This impressive neoclassical hotel has mahogany
★   floors and pyramid skylights. It's five minutes from town and faces the Kolding Fjord and 50 acres of countryside. The rooms vary in size (with 39 in a separate annex), but all have pale wood beds and bright prints. There's also an excellent French-Danish restaurant. ⊠ *Fjordvej 154, DK–6000 Strandhuse,* ☎ *75/51–00–00,* ᴲᴬˣ *75/51–00–51. 114 rooms, 6 suites. Restaurant, bar, indoor pool, sauna, tennis court, health club. AE, DC, MC, V.*

Jylland

Ribe

★ ⑥⑥ *60 km (36 mi) southwest of Kolding, 150 km (103 mi) southwest of Århus.*

In the southeastern corner of Jylland, the country's oldest town is well worth the detour for its medieval center preserved by the Danish National Trust. From May to mid-September, a night watchman circles the town, recalling its history and singing traditional songs. If you want to accompany him, gather at the main square at 10 PM.

The **Ribe Domkirke** (Cathedral) stands on the site of one of Denmark's earliest churches, built around AD 860. The present structure dates from the 12th century, with a 14th-century bell tower. Note the Cat Head Door, said to be for the exclusive use of the devil. ⊠ *Torvet 15,* ☎ *75/42–06–19.* ⊡ *Dkr 10.* ⊘ *May and Sept., Mon.–Sat. 10–5, Sun. noon–5; June–Aug., Mon.–Sat. 10–6, Sun. noon–6; Oct. and Apr., Mon.–Sat. 11–4, Sun. noon–3; Nov.–Mar., Mon.–Sat. 11–3, Sun. noon–3. Call first to confirm hours.*

The **Ribes Vikinger** (Museum for the Viking Period and the Middle Ages) chronicles Viking history with conventional exhibits of household goods, tools, and clothing. There's a multimedia room, with an interactive computer screen where you can search for more Viking information in the form of text, pictures, and videos. ⊠ *Odinspl.,* ☎ *76/88–11–33.* ⊡ *Dkr 45.* ⊘ *June–Aug., daily 10–5; Apr.–May and Sept.–Oct., daily 10–4; Nov.–Mar., Tues.–Sun. 10–4.*

Take Bus 52 (confirm with the driver) from the railway station across the street from the Ribes Vikinger 2 km south, and you'll arrive at the **Viking Center,** an outdoor exhibit detailing how the Vikings lived day-to-day, with demonstrations about homes, food, and crafts by real people. ⊠ *Lustrupsholm, Lustrupvej 4,* ☎ *75/41–16–11.* ⊡ *Dkr 45.* ⊘ *May 5–June, weekdays 11–4; July–Sept., daily 11–4.*

Dining and Lodging

$ ✕ **Sælhunden.** This 300-year-old canal-side "Male Seal" tavern barely fits a dozen tables, but its cozy atmosphere draws wayfarers and locals. The only seal mementos left are a few skins and pictures, but you can still order a "seal's special" of cold shrimp, sautéed potatoes, and scrambled eggs or—an old Danish favorite—fat strips of pork served with cream gravy and boiled potatoes, only served Wednesday in the winter. Console yourself in summer with *rød grød med fløde* (red porridge with cream); the pronunciation of the dessert—which defies phonetic spelling—is so difficult Danes get a kick out of making foreigners pronounce it. ⊠ *Skibbroen 13,* ☎ *75/42–09–46. DC, MC, V. Closed for dinner after 8:45.*

$$$ ✕🏨 **Hotel Dagmar.** In Ribe's quaint center, this cozy half-timber hotel
★ encapsulates the charm of the 16th century—with stained-glass windows, sloping wooden floors, and carved chairs. The lavish rooms are all appointed with antique canopy beds, fat armchairs, and chaise longues. The fine French restaurant serves such specialties as fillet of salmon in sorrel cream sauce. ⊠ *Torvet 1, DK–6760,* ☎ *75/42–00–33,* FAX *75/42–36–52. 48 rooms. Restaurant, bar, meeting rooms. AE, DC, MC, V.*

$ 🏨 **Ribe Family and Youth Hostel.** In town center, this plain, redbrick hostelry is run by helpful wardens Jens Philipsen and Gudrun Rishede. Six- and four-bed family rooms are arranged in clusters of two, each with its own private bath and toilet in a small hallway. There are also eight four-bed rooms with completely private facilities. They are functional and childproof, with pine bunks and industrial carpeting. A kitchen is available for use. ⊠ *Ribehallen, Skt. Pedersg. 16, DK–6760,* ☎ *75/*

42–06–20, ☎ *75/42–42–88. 152 beds in 34 family rooms. Cafeteria. No credit cards. Closed Dec. and Jan.*

Sønderho

⑥⑦ *30 km (19 mi) northwest of Ribe, plus 12-min ferry from Esbjerg, 153 km (96 mi) southwest of Århus, plus 12-min ferry from Esbjerg.*

During the 19th century, the tiny island of **Fanø** had an enormous ship-building industry and a fleet second only to Copenhagen's. The shipping industry deteriorated, but the proud maritime heritage remains.

From Fanø's ferry port in Nordby, take a bus south to Sønderho. Along the tiny winding lanes are thatched cottages decorated with ships' relics, figureheads, painted doors, and brass lanterns. You may even see people wearing the traditional costumes, especially on *Sønderhodag,* a town festival held on the third Sunday in July.

Dining and Lodging

$$ ✕☷ **Sønderho Kro.** Just 13 km (8 mi) from Fanø's main town of
★ Nordby, this 270-year-old thatched inn is one of Jylland's finest, its charm preserved with a beamed foyer, painted doors, and timbered ceilings. Rooms are jazzed up with four-poster beds, elegant tapestries, and gauzy curtains. The French-Danish restaurant serves excellent seafood on its old tables. ⊠ *Kropl. 11, DK–6720, Sønderho,* ☎ *75/16–40–09. 6 rooms, 2 suites. Restaurant. AE, DC, MC, V. Closed Feb. and weekdays Nov.–Jan.*

Billund

⑥⑧ *101 km (63 mi) southwest of Århus.*

★ ☺ Billund's only claim to fame is **Legoland,** an amusement park in which everything is constructed from 45 million plastic Lego bricks. Among its incredible structures are scaled-down versions of cities and villages, working harbors and airports, a Statue of Liberty, statue of Sitting Bull, Mount Rushmore, safari park, and Pirate Land. Grown-ups might marvel at toys from pre-Lego days, the most exquisite of which is Titania's Palace, a sumptuous dollhouse built in 1907 by Sir Neville Wilkinson for his daughter. The Lego empire is expanding: the company's goal is to open one park globally every three years, but Danes maintain that theirs, the original, will always be the best. The park also has a massive theme building–ride–restaurant extravaganza that's much better experienced than described. It all takes place within the double–football field size Castleland, where guests arrive via a serpentine dragon ride. Naturally, everything inside is made of the ubiquitous bricks, including the wizards and warlocks, dragons, and knights that inhabit it. That is until you get to the theme restaurant, The Knight's Barbecue, where waiters in Middle Ages garb hustle skewered haunches of beef, "loooong sausages," and typical fare of the period. ⊠ *Billund,* ☎ *75/33–13–33.* ▣ *Dkr 130.* ☻ *Mid-Apr.–Oct., daily 10–8.*

Vejle

⑥⑨ *40 km (25 mi) east of Billund, 73 km (46 mi) southwest of Århus.*

On the east coast, Vejle is beautifully positioned on a fjord, amid forest-clad hills. You can hear the time of day chiming on the old **Dominican monastery clock**; the clock remains, but the monastery long ago gave way to the town's imposing 19th-century city hall.

In town center, at Kirke Torvet, is **Skt. Nikolai Kirke** (St. Nicholas Church). In the left arm of the cross-shape church, lying in a glass Em-

pire-style coffin, is the body of a bog woman found preserved in a peat
marsh in 1835; she dates to 500 BC. The church walls contain the skulls
of 23 thieves executed in the 17th century. ⊠ *Kirke Torvet,* ☎ *75/82–
41–39.* ⊙ *May–Sept., weekdays 9–5, Sat. 9–noon, Sun. 9–11:30.*

Lodging

$$$$ 🏨 **Munkebjerg Hotel.** Seven kilometers (4½ miles) southeast of town,
surrounded by a thick beech forest and majestic views of the Vejle Fjord,
this elegant hotel attracts guests who prefer privacy. Beyond the rustic lobby, rooms furnished in blond pine and soft green overlook the
forest. There are also two top-notch French-Danish restaurants and a
swank casino. ⊠ *Munkebjergvej 125, DK–7100,* ☎ *75/72–35–00,* FAX
*75/72–08–86. 145 rooms, 2 suites. 2 restaurants, room service, indoor
pool, sauna, tennis court, health club, casino, meeting rooms, helipad.
AE, DC, MC, V.*

Nightlife

The casino at the **Munkebjerg Hotel** (☞ *above*) has blackjack, roulette,
baccarat, and slot machines.

Jelling

⑩   *10 km (6 mi) northwest of Vejle (via Rte. 18), 83 km (52 mi) southwest of Århus.*

In Jelling, two 10th-century burial mounds mark the seat of King
Gorm and his wife, Thyra. Between the mounds are two **Runestener**
(runic stones), one of which is Denmark's certificate of baptism, showing the oldest known figure of Christ in Scandinavia. The inscription
explains that the stone was erected by Gorm's son, King Harald Bluetooth, who brought Christianity to the Danes in AD 960.

The most scenic way to get to Jelling is via the **vintage steam train** that
runs from Vejle every Sunday in July and the first Sunday in August.
Call the Jelling tourist office for schedules.

Silkeborg

⑪   *60 km (38 mi) north of Jelling, 43 km (27 mi) west of Århus.*

At the banks of the River Gudenå begins Jylland's lake district. Stretching from Silkeborg in the west to Skanderborg in the east, this area
contains some of Denmark's loveliest scenery and most of its meager
mountains, including the 438-ft **Himmelbjerget**, at Julsø (Lake Jul). You
can climb the narrow paths through the heather and trees to the top,
where an 80-ft tower stands sentinel, placed there on Constitution Day
in 1875 in memory of King Frederik VII.

The best way to explore the lake district is by water, as the Gudenå
winds its way some 160 km (100 mi) through lakes and wooded hillsides down to the sea. Take one of the excursion boats or the world's
last coal-fired paddle steamer, *Hjejlen,* which departs in summer from
Silkeborg Harbor. Since 1861 it has paddled its way through narrow
stretches of fjord, where the treetops meet overhead, to the foot of the
Himmelbjerget. ⊠ *Havnen, Silkeborg,* ☎ *86/82–07–66 (reservations).*
🎫 *Dkr 76 round-trip.* ⊙ *Mid-June–early Aug., Sun. 10 and 1:45.*

★   Silkeborg's main attractions are housed in the **Kulturhistoriske Museum**
(Museum of Cultural History): the 2,200-year-old Tollund Man and
Elling Girl, two bog people preserved by natural ingredients in the soil
and water. Discovered in 1950, the Tollund Man remains the best-pre-

served human face from the Iron Age. He was killed by strangulation—the noose remains around his neck—with a day's worth of stubble that can still be seen on his hauntingly serene face. ⊠ *Hovedgådsvej 7,* ☎ *86/82–15–78.* ☐ *Dkr 20.* ☉ *Apr. 15–Oct. 23, daily 10–5; Oct. 24–Apr. 14, Wed. and weekends noon–4.*

Dining

$$ ✕ **Spisehuset Christian VIII.** Cut off from Silkeborg's center by a highway, this tiny crooked building seems transported from another time. Inside it's elegant and busy, with an international group of diners occupying the dozen cramped tables. The inventive menu includes tournedos of guinea fowl with mushrooms, and fish specialties such as poached turbot with scallops and spring onions. ⊠ *Christian VIII Vej 54,* ☎ *86/82–25–62. AE, DC, MC, V. Closed Sun.*

Århus

72 *40 km (24 mi) east of Silkeborg.*

Århus is Denmark's second-largest city, and, with its funky arts and college community, one of its most pleasant. The town is liveliest during the 10-day **Århus Festival** in September, which combines everything from concerts, theater, and exhibitions to beer tents and sports. In addition, the **Århus International Jazz Festival** in early or mid-July bills international and local greats. In July, the **Viking Moot** draws aficionados to the beach below the Museum of Prehistory at Moesgård. Activities and exhibits include market booths, ancient defense techniques, and rides on Viking ships.

A good starting point is the **Rådhus,** probably the most unusual city hall in Denmark. Built in 1941 by noted architects Arne Jacobsen and Erik Møller, the pale Norwegian-marble block building is controversial but cuts a startling figure when illuminated in the evening. ⊠ *Park Allé,* ☎ *89/40–20–00.* ☐ *City hall Dkr 10, tower Dkr 5.* ☉ *Guided tours in Danish only mid-June–early Sept., weekdays at 11; tower tours weekdays at noon and 2.*

★ Don't miss the town's open-air museum, known as **Gamle By** (Old Town). Its 70 half-timber houses, mill, and millstream were carefully moved from locations throughout Jylland and meticulously re-created, inside and out. ⊠ *Viborgvej,* ☎ *86/12–31–88.* ☐ *Dkr 55.* ☉ *June–Aug., daily 9–6; Apr., May, Sept., and Oct., daily 10–5; Jan.–Mar., daily 11–3; Nov. and Dec., daily 10–4. Grounds always open.*

In a 250-acre forest south of Århus is the **Moesgård Forhistorisk Museum** (Prehistoric Museum), with exhibits on ethnography and archaeology, including the famed Grauballe Man, a 2,000-year-old corpse so well bog-preserved that scientists could determine his last meal. Also, take the Forhistoriskvej (Prehistoric Trail) through the forest, which leads past Stone- and Bronze-Age displays to reconstructed houses from Viking times. ⊠ *Moesgård Allé,* ☎ *89/42–11–00.* ☐ *Dkr 35.* ☉ *Mid-Mar.–Sept., daily 10–5; Oct.–mid-Mar., Tues.–Sun. 10–4.*

☺ If you are visiting Århus with children, visit its provincial **Tivoli,** with rides, music, and lovely gardens. ⊠ *Skovbrynet,* ☎ *86/14–73–00.* ☐ *Dkr 35.* ☉ *Late-Apr.–mid-June, daily noon–10; mid-June–early Aug. noon–11.*

Be sure to ask at the tourist office about the **Århus Pass,** which affords free passage on buses, free or discounted admission to museums and sites, and tours. A one-day pass is Dkr 88, a two-day pass is Dkr 110, and a seven-day is Dkr 155.

Dining and Lodging

$ ✗. **Rio Grande.** Full of the standard-issue blankets, straw hats, and bright colors ubiquitous in Mexican restaurants the world over, Rio Grande is a favorite with youngsters, families, and even businesspeople. Heaping plates of tacos, enchiladas, and chili are a good value—and tasty, too. ✉ *Vesterg. 39,* ☎ *86/19–06–96. AE, MC, V.*

$$$ 🏨 **Royal Hotel.** In operation since 1838, Århus's grand hotel has welcomed such greats as Arthur Rubinstein and Marian Anderson. Well-heeled guests are welcomed into a stately lobby appointed with Chesterfield sofas, modern paintings, and a winding staircase. Plush rooms vary in style and decor, but all have rich drapery, velour and brocade furniture, and marble bathrooms. ✉ *Store Torv 4, DK–8100 Århus C,* ☎ *86/12–00–11,* 🆉 *86/76–04–04. 105 rooms, 7 suites. Restaurant, bar, sauna, casino, business services. AE, DC, MC, V.*

$ 🏨 **Youth Hostel Pavilionen.** As in all Danish youth and family hostels, the rooms here are clean, bright, and functional. The secluded setting in the woods near the fjord is downright beautiful. Unfortunately, the hostel can get a bit noisy. You can have use of the kitchen. ✉ *Marienlunsdvej 10, DK–8100,* ☎ *86/16–72–98,* 🆉 *86/10–55–60. 32 rooms, 11 with private shower, 4 shared showers and toilets. Cafeteria (breakfast only). AE, MC, V. Closed mid-Dec.–mid-Jan.*

Nightlife and the Arts

There's no better time to visit Århus than during the 10-day **Århus Festival Week** in late August, when jazz, classical, and rock concerts are nonstop, in addition to drama, theater, and dance.

BARS, LOUNGES, AND DISCOS

The **Café Mozart** (✉ Vesterport 10, ☎ 86/18–55–63) plays classical music and serves homemade organic Middle Eastern and other ethnic specialties, including what it claims as the world's biggest pita bread. The **Hotel Marselis** (✉ Strandvejen 25, ☎ 86/14–44–11) attracts a varied crowd to its two venues: the **Beach Club** with danceable rock and disco and the more elegant **Nautilas** piano bar for an older crowd. As in most other towns, the local discos open and close with remarkable frequency; stop by at a local café for the latest on what's happening.

CASINO

The **Royal Hotel** (✉ Store Torv 4, ☎ 86/12–00–11) is the city's casino with blackjack, roulette, baccarat, and slot machines.

JAZZ CLUBS

For jazz, head to **Bent J's** (✉ Nørre Allé 66, ☎ 86/12–04–92), a small club with free-admission jam sessions three times a week and occasional big-name concerts. **Glazz Huset** (✉ Åboulevarden 35, ☎ 86/12–13–12) is Århus's big jazz club, attracting some international stars.

Ebeltoft

🕖 *45 km (28 mi) east of Århus.*

Drive northeast to the tip of what Danes call Jylland's nose, Ebeltoft, a town of crooked streets, sloping row houses, and local crafts shops. Danish efficiency is showcased beside the ferry, at the **Vindmølleparken,** one of the largest windmill parks in the world, where 16 wind-powered mills on a curved spit of land generate electricity for 600 families. ✉ *Færgehaven,* ☎ *86/34–12–44.* 🎫 *Free.* ☉ *Daily.*

You can't miss the *Frigate Jylland,* dry-docked on the town's main harbor. The renovation of the three-masted tall ship was financed by Danish shipping magnate Mærsk McKinney Møller, and it's a testament to Denmark's seafaring days of yore: Wander through to examine the bridge, gun deck, galley, captain's room, and perhaps most impressive of all, the 10½-ton pure copper and pewter screw, and view the voluptuous Pomeranian pine figurehead. ⊠ *Strandvejen 4,* ☎ *86/34–10–99.* ☞ *Dkr 50.* ⊙ *Daily 10–5.*

Also on the Ebeltoft harbor is the small, light, and airy **Glasmuseum.** The setting is perfect for the collection, ranging from mysterious symbol-imbedded monoliths of Swedish glass sage Bertil Vallien to the luminous gold pavilions of Japanese artist Kyohei Fujita. Once a customs and excise house, the museum has a glass workshop where international students come to study. Functional pieces, art, and books are sold at the shop. ⊠ *Strandvejen 8,* ☎ *86/34–17–99.* ☞ *Dkr 40.* ⊙ *Mid-May–mid-Sept., daily 10–5; mid-Sept.–mid-May, daily 1–4.*

Viborg

🗗 *60 km (36 mi) west of Randers, 66 km (41 mi) northwest of Århus.*

Viborg dates to at least the 8th century, when it was a trading post and a place of pagan sacrifice. Later it became a center of Christianity, with monasteries and an episcopal residence. The 1,000-year-old **Hærvejen,** the old military road that starts near here, was once Denmark's most important connection with the outside world—though today it lives on as a bicycle path. Legend has it that in the 11th century, King Canute set out from Viborg to conquer England; he succeeded, of course, and ruled from 1016 to 1035. Today you can buy reproductions of a silver coin minted by the king, embossed with the inscription "Knud, Englands Kong" (Canute, King of England).

Built in 1130, Viborg's **Domkirke** (Cathedral) was once the largest granite church in the world. Today only the crypt remains of the original building, restored and reopened in 1876. The dazzling early 20th-century biblical frescoes are by Danish painter Joakim Skovgard. ⊠ *Mogensg.,* ☎ *86/62–10–60.* ☞ *Free.* ⊙ *June–Aug., Mon.–Sat. 10–4, Sun. noon–5; Sept. and Apr.–May, Mon.–Sat. 11–4, Sun. noon–4; Oct.–Mar., Mon.–Sat. 11–3, Sun. noon–3.*

Aalborg

🗗 *80 km (50 mi) northeast of Viborg, 112 km (70 mi) north of Århus.*

The gentle waters of the Limfjord sever Jylland completely. Clamped to its narrowest point is Aalborg, Denmark's fourth-largest community. The town celebrated its 1,300th birthday with a year of festivities in 1992—once and for all cementing the town's party reputation. The gateway between north and south Jylland, the city is a charming combination of new and old: twisting lanes filled with medieval houses and, nearby, broad modern boulevards.

★ The local favorite site is the magnificent 17th-century **Jens Bang Stenhus** (Jens Bang's Stone House), built by a wealthy merchant. Chagrined he was never made a town council member, the cantankerous Bang avenged himself by caricaturing his political enemies in gargoyles all over the building and then adding his own face, its tongue sticking out at town hall. The five-story building dating from 1624 has a vaulted stone beer-and-wine cellar, one of the most atmospheric in the country (☞ Nightlife and the Arts, *below*). ⊠ *Østerå 9.*

The Baroque **Budolfi Kirke** (Budolfi Cathedral) is dedicated to the English saint Botolph. The church, originally made of wood, has been rebuilt several times in its 800-year history and is now made of stone. It includes a copy of the original tower of the Rådhus in Copenhagen, which was taken down about a century ago. The money for the construction was donated to the church by a generous local merchant and his sister, both of whom, locals say, had no other family on which to lavish their wealth. ⊠ *Gammel Torv.*

Next to Budolfi Kirke is the 15th-century **Helligaandsklosteret** (Monastery of the Holy Ghost). One of Denmark's best-preserved monasteries—and perhaps the only one that admitted both nuns and monks—it is now a home for the elderly; unfortunately, it is generally not open to the public. During World War II the monastery was the meeting place for the Churchill Club, a group of Aalborg schoolboys who became world-famous for their sabotage of the Nazis, even after the enemy thought they were locked up. ⊠ *C. W. Obels Plads, Gammel Torv,* ☎ *98/12–02–05.*

In the center of the old town is **Jomfru Ane Gade,** named, as the story goes, for an aristocratic maiden accused of being a witch, then beheaded. Now the street's fame is second only to that of Copenhagen's Strøget. Despite the flashing neon and booming music of about 30 discos, bars, clubs, and eateries, the street attracts a thick stream of mixed pedestrian traffic and appeals to all ages.

The only Fourth of July celebrations outside the United States annually blast off in nearby **Rebild Park,** a salute to the United States for welcoming some 300,000 Danish immigrants. The tradition dates back to 1912.

Just north of Aalborg at Nørresundby (still considered a part of greater Aalborg) is **Lindholm Høje,** a Viking and Iron Age burial ground where stones placed in the shape of a ship enclose many of the site's 682 graves and sheep often outnumber tourists. At its entrance there's a museum that chronicles Viking civilization and recent excavations. ⊠ *Hvorupvej,* ☎ *98/17–55–22.* 🏛 *Museum Dkr 20; burial-ground free.* ☉ *Easter–mid-Oct., daily 10–5; mid-Oct–Easter, daily 10–4.*

Dining and Lodging

$$ ✕ **Restaurant Dufy.** Light and bright on an old cobbled street, this is one of the most popular eateries in town. Downstairs, it has a French-style bistro ambience, with marble-topped tables, engraved mirrors, and windows overlooking Jomfru Ane Gade. The upstairs is more elegant and quieter. The French menu includes lobster-and-cognac soup for two, sliced roast duck with Waldorf salad, and beef fillet. ⊠ *Jomfru Ane G. 8,* ☎ *98/16–34–44. AE, DC, MC, V.*

$$ ✕ **Restaurant Knive og Gaffel.** In a 400-year-old building parallel to
★ Jumfru Ane Gade, this busy restaurant is crammed with oak tables, crazy slanting floors, and candlelight; the year-round courtyard is a veritable greenhouse. Young waitresses negotiate the mayhem to deliver inch-thick steaks, the house specialty. ⊠ *Maren Turisg. 10,* ☎ *98/16–69–72. DC, MC, V. Closed Sun.*

$ ✕ **Duus Vinkælder.** Most people come to this cellar—part alchemist's
★ dungeon, part neighborhood bar—for a drink, but you can also get a light bite. In summer enjoy smørrebrød, in winter sup on grilled specialties like frikadeller and *biksemad* (a meat-and-potato hash), and the restaurant's special liver pâté. ⊠ *Østerä 9,* ☎ *98/12–50–56. DC, V. Closed Sun.*

$$$$ 🏨 **Helnan Phønix.** In a central and sumptuous old mansion, this hotel is popular with international and business guests. The rooms are luxuriously furnished with plump chairs and polished, dark-wood furniture; in some the original raw beams are still intact. The Brigadier serves excellent French and Danish food. ⊠ *Vesterbro 77, DK–9000,* ☎ *98/12–00–11,* 🇫🇦🇽 *98/16–31–66. 185 rooms, 3 suites. Restaurant, bar, café, room service, sauna, meeting room. AE, DC, MC, V.*

Nightlife and the Arts

BEER-WINE CELLAR

Duus Vinkælder (☞ *above*) is extremely popular, one of the most classic beer and wine cellars in all of Denmark.

CASINO

The city's sole casino is at the **Limsfjordshotellet** (⊠ Ved Stranden 14–16, ☎ 98/16–43–33) with blackjack and more.

MUSIC AND DISCOS

Aalborg doesn't have a regular jazz club, but local musicians get together at least once a week for **jam sessions.** Ask the tourist board for details. If you're there in the fall or winter, head to the harbor-side **Kompasset** (⊠ Vesterbådehavn, ☎ 98/13–75–00), where live jazz is paired with a Saturday-afternoon lunch buffet. **Gaslight** (⊠ Jomfrue Ane G. 23, ☎ 98/10–17–50) plays rock and grinding dance music to a young crowd. **Rendez-Vous** (⊠ Jomfrue Ane G. 5, ☎ 98/16–88–80) has an upstairs dance floor packed with 18- to 25-year-olds dancing to standard disco. **Ambassadeur** (⊠ Vesterbro 76, ☎ 98/12–62–22), with four dance restaurants and live music, is popular with a mature audience.

Skagen

76 *88 km (55 mi) northeast of Aalborg, 212 km (132 mi) north of Århus.*

At the windswept northern tip of Jylland is Skagen (pronounced *skane*), a very popular summer beach area for well-heeled Danes, where, historically, the long beaches and luminous light have inspired painters and writers alike. The 19th-century Danish artist Holger Drachmann (1846–1908) and his friends, including the well-known P. S. Kroyer, founded the Skagen School of painting, which captured the special quality of northern light; you can see their efforts on display in the **Skagen Museum.** ⊠ Brøndumsvej 4, ☎ 98/44–64–44. ☞ Dkr 40. ☉ June–Aug., daily 10–6; May and Sept., daily 10–5; Apr. and Oct., Tues.–Sun. 11–4; Nov.–Mar., Wed.–Fri. 1–4, Sat. 11–4, Sun. 11–3.

Danes say that in Skagen you can stand with one foot on the Kattegat, the strait between Sweden and eastern Jylland, the other in the Skagerrak, the strait between western Denmark and Norway. The point is so thrashed by storms and clashing waters that the 18th-century **Tilsandede Kirke** (Sand-Buried Church), 2 km (1 mi) south of town, is completely covered by dunes.

Even more famed than the Buried Church is the west coast's dramatic ★**Råbjerg Mile,** a protected migrating dune that moves about 33 ft a year and is accessible on foot from the Kandestederne.

Dining and Lodging

$$$ ✕🖫 **Brøndums Hotel.** A few minutes from the beach, this 150-year-old gabled inn is furnished with antiques and Skagen School paintings, and although it is charming, it is beginning to show its age. The very basic 21 guest rooms in the main building are old-fashioned and include wicker chairs, Oriental rugs, and pine four-poster beds. The 25 annex rooms are more modern. The fine French-Danish restaurant, where the Skagen School often gathered, has a lavish cold table. ⊠ Anchersvej 3, DK–9990, ☎ 98/44–15–55, FAX 98/45–15–20. 46 rooms, 12 with bath. Restaurant, meeting rooms. AE, DC, MC, V.

★ ✕🖫 **Strand Hotel.** In the old part of Skagen, this bright and romantic hotel is the perfect foil to the wild, windy sea- and sandscapes nearby. Filled with gently curved wicker furnishings, painted woods, and original art, the hotel's rooms are simple and restful, the staff friendly and accommodating. Sømærket, the traditional Danish fish restaurant, is open only between April and October, but breakfast, which includes healthful and fortifying fresh breads and berries, is available year-round. ⊠ *Jeckelsvej 2, DK–9990,* ☎ *98/44–34–99,* FAX *98/44–59–19. 21 rooms; 6-person house. Restaurant, meeting rooms. AE, DC, MC, V.*

Jylland A to Z

Arriving and Departing

BY CAR AND FERRY

Getting around Denmark these days is much easier than in the past thanks to bridges that connect the kingdom to both Sweden and the continent; that said, for the visitor, it's best to confirm all passage with either a local tourist board or FDM (the Danish Motoring Association) before setting out—you'll avoid confusion caused by ferry mergers and discontinued routes. Nonetheless, more than 20 ferry routes still connect the peninsula to the rest of Denmark (including the Faroe Islands), as well as England, Norway, and Sweden, with additional connections to Kiel and Puttgarden, Germany, the Baltics, Poland, and Russia. Most travelers, however, drive north from Germany, or arrive from the islands of Sjælland or Fyn. Ferry prices can get steep and vary according to how many are traveling and the size of the vehicle. For most ferries you can get information and make reservations by calling **FDM,** the Danish automobile association (☎ 35/43–02–00).

From Copenhagen or elsewhere on Sjælland, you can drive the approximately 110 km (69 mi) across the island, then cross the world's second longest suspension bridge, the Storebæltsbro, to Knudshoved. You then drive the 85 km (53 mi) across Fyn and cross from Middelfart to Fredericia, Jylland over the Lillebæltsbro (Little Belt Bridge). More choices abound here, since two bridges link Middelfart to Fredericia. The older, lower bridge (2 km/1 mi) follows Route 161, whereas the newer suspension bridge (1 km/½ mi) on E20 is faster. For direct Sjælland to Jylland passage, you can take a car-ferry hydrofoil between Sjællands Odde and Ebeltoft (45 minutes) or Århus (1 hour). For ferry schedules and information, call **Mols Line** (☎ 70/10–14–18).

For general route information, call **FDM** (☎ 35/43–02–00). Other major routes include those of **Scandinavian Seaways** (Esbjerg, ☎ 79/17–79–17; Copenhagen, ☎ 33/42–30–00), which links England's Harwich to Esbjerg in the southwest. There are ferries from Göteborg (3¼ hours), on Sweden's west coast and Oslo, Norway (10 hours), to Frederikshavn in the northeast. Call **Stena Line** (☎ 96/20–02–00) for both.

BY PLANE

Billund Airport, 2 km (1 mi) southwest of downtown, receives flights from London, Stockholm, Brussels, Amsterdam, Frankfurt, Oslo, Manchester, Paris, Nice, Bergen, and the Faroe Islands on **Mærsk Air** (☎ 75/33–28–44). **Sunair** (☎ 75/33–16–11) serves Billund, Århus, Oslo, Stockholm, and Göteborg. Several domestic airports, including Aalborg, Århus, and Esbjerg, are served by Mærsk and **SAS** (☎ 32/32–00–00), both of which have good connections to Copenhagen. **Cimber Air** (☎ 74/42–22–77) links Sønderborg, just north of the German border with Copenhagen.

BY TRAIN

DSB (☎ 70/13–14–15) makes hourly runs between Copenhagen and Fredericia. The 3½-hour trip includes train passage aboard the Store Bælt's bridge between Korsør, on west Sjælland, and Nyborg, on east Fyn.

Getting Around

At the Århus tourist office, check out the **Århus Pass,** which affords free bus travel, free or discounted admission to museums and sites, and tours.

BY BICYCLE

Jylland has scores of bike paths, and many auto routes also have cycle lanes. Keep in mind that distances are much longer here than elsewhere in the country, and that even these humble hills are a challenge for children and novice cyclists. Consider prearranged package holidays, which range from island day trips to eight-day excursions. Among the offices that can help with bike tips are the tourist boards in Viborg, Silkeborg, and Vejen (☞ Visitor Information, *below*), or the **County of North Jylland** tourist office (⊠ Niels Bohrsvej, Box 8300, DK–9220 Aalborg, ☎ 96/35–10–00).

Bike rentals are available in most towns from the tourism board, which can also supply maps and brochures. In the west, the **Vestkyst-stien** (west-coast path) goes from Skagen in the north to Bulbjerg in the south. In the east, the **Vendsyssel-stien** (winding path) goes from Frederikshavn to the mouth of the Limfjord. The **Østkyst-stien** (east-coast path) follows and leads to the south of the Limfjord. In the south, much of the 1,000-year-old **Hærvejen** (Old Military Road) has been converted into a network of picturesque cycling lanes. It's signposted for all 240 km (145 mi) through the center of Jylland, from Padborg in the south to Viborg in the north.

BY BUS

Intercity buses are punctual but slower than trains. Passengers can buy tickets on the bus and pay according to destination. For schedules and fares, call the local tourist office, as a network of different bus companies covers the peninsula. For most intercity travel, schedules are posted at all bus stops and fares are usually under Dkr 10.

BY CAR

Although train and bus connections are excellent, sites and towns in Jylland are widely dispersed, and the peninsula is best explored by car. Whether you decide to take speedy, modern highways or winding old roads, traffic is virtually nonexistent.

BY TRAIN

For long trips, the **DSB** (☎ 70/13–14–15) trains are fast and efficient, with superb views of the countryside. Smaller towns do not have innercity trains, so you'll have to switch to buses once you arrive.

Contacts and Resources

EMERGENCIES

Ambulance, fire, or police (☎ 112).

Doctor: Aalborg (☎ 98/13–62–11). **Århus** (☎ 86/20–10–22).

Pharmacies: Aalborg (⊠ Budolfi Apotek, corner of Vesterbro and Algade, ☎ 98/12–06–77). **Århus** (⊠ Løve Apoteket, Store Torv 5, ☎ 86/12–00–22).

GUIDED TOURS

Guided tours are few and far between, but check with the local tourism offices for tips and reservations. Some carry brochures that describe walking tours.

Legoland Tours: Between mid-June and mid-August, the tour departs from Copenhagen at 8 AM on Thursdays and Saturdays (call ☎ 32/55–44–22 or 32/54–06–06 to reserve) and costs Dkr 450, including park admission. The trip takes about 12 hours, with four hours spent at the park.

Walking Tours: The **Århus Round the City** tour (2½ hours) begins at the tourist office and includes Den Gamle By, the Domkirke, concert hall, university, and harbor. **Aalborg's City Tour** (two hours) departs from Adelgade and includes most of the town museums, the Budolfi Cathedral, Monastery of the Holy Ghost, Town Hall, the Jens Bang Stone House, and Jomfru Ane Gade.

VISITOR INFORMATION

County of North Jylland tourist office (✉ Niels Bohrsvej 13, Box 8300, DK–9220 Aalborg, ☎ 96/35–10–00).

Aalborg (✉ Østerå 8, ☎ 98/12–60–22). **Århus** (✉ Park Allé,, ☎ 89/40–67–00). **Billund** (✉ c/o Legoland A/S, by the park, ☎ 76/50–00–55). **Jelling** (✉ Gormsg. 4, ☎ 75/87–13–01). **Randers** (✉ Tørve-briggen 12, ☎ 86/42–44–77). **Ribe** (✉ Torvet 3–5, ☎ 75/42–15–00). **Silkeborg** (✉ Havnen 8A, ☎ 86/82–19–11). **Vejen** (✉ Banegården, ☎ 75/36–26–96). **Vejle** (✉ Sønergade 14, ☎ 75/82–19–55). **Viborg** (✉ Nytorv 9, ☎ 86/61–16–66).

6 BORNHOLM

CALLED THE PEARL OF THE BALTIC for its natural beauty and winsomely rustic towns, Bornholm, 177 km (110 mi) southeast of Sjælland, is geographically unlike the rest of Denmark. A temperate climate has made this 588-square-km (436-square-mi) jumble of granite bluffs, clay soil, and rift valleys an extravagance of nature. Rich plantations of fir bristle beside wide dunes and vast heather fields; lush gardens teem with fig, cherry, chestnut, mulberry, and blue-blooming Chinese Emperor trees; and meadows sprout 12 varieties of orchids. Denmark's third-largest forest, the Almindingen, crowns the center; the southern tip is ringed with some of Europe's whitest beaches.

During the Iron and Bronze ages, Bornholm was inhabited by seafaring and farming cultures that peppered the land with burial dolmens and engravings. From the Middle Ages to the 18th century, the Danes battled the Swedes for ownership of the island, protecting it with strongholds and fortified churches, many of which still loom over the landscape.

Today Bornholmers continue to draw their livelihood from the land and sea—and increasingly from tourism. Chalk-white chimneys rise above the rooftops, harbors are abob with painted fishing boats, and in spring and summer fields blaze with amber mustard and grain.

Certainly, few people come to Bornholm to stay indoors. Long, silky beaches, rolling hills, and troll-inspiring forests make this a summer haven for walking, hiking, and swimming—particularly for families, many of whom take their summer vacations by packing provisions and children onto a pair of bikes, and winding throughout the island.

Bornholm is famous throughout Scandinavia for its craftspeople, especially glassblowers and ceramicists, whose work is often pricier in Copenhagen and Stockholm. In the center of each town (especially Gudhjem and Svaneke), you'll find crafts shops and *værksteder* (workshops). When you're on the road, watch for *keramik* (ceramics) signs, which direct you to artists selling from home.

Fishing
Cod, salmon, and herring fishing are excellent in season, though better from a boat than from shore. Licenses cost Dkr 25 per day, Dkr 75 per week, and Dkr 100 per year. Contact the tourist board for details and information on charter trips.

Hiking
In contrast to the rest of Denmark, Bornholm is hilly and rugged. Marked trails crisscross the island, including three 4-km (2½-mi) hikes through the Almindingen Forest and several more through its Ekkodalon (Echo Valley). The northern coastline is beautiful but a rocky and more strenuous walk. Ask for a map, routes, and tips from any tourism office. The *Bornholm Green Guide*, available in shops and tourism offices, offers suggestions for walking and hiking tours.

Swimming
Beach worshipers thrive in Bornholm. The swimming and sunning are best south, between Pedersker and Snogebæk, where the dunes are tall and the beaches wide. As elsewhere in Denmark, topless bathing is common and nude bathing is tolerated.

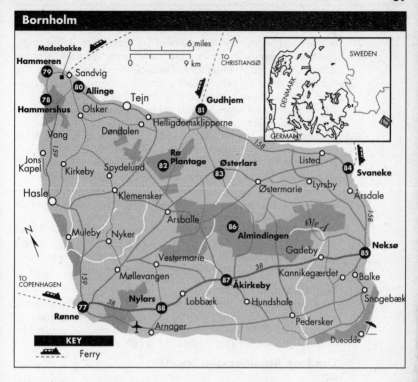

Bornholm

Rønne

㊐ *190 km (120 mi) southeast of Copenhagen (7 hrs by ferry).*

Borhholm's capital, port, and largest town is Rønne, a good starting point for exploring northward or eastward. East of Nørrekås Harbor on Laksegade, you'll find an enchanting area of rose-clad 17th- and 18th-century houses, among them the tile-roof **Erichsens Gård** (farm). The home of the wealthy Erichsen family, whose daughter married the Danish poet Holger Drachmann, it is preserved with paintings by Danish artist Kristian Zahrtmann, period furnishings, and a lovely garden. ⊠ *Lakseg. 7,* ☎ *56/95–87–35.* ☞ *Dkr 25.* ☉ *June–Aug., Tues.–Sat. 10–5.*

Near Store Torv, the main square, is the **Bornholm Museum,** which features local geologic and archaeological exhibits in addition to more than 4,500 pieces of ceramics and glass. The museum also displays 25 18th-century *Bornholmure* (Bornholm Clocks), as characteristic of the island as smoked herring. In 1744, a Dutch ship was wrecked on Bornholm, and the English grandfather clocks it carried became the models for the island's clocks. ⊠ *Skt. Mortensg. 29,* ☎ *56/95–07–35.* ☞ *Dkr 25.* ☉ *May–Oct., Tues.–Sat. 10–5; Nov.–Apr., Tues., Thurs., and Sat. 1–4.*

Dining and Lodging

$$ ✕ **Rådhuskroen.** With exposed timbers, comfortable armchairs, and close-set tables, this restaurant provides a softly lit change from Rønne's busy streets. The menu has changed in recent years to highlight substantial beef dishes like pepper steak with wine and cream sauce, but you can still get a couple of local fish specialties—like poached Baltic salmon or grilled fillet of sole, both served with lobster sauce. ⊠ *Nørreg. 2,* ☎ *56/95–00–69. AE, DC, MC, V.*

$$$ 🏨 **Fredensborg.** The island's standard for luxury is set at this hotel, situated on a curve of forest near a small beach. The glass-and-tile lobby is spare and sunny, the staff pleasant and eager. The dozen ample apartments have full kitchens, and guest rooms are done in pastel schemes, with modern furniture and balconies overlooking the sea. The rustic restaurant, De Fem Ståuerne, serves traditional French-Danish food. ⊠ *Strandvejen 116, DK–3700,* ☎ *56/95–44–44,* ℻ *56/95–03–14. 60 rooms, 12 apartments. Restaurant, bar, room service, hot tub, sauna, tennis court, meeting rooms. AE, DC, MC, V.*

$$$ 🏨 **Hotel Griffen.** Just off a busy street and the Rønne harbor, this is one of Bornholm's largest and most modern hotels. It's three stories tall, with plenty of windows and views of the sea on one side and Rønne on the other. The rooms, done in deep-brown tones, have every modern convenience. ⊠ *Kredsen 1, DK–3700,* ☎ *56/95–51–11,* ℻ *56/95–52–97. 140 rooms, 2 suites. Restaurant, bar, room service, indoor pool, sauna, dance club, meeting rooms. AE, DC, MC, V.*

$ ⛺ **Galløkken Camping.** This site is just a short walk from the Rønne center, near an old military museum. The grounds are open, but trees surround the perimeter. There are good shower and cooking facilities. ⊠ *Strandvejen 4, DK–3700 Rønne,* ☎ *56/95–23–20.*

Nightlife and the Arts

Bornholm's nightlife is limited to a handful of discos and clubs in Rønne, which open and close frequently as tastes change. **Stemmegaffeln** (⊠ Svaneke Torv 5, ☎ 56/49–73–21), in a bright square surrounded by shops, is popular for light meals and live folk music.

Outdoor Activities and Sports

GOLF

The **Bornholm Golf Club** near Rønne (☎ 56/95–68–54) is an 18-hole park course in a natural setting with plenty of wildlife and fauna—the brochure even boasts that you can enjoy nightingales and wild orchids along the course. There's also a restaurant and pro shop.

Shopping

CLOCKS

A Bornholmure is a type of grandfather clock handmade on the island. Antique versions cost from Dkr 10,000 to Dkr 80,000 and more. The clocks often have round faces but can be rectangular as well and are completely hand-painted. On the hour, the modern clocks sound the hour with music—which ranges from Mozart and Verdi to Sondheim and Andrew Lloyd Webber. New reproductions modeled from museum originals are custom-made by **Bornholmerure** (⊠ Torneværksvej 26, Rønne, ☎ 56/95–31–08). A handmade custom clock costs, on the average, Dkr 37,000.

CLOTHING

You can pick up unusual gifts and one-of-a-kind clothing made of hand-printed textiles at **Bente Hammer** (⊠ Nyker Hovedg. 32, Rønne, ☎ 56/96–33–35).

MARKET

There is a large **vegetable and fruit market** on Wednesday and Saturday mornings in Store Torv, the main square in Rønne.

En Route   Fourteen kilometers (8½ miles) north of Rønne is the bluff known as **Jons Kapel.** A medieval legend has it that a monk, Brother Jon, lived in a cave and used these treacherous sea cliffs as a pulpit for his impassioned sermons. Wear rubber-sole hiking boots to climb the stairs that lead to the pulpit, where the agile friar stood atop the dramatic 72-ft-high cliffs that loom over the crashing waves.

Hammershus

★ ⑦⑧ *8 km (5 mi) north of Jons Kapel, 30 km (19 mi) north of Rønne.*

The ruins of the **fortress of Hammershus** constitute northern Europe's largest stronghold. The hulking fortress was begun in 1255 by the archbishop of Lund (Sweden), and became the object of centuries of struggle between Denmark and Sweden. In 1658 Danes under Jens Kofoed killed its Swedish governor, and the castle was given back to Denmark. Used until 1743, it became a ruin when it was quarried for stone to fortify Christiansø and that island's buildings. The government finally intervened in 1822, and the site is now a mass of snaggletoothed walls and towers atop a grassy knoll. During restoration work in 1967, 22 gold German guilders were found. Occasionally, concerts and other performances are held at the ruins. ⊠ *Free.*

Nightlife and the Arts

They don't happen nearly enough, but check with the local tourism office (☞ Bornholm A to Z, *below*) to see if any special events are planned at or near Hammershus: the ruins add a spectacular dimension to classical music and the performing arts.

Hammeren

⑦⑨ *5 km (3 mi) north of Hammershus, 36 km (23 mi) north of Rønne.*

Despite constant Baltic winds, rare plants and trees grow on the warm, granite-scattered Hammeren (the Hammer), including radiant anemones. The knuckle of land jutting from the island's northern tip is nearly separated from the island by a deep rift valley and the Hammer Sø (Hammer Lake). Look across the water south of the tip to the stone formation known as the Camel Heads.

En Route A little more than 3 km (2 mi) southeast of Hammeren, **Madsebakke** is the largest collection of Bronze Age rock carvings in Denmark. They are presumed to be ceremonial carvings, which ancient fishermen and farmers hoped would bring good weather and bountiful crops. The most interesting of them depicts 11 ships, including one with what's called a sun wheel.

Allinge

⑧⓪ *3 km (2 mi) east of Madsebakke, 21 km (13 mi) north of Rønne.*

In Allinge and its twin town Sandvig, you'll find centuries-old neighborhoods and, particularly in Allinge, half-timber houses and herring smokehouses sprouting tall chimneys. Just south is a wood that the islanders call the **Trolleskoven** (Troll Forest). Legend says trolls live in the woods, and when they "brew" fog, they escape the heat in the kitchen and go out looking for trouble. The most mischievous is the littlest troll, Krølle Bølle.

Lodging

$$ 🏨 **Strandhotellet.** Romantic old-world charm is the draw at this venerable hotel. On a corner across from the harbor, it has a white arched entry into a stone-and-whitewashed lobby. The rooms are furnished in plain beech furniture with woolen covers and pastel colors. ⊠ *Strandpromenaden 7, Sandvig, DK–3770,* ☎ *56/48–03–14,* ⅿ𝔸𝕏 *56/48–02–09. 50 rooms, 1 suite. Restaurant, bar, sauna, steam room, health club. AE, DC, MC, V. Closed mid-Oct.–mid-Apr.*

$ ⛺ **Sandvig Familie Camping.** This site is pleasantly close to the beach, so that most of its sites enjoy a view of the water. The large kitchen and bathing facilities were renovated a few years ago. ⊠ *Sandlinien 5, DK–3770 Allinge,* ☎ *56/48–04–47 or 56/48–00–01.*

En Route   Eight kilometers (5 miles) southeast of Allinge along the coastal path, you'll come upon the grottoes and granite cliffs of the **Helligdomsklipperne** (Cliffs of Sanctuary), which contain a well-known rock formation best seen from the boats that ply the nearby waters in summer. In the Middle Ages, people used to visit these waters, believing that they had holy, healing powers—hence the name.

Just southeast of the Helligdomsklipperne, a pastoral coastal path leads to the tiny, preserved **Døndalen Forest.** Its fertile soil bears a surprising array of Mediterranean vegetation, including fig and cherry trees. During rainy periods look for a waterfall at the bottom of the dale.

Gudhjem

★ ⑧   *18 km (11 mi) east of Allinge, 33 km (21 mi) northeast of Rønne.*

Especially at the height of summer, Gudhjem (God's Home) is perhaps the most tourist-packed town on Bornholm—and the reason is obvious. Tiny half-timber houses and gift shops with lace curtains and clay roofs line steep stone streets that loop around the harbor. The island's first smokehouses still produce alder-smoked golden herring.

★ ♺   Walk down Brøddegade, which turns into Melstedvej; here you'll find the **Landsbrugs Museum** (Agricultural Museum) and Mestedgaard, a working farm with cows, horses, sheep, pigs, geese, and wandering kittens. The farm includes the well-kept house and garden of a 19th-century farm family. Notice the surprisingly bright colors used on the interior of the house, and leave time to visit the old shop, where you can buy locally produced woolen sweaters, wooden spoons, and even homemade mustard. ⊠ *Melstedvej 25,* ☎ *56/48–55–98.* ⊡ *Dkr 25.* ☉ *Mid-May–mid-Oct., Tues.–Sun. 10–5.*

OFF THE BEATEN PATH   **BORNHOLM KUNST MUSEUM –** Follow the main road, Hellidomsvej, out of town in the direction of Allinge/Sandvig, and you'll come to Bornholm's art museum, an excellent example of the Danes' ability to integrate art, architecture, and natural surroundings. Built by the architectural firm of Fogh and Følner, the white-painted brick, granite, and sandstone building is centered by a thin stream of "holy" trickling water that exits the building and leads the visitor to a walkway and overlook above the Helligdomsklipperne (☞ above). Throughout, the walls of the museum are punched out by picture windows overlooking nearby grazing cows and the crashing Baltic: a natural accompaniment to the art. Most of the works are by Bornholmers, including a body of Modernist work by Olaf Høst, Karl Esaksen, and Olaf Rude, who recognized a particular ability in Bornholm's sea-surrounded light to bring out the poignancy in abstract scenes of local life. The museum also displays some sculpture and glass, as well as a survey of more historical paintings. Check out the restaurant and shop. ⊠ *Hellidomsvej 95,* ☎ *56/ 48–43–86.* ⊡ *Dkr 30.* ☉ *May–mid-Oct., Tues.–Sun. 10–5; mid-Oct.– Apr., Tues., Thurs., Sun. 1–5.*

Lodging

$ ⚏ **Skt. Jørgens Gård Vandrehjem.** In a half-timber 100-year-old former manor house, this hostel in the middle of Gudhjem offers single-to eight-bed rooms with standard Danish hostel style: pine bunks and industrial carpeting. There are six kitchens available for use. ⊠ *Gudhjem Vandrehjem, DK–3760,* ☎ *56/48–50–35,* ℻ *56/48–56–35. 52 rooms, 26 with bath. Restaurant. No credit cards.*

Shopping

Baltic Sea Glass (✉ Melstedvej 47, Gudhjem, ☎ 56/48–56–41), on the main road just on the outskirts of town, offers high-quality, bright, and imaginative decanters, glasses, candlesticks, and one-of-a-kind pieces, including an old-fashioned contraption to catch flies. In town, see the delicate porcelain bowls of **Per Rehfeldt** (✉ Kastenievej 8, ☎ 56/48–54–13). Unique, hand-thrown ceramic work is available from and by **Julia Manitius** (✉ Holkavej 12, ☎ 56/48–55–99).

OFF THE BEATEN PATH

CHRISTIANSØ – A 45-minute boat ride northeast from Gudhjem will bring you to the historic island of Christiansø. Though it was originally a bastion, the Storetårn (Big Tower) and Lilletårn (Little Tower) are all that remain of the fort, built in 1684 and dismantled in 1855. The barracks, street, and gardens, for which the earth was transported in boats, have hardly changed since that time. They remain under the jurisdiction of the defense ministry, making this a tiny tax-free haven for its 100 inhabitants. Nearby, the rocky, uninhabited island of **Græsholmen** is an inaccessible bird sanctuary—the only place in Denmark where the razorbill and guillemot breed.

Rø Plantage

82 *6 km (4 mi) southwest of Gudhjem, 24 km (15 mi) northeast of Rønne.*

Rø Plantation is a new but dense forest that serves as a quiet foil to the hubbub of Gudhjem. A century ago it was a heather-covered grazing area, but after stone dikes were erected to keep the cattle out, spruce, pine, larch, and birch were cultivated. The cool refuge now consists largely of saplings and new growth—the result of devastating storms in the late '50s and '60s.

Outdoor Activities and Sports

GOLF

Rø Golfbane (✉ Spellingevej 3, ☎ 56/48–40–50) has won various European and Scandinavian awards for its natural beauty—and challenges. Its 18 holes are set close to the coastal cliffs, and enjoy views of the sea. It has a pro shop and restaurant.

Østerlars

83 *5 km (3 mi) southeast of Rø Plantage, 22 km (14 mi) northeast of Rønne.*

The standout attraction here is the **Østerlars Kirke.** The largest of the island's four round churches, it was built in about 1150; extensions, including the buttresses, were added later. Constructed from boulders and slabs of limestone, the whitewashed church was part spiritual sanctuary, part fortification, affording protection from enemy armies and pirates. Inside is the island's only painted tympanum, with a faded image of a cross and decorative foliage. Several Gothic wall paintings—including depictions of the Annunciation and Nativity—have survived from the 1300s. ✉ *Gudhjemsvej 28,* ☎ *56/49–82–64.* ✈ *Dkr 4.* ☉ *Apr.–mid-Oct., Mon.–Sat. 9–5.*

Svaneke

84 *21 km (13 mi) east of Østerlars, 49 km (31 mi) northeast of Rønne.*

The coastal town of Svaneke, Denmark's easternmost settlement, is an enchanting hamlet of 17th- and 18th-century houses, winding cobbled streets, and a harbor sliced from the rocky earth. Once a fishing village, it is now immaculately preserved and home to a thriving artists' community.

Dining and Lodging

$$ ✕⌂ **Siemsens Gaard.** Built in a 270-year-old merchant house, this U-shape hotel with a gravel-courtyard café overlooks the harbor. The inside is cushy, with Chesterfield sofas below severe black-and-white prints and antiques. The rooms differ, but all are done up in stripped pine and soft colors. The bright, modern restaurant serves French-Danish food, with a menu of 125 options—from club sandwiches to smoked Baltic salmon to smørrebrød. ⌂ *Havnebryggen 9, DK–3740,* ☎ *56/49–61–49,* ℻ *56/49–61–03. 50 rooms. Restaurant, café, sauna, health club. AE, DC, MC, V.*

$$ ⌂ **Hotel Østersøen.** Across from the harbor, this hotel has a provin-
★ cial facade and a Key West courtyard with palm trees and a pool. Industrial carpets and century-old beams line the modern lobby, and the stark apartments (rented by the week) are appointed with leather sofas, swanky teak dinette sets, and streamlined furniture. The hotel is well suited for families and couples traveling in pairs. ⌂ *Havnebryggen 5, DK–3740,* ☎ *56/49–60–20,* ℻ *56/49–72–79. 21 apartments. Pool, business services. AE, DC.*

Shopping

Stroll through the ateliers and boutiques in the central Glastorvet in Svaneke. Among them is the studio of **Pernille Bülow** (⌂ Glastorvet, Brænderigænget 8, ☎ 56/49–66–72), one of Denmark's most famous glassblowers. Her work is sold in Copenhagen's best design shops. Even if you buy directly from her studio, don't expect bargains—though you may be lucky to find seconds—but do expect colorful, experimental work. **Askepot** (⌂ Postg. 5, Svaneke, ☎ 53/99–70–42), whose name means Cinderella, sells handmade leather hats, jackets, shoes, bags, belts, and wallets.

Neksø

⑧⑤ *9 km (5½ mi) south of Svaneke, 48 km (30 mi) northeast of Rønne.*

Neksø (or Nexø) bustles with visitors and locals who shop and live around its busy harbor, lined with fishing boats from throughout the Baltics and Eastern Europe. It might seem like a typical 17th-century town, but it was rebuilt almost completely after World War II, when the Russians bombed it to dislodge stubborn German troops who refused to surrender—three days after the rest of Denmark had been liberated. The Russians lingered on the island until April 1946.

Wander down to the harbor to find, in a mustard-yellow building, the **Neksø Museum** with its fine collection of fishing and local history exhibits. The museum also houses photographs and memorabilia of Danish author Martin Andersen Hansen (1909–55), who changed his last name to Nexø after his beloved town. A complicated and vehement socialist, he wrote, among other works, *Pelle the Conqueror,* set in Bornholm at the turn of the century, when Swedish immigrants were exploited by Danish landowners. The story was turned into an Academy Award–winning film. ⌂ *Havnen,* ☎ *56/49–25–56.* ⊡ *Dkr 10.* ☉ *May–Oct., Tues.–Sun. 10–4.*

Outdoor Activities and Sports

GOLF

The 18-hole **Nexø Golf Club** (☎ 56/48–89–87) is close to the island's best sandy, rock-free beaches.

WINDSURFING

The best windsurfing beaches are on the southern sandy coast, where the winds are strong and the beaches sandy (the shores are rockier north

TAKE PICTURES. FURTHER.™

© Eastman Kodak Company, 1999. Kodak, Max and Take Pictures. Further. are trademarks.

Ever see someone

waiting for the sun to come out

while trying to photograph

a charging rhino?

New!
Kodak Max film:

Now with better color,
Kodak's maximum
versatility film gives
you great pictures in
sunlight, low light,
action or still.

WITH KODAK MAX
photos taken on Kodak Max 400 film

It's all you need
to know about film.

www.kodak.com

Fodor's

Distinctive guides packed with up-to-date expert advice and smart choices for every type of traveler.

Fodor's. For the world of ways you travel.

of Neksø). **Windsurfing ved Balke Strand** (☎ 56/95–00–77), 4 km (2½ mi) south of Neksø, offers classes and board rentals.

Shopping

For exquisite woodwork see **Bernard Romain** (✉ Rønnevej 54, Neksø, ☎ 56/48–86–66).

Almindingen

86 *23 km (14 mi) west of Neksø, 27 km (17 mi) northeast of Rønne.*

The lush Almindingen, Denmark's third-largest forest, is filled with ponds, lakes, evergreens, well-marked trails, and blooms with lily of the valley in spring. Within it, the oak-lined **Ekkodalen** (Echo Valley)— where children love to hear their shouts resound—is networked with trails leading to smooth rock faces that soar 72 ft high. At the northern edge, near the road to Østermarie, stood one of Bornholm's most famous sights until 1995: seven evergreens growing from a single trunk. The tree fell that year, but pass by, and you might see the remains of its curious trunk.

Outdoor Activities and Sports

HIKING

Check with the tourist board for a map delineating three 4-km (2½-mi) hikes through the Almindingen Forest and several more through its Echo Valley. The *Bornholm Green Guide,* available in shops and tourism offices, offers walking and hiking routes.

Åkirkeby

87 *5 km (3 mi) south of Almindingen, 24 km (15 mi) east of Rønne.*

Åkirkeby is the oldest town on the island, with a municipal charter from 1346. The town's church, the **Åkirke,** is Bornholm's oldest and largest, dating from the mid-13th century. Though it is not a round church, both walls and tower were well suited for defense. The altarpiece and pulpit are Dutch Renaissance from about 1600, but the carved sandstone font is as old as the church itself. ✉ *Torvet,* ☎ *56/ 97–41–03.* 🎫 *Dkr 5.* ⊙ *Mon.–Sat. 10–4.*

Nylars

88 *8 km (5 mi) west of Åkirkeby, 9 km (6 mi) east of Rønne.*

Like the Østerlars church, the round **Nylars Kirke** dates from 1150. The chalk paintings from the Old Testament on its central pillar are the oldest on the island, possibly dating from 1250. Even older are the runic stones on the church's porch. Both are of Viking origin. ✉ *Kirkevej,* ☎ *56/97–20–13.* 🎫 *Suggested donation Dkr 3.* ⊙ *Mid-May–mid-Sept., Mon.–Sat. 9–5.*

Bornholm A to Z

Arriving and Departing

BY BUS

A *Gråhund* (Greyhound) No. 866 bus from Copenhagen's main station travels to Dragør, boards a ferry to Limhamn, and then continues to Ystad, where it connects with a ferry to Rønne. Buses depart twice daily, once in the morning and again in late afternoon. Call **Bornholm Bussen** (☎ 44/68–44–00).

BY CAR FERRY AND HYDROFOIL

The *Bornholmstrafikken* car ferry from Copenhagen's Kvæsthusbro Harbor (near Nyhavn) departs at 11:30 PM year-round and from June through July daily (except Wednesday) at 8:30 AM. The trip takes seven hours. To avoid delays, make reservations. Comfortable sleeping bunks in a massive hall are also available for an extra cost.

The Nordbornholms Turistbureau (North Bornholm Tourist Board, ☎ 56/48–00–01) is the agent for a summer ferry that links Neu Mukran (3½ hours) and Sassnitz (3½ hours) on the island of Rügen in Germany. **Bornholmstrafikken** (☎ 56/95–18–66), a competing company, offers passage aboard the ferry to Neu Mukran (3½ hours), just 5 km (3 mi) from Sassnitz. Prices vary according to the number of people traveling and the size of the vehicle. There is also a boat between Świnoujście, Poland and Rønne (seven hours); call **Polferries** (☎ 48/97–32–1614–0) in Poland. A hydrofoil from Nyhavn goes to Malmö, Sweden, where it connects with a bus to Ystad and a ferry to Rønne. The four-hour voyage runs twice daily, usually in the morning and again in the late afternoon. Call **Flyve Bådene** (☎ 33/12–80–88).

BY PLANE
The **airport** is 5 km (3 mi) south of Rønne at the island's southwestern tip. **Mærsk Air** (☎ 56/95–11–11) makes several daily flights only from Copenhagen. **Lufthansa** (☎ 33/37–73–33) flies from Berlin and Hamburg; **Eurowings** (☎ 49/231–924–5306) from Dortmund and Osnabrück.

Getting Around
BY BICYCLE
Biking is eminently feasible and pleasant on Bornholm, thanks to a network of more than 200 km (125 mi) of cycle roads, including an old railway converted to a cross-island path. Rentals of sturdy two-speeds and tandems are available for about Dkr 50 a day at more than 20 different establishments all over the island—near the ferry, at the airport, and in Allinge, Gudhjem, Hasle, Pedersker (near Åkirkeby), Rønne, Svaneke, and most other towns. Try **Bornholms Cykeludlejning** (⌂ Nordre Kystevej 5, ☎ 56/95–13–59) or **Cykel-Centret** (⌂ Sønderg. 7, ☎ 56/95–06–04), both in Rønne.

BY BUS
Though bus service is certainly not as frequent as in major cities, there are regular connections between towns. Schedules are posted at all stations, and you can usually pick one up on board. The fare is Dkr 8 per zone, or you can buy a klip kort (punch ticket) of 10 klips for Dkr 64. A 24-hour bus pass costs Dkr 100. Children 5–11 pay half-price.

BY CAR
There are excellent roads on the island, but be alert for cyclists and occasional leisurely paced cows.

Contacts and Resources
EMERGENCIES
Ambulance, accident, or fire (☎ 112). **Bornholm's Central Hospital** (⌂ Sygehusvej, Rønne, ☎ 56/95–11–65). **Rønne Apotek** (Rønne Pharmacy, ⌂ Store Torveg. 12, Rønne, ☎ 56/95–01–30).

GUIDED TOURS
Aerial Tours: An aerial tour in a Cessna or Piper plane (20–45 min) covers either the entire coast or the northern tip. Call **Klippefly** (☎ 56/95–35–73 or 56/48–42–01).

BAT Tours: The **BAT** (Bornholm Municipality Traffic Company, ☎ 56/95–21–21) offers some inventive summer tours. All are offered Tuesday through Friday, from mid-July until early August. All begin at the red bus terminal at Snellemark 30 in Rønne at 10 AM and cost Dkr 100. (You can also buy a 24-hour bus card for Dkr 100, or a five- or seven-day card for Dkr 350, good for both the regional buses and the tours.) Tour prices do not include some Dkr 5–Dkr 10 admissions or lunch at a herring smokehouse. The five-hour **Kunstoghåndværk** (**Arts and Crafts**) tour includes stops at glass, pottery, textile, and silver studios. In summer, different studios are visited each day. The **Grønne Bus** (Green Bus) visits sights that illustrate the ways in which the island's exquisite flora and fauna are being preserved. **Bonndegårdsbussen** (Farm Bus) visits chicken, cow, and pig farms, as well as a "free-range" pig farm, to show the differences in practice and attitude between conventional and progressive farming. The **Veteranbus** (Veteran Bus), a circa World War II Bedford, connects some of Bornholm's oldest industries, including a clockmaker, water mill, and Denmark's last windmill used for making flour.

Boat Tours: From mid-June to mid-September, boats to the Helligdomsklipperne (Sanctuary Cliffs) leave Gudhjem at 10:30, 1:30, and 2:30, with extra sailings mid-June to mid-August. Call **Thor Båd** (☎ 56/48–51–65). Boats to Christiansø depart from Svaneke at 10 AM daily year-round; May to September daily at 10:20 from Gudhjem, and at 1 from Allinge; between mid-June and August, an additional boat leaves Gudhjem weekdays at 9:40 and 12:15. Call **Christiansø Farten** (☎ 56/48–51–76) for additional information.

Sightseeing Tours: The **Bornholmrund** (Round Bornholm) bus tour (8½ hours), beginning at 9:30 Tuesday and Thursday, includes Rønne, Hammershus, Allinge, Gudhjem, Østerlars Church, Svaneke, Nexø, Balka, Åkirkeby, and the Almindingen Forest. To make reservations, call the Bornholm tourist board (☞ *below*).

VISITOR INFORMATION

Nordbornholms Turistbureau (North Bornholm Tourist Board, ☎ 56/ 48–00–01). **Bornholm's Main Tourist Office** (⊠ Nordre Kystvej 3, Rønne, ☎ 56/95–95–00.

Allinge (⊠ Kirkeg. 4, ☎ 56/48–00–01). **Åkirkeby** (⊠ Torvet 2, ☎ 56/ 97–45–20). **Gudhjem** (⊠ Åbog. 9, ☎ 56/48–52–10). **Hasle** (⊠ Havneg. 1, ☎ 56/96–44–81). **Nexø,** (⊠ Åsen 4, ☎ 56/49–32–00). **Svaneke** (⊠ Storeg. 24, ☎ 56/49–63–50).

7 GREENLAND

WHEN ERIC THE RED discovered Greenland (Kalaallit Nunaat in Greenlandic, Grønland in Danish) a thousand years ago, his Norsemen thought they had reached the edge of the world. After it, there was only *Ginnungagap,* the endless abyss.

Greenland still commands awe from the growing number of visitors who venture off the usual Scandinavian path to explore the world's largest island. Measuring more than 1.3 million square km (840,000 square mi), it's larger than Italy, France, Great Britain, unified Germany, and Spain combined. The coastal regions are sparsely populated with about 7,500 Danes and 48,000 Inuit—the indigenous people, whose roots can be traced to the native inhabitants of Canada's Arctic, and farther back to the people of Alaska. More than 80% of the land is eternally frozen beneath an ice cap that, at its deepest, reaches a thickness of 3 km (2 mi). If it melted, sea levels around the world would rise nearly 20 ft.

The number of tourists is growing at an enormous rate, from just 3,000 in 1993 to 18,000 in 1997. But relatively speaking, with these few tourists (almost all on package tours), Greenland remains one of the world's least developed regions. By its nature, the region is far more difficult to explore than dwarfed mother Denmark. Travel is possible only by helicopter or coastal boat, since there are few roads and no railroads. However, the southern and western towns—trimmed with building-block red-and-green houses and well-used harbors—have adequate hotels, airfields, and helicopter pads, and regular summertime ferry service. Man-made luxuries are few, but the rewards of nature are savagely beautiful. Below the Arctic Circle, the draws include Norse ruins, Ice Age–gouged mountains, and jagged fjords. Farther north, dogsleds whip over icy plains, and ferries glide past icebergs as big as city blocks.

Greenland's first inhabitants probably arrived some 4,000 years ago from what is today Canada. Various Inuit peoples continued to migrate to and roam across the island, but current Greenlanders are descendants of a particular Canadian Inuit culture that arrived around AD 1000. Greenland's recorded history began at about the same time, in AD 982, when Eric and his Norse settlers claimed the land, but after 400 years of colonization they mysteriously disappeared. During this period Denmark and Norway were joined under the Danish crown, a union that muddled ownership of Greenland until 1933, when the International High Court awarded Denmark complete sovereignty. (Until 1997, this dual heritage led every town to have both a Greenlandic and a Danish name; today the Greenlandic names are used on modern maps with the Danish included in brackets.) Geographically isolated and increasingly politically independent, Greenlanders are intent on redefining their ethnic identity in a modern world. They refer to themselves as Inuit, in solidarity with native peoples of Canada, Alaska, and the former Soviet Union, and speak their own language in addition to Danish.

In 1978 Denmark granted Greenland home rule, vesting its tiny Landsting (parliament) in the capital Nuuk/Godthåb with power over internal affairs. Though Denmark continues to devolve power, it still administers foreign policy and provides financial aid to an economy based on fishing, animal husbandry, construction, and tourism.

Since most travelers follow preset routes, towns and sites are arranged south to north in geographic order and not necessarily in the order they would be visited. Perhaps only one major museum or site is noted per village, but there is much more to see in Greenland's changeable nature. Venture along the wooden stairs and boardwalks that connect most private homes and provide inner-village walking paths. Cruise beneath the expanse of an iceberg and listen to it moan. Rise at 3 AM to take a stroll through the sunshine. There is no private property in Greenland—nature is free for all to enjoy, and in Greenlandic fashion, it is best savored slowly. Those who love this island do not move through it at a clip: it's more gratifying to let it move you.

Fishing

Visitors can buy fishing licenses (Dkr 200) from the local police, major hotels, and tourism offices. Call the local tourist board for details.

Hiking

Hiking in Greenland appears unlimited, but the tourist board does try to control hikers, for their own saferty, via marked maps. Keep in mind, however, that it's wiser to join an organized hike with an experienced guide than to attempt a solo expedition, since it's not uncommon for rescue crews to have to go out in search of lost hikers. Organized excursions are available in Nuuk/Godthåb and Narsarsuak for about Dkr 150 for a half day, Dkr 300 for a full day. The tourist offices of Qaqortoq/Julianehåb and Sisimiut/Holsteinsborg arrange hikes on request and charge according to the number of participants. For the most popular hiking areas in Greenland, new topographic maps at 1:50,000 are available. In these areas, experienced hikers can find their way without a guide. To cross the polar ice cap or to enter Greenland's national parkland—which is the size of Great Britain and France combined—you must obtain a license. Contact the **Danish Polar Center** (✉ Strandg. 100H, DK–1401 KBH K, ☎ 32/88–01–00, FAX 32/88–01–01).

Narsarsuaq

89 *4 hrs, 50 min northwest of Copenhagen by plane.*

Narsarsuaq, meaning Great Plain in English, aptly describes the wide, smooth land harboring one of Greenland's largest civilian airports. The town is accessible from Copenhagen, Reykjavík, and Kangerlussuaq only by plane, and from Nuuk/Godthåb by plane and boat—though boats are booked months in advance.

Not far from the edge of town, visitors can take a 10-km (6-mi) boat ride from the Narsarsuaq harbor to an area where icebergs have broken off from a nearby glacier. There they are invited to collect glacial ice for the cocktails served on board.

Also near Narsarsuaq is the point locals call **Hospitalsdalen** (Hospital Valley), a controversial area named for an alleged American hospital where Korean War wounded were said to have been hidden away so as not to weaken morale back home. Though most history books deny the story, many locals swear it's true.

Qaqortoq/Julianehåb

90 *6 hrs south of Narsarsuaq by ferry.*

With a population of 3,600, this is the largest town in southern Greenland and one of the loveliest. In the town square you'll see the island's only fountain, surrounded by half-timber and brightly colored houses. Though the oldest building in town is the cooper shop, which dates from 1797, the most interesting is the smithy, from 1871, which now houses the **Julianehåb Museum.** Inside are handmade hunting tools, kayaks, Inuit clothing, and a furnished sod house you can enter. A traditional dwelling, it remained cozy and warm even during the harsh winter. ✉ *Free.* ☉ *Weekdays 11–4.*

Greenland

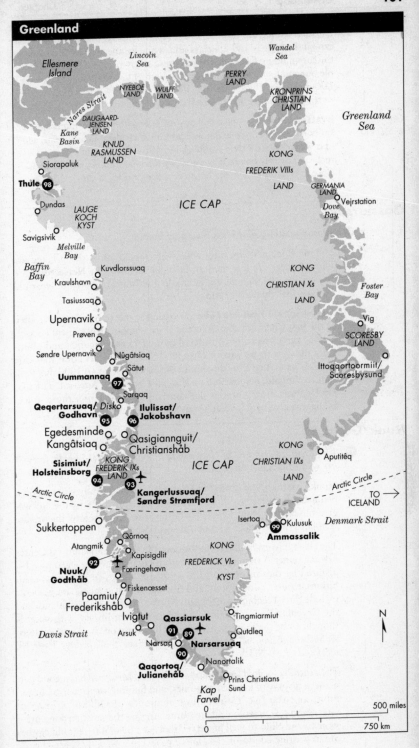

Ellesmere
Island

Lincoln
Sea

Wandel
Sea

*NYEBOE
LAND*   *WULFF
LAND*

PERRY
LAND

KRONPRINS
CHRISTIAN
LAND

Nares Strait

DAUGAARD-
JENSEN
LAND

Kane
Basin

KNUD
RASMUSSEN
LAND

Greenland
Sea

Siorapaluk

Thule 98

KONG

FREDERIK VIIIs

LAND

GERMANIA
LAND

Vejrstation

Dundas

*LAUGE
KOCH
KYST*

ICE CAP

Dove
Bay

Savigsivik

*Melville
Bay*

*Baffin
Bay*

Kuvdlorssuaq

KONG

CHRISTIAN Xs

LAND

Foster
Bay

Kraulshavn

Tasiussaq

Upernavik

Prøven

Søndre Upernavik

Nûgâtsiaq

Sätut

Uummannaq 97

Sarqaq

Vig

*SCORESBY
LAND*

Ittoqqortoormiit/
Scoresbysund

**Qeqertarsuaq/
Godhavn** 95

Disko

**Ilulissat/
Jakobshavn**
96

Egedesminde
Kangâtsiaq

Qasigiannguit/
Christianshåb

**Sisimiut/
Holsteinsborg**
94

*KONG
FREDERIK IXs
LAND*

93

KONG

CHRISTIAN IXs

LAND

Aputitêq

ICE CAP

Arctic Circle

Arctic Circle

**Kangerlussuaq/
Søndre Strømfjord**

Sukkertoppen

Qôrnoq

Isertoq

Kulusuk

Denmark Strait

99

Ammassalik

TO
ICELAND →

Atangmik

Kapisigdlit

**Nuuk/
Godthåb**
92

Føringehavn

KONG

FREDERICK VIs

KYST

Fiskenæsset

**Paamiut/
Frederikshåb**

Ivigtut

Arsuk

Davis Strait

Qassiarsuk

91

Narsaq

89

Narsarsuaq

Tingmiarmiut

Qutdleq

90

**Qaqortoq/
Julianehåb**

Nanortalik

Prins Christians
Sund

*Kap
Farvel*

N

500 miles
0

0   750 km

Lodging

$$ 🏨 **Hotel Qaqortoq.** Built in 1987, this hotel is among the more modern on the huge island. Its glass-and-white facade atop a hill overlooks the surrounding fjord and the picturesque town center. Rooms are simple but comfortable, all with private bath, TV, and phone. ✉ *Box 155, DK–3920,* ☎ *299/64–22–82,* FAX *299/64–12–34. 50 rooms. Restaurant, bar, billiards. DC, MC, V.*

OFF THE
BEATEN PATH

HVALSEY CHURCH – A nice half-day excursion from Qaqortoq is the 14½-km (9-mi) sailboat ride to the well-preserved Hvalsey Church ruins, site of a well-attended Norse wedding in 1408—the community's last recorded activity before it mysteriously disappeared. As the church is close to a rocky beach, the hardy can opt for a frigid dip.

Qassiarsuk

🄑 *30 min northwest of Narsarsuaq by boat.*

The main focus of the tiny village of Qassiarsuk is sheep breeding. Though there are few modern facilities in town, the **Norse ruins** are fascinating and include, for example, the Brattahlíð—1,000-year-old ruins of Eric the Red's farm.

The remains of **Tjodhilde Kirke** are especially intriguing: this was touted as the first Christian church on the North American continent (Greenland is geographically considered part of North America and politically thought to be part of Europe). It was from this point that Eric the Red's son, Leif Ericsson, began the expedition in AD 1000 that took him to Vinland, somewhere on the coast of North America. The first Greenlandic Ting (outdoor parliament), fashioned after those in Iceland, was also held here at about the same time.

Nuuk/Godthåb

🄒 *1 hr, 25 min northwest of Narsarsuaq by small plane (15 hrs by ferry),7 hrs east of Ottawa by plane.*

Nuuk/Godthåb, the capital of Greenland, is beautifully situated on a peninsula between two fjords. It was founded in 1728 by the Norwegian missionary Hans Egede; his harbor-side home is now the private residence of the island's home-rule premier.

The city's newest landmark is **Katuaq,** the Greenland Cultural Center in town center. A triangular-shape construction fronted by a wavy wall—inspired by the Aurora Borealis—contains spaces for concerts, exhibitions, theater, conventions, and cinema, as well as a café. Its residents include the Greenland Art School, Nordic Institute on Greenland, and the Groenlandica Collection, a modern lending library with what is thought to be the largest collection of literature on the Arctic regions. ✉ *Skibshavnsvej,* ☎ *299/32–33–00.* 🎫 *Free.* ☉ *Weekdays 10–9:30, weekends 1:30–9:30.*

The centrally located **Landsmuseet** (National Museum) has a good permanent display of kayaks, costumes, and hunting weapons, an art exhibit, and the five 15th-century mummies of Qilakitsoq, one of Greenland's archaeological treasures. Among the most striking are a woman and child so well preserved that even their 500-year-old clothes are in pristine condition. ✉ *Hans Egede Vej 8,* ☎ *299/32–26–11.* 🎫 *Free.* ☉ *Tues.–Sun. 1–4.*

Dining and Lodging

$$$$ ✕🏨 **Hotel Hans Egede.** This hotel is the largest in Greenland. The rooms are plain and functional but have such extras as minibars, TVs, VCRs, and phones. The sixth-floor Sky Top Restaurant, known for its lovely view of the fjords and its inventive nouveau Greenlandic menu, prepares local fish employing French methods. ✉ *Box 289, DK–3900,* ☎ *299/32–42–22,* 🆔 *299/32–44–87. 108 rooms. Restaurant, pub, dance club, meeting rooms. DC, MC, V.*

Kangerlussuaq/Søndre Strømfjord

93 *1 hr northeast of Nuuk/Godthåb by plane, 4 hrs, 20 min northwest of Copenhagen by plane.*

Kangerlussuaq/Søndre Strømfjord is at the head of one of the longest and deepest fjords in the world. The airport, Greenland's most vital, lies just 25 km (15½ mi) from the ice cap. Until World War II, nobody lived here permanently, but Greenlanders came in the spring to hunt reindeer. During the war, the U.S. Air Force chose its dry, stable climate for an air base, called Bluie West Eight. The military moved out in the fall of 1992, selling all the facilities to the local government for the sum of $1.

Sisimiut/Holsteinsborg

94 *40 min west of Kangerlussuaq/Søndre Strømfjord by helicopter.*

On the Davis Strait, this hilltop town is full of Danish-style wooden houses—a local luxury, as all wood is imported. A favorite area for dogsledging, during which you are pulled by a team of half-wild wolf-dogs; they are harnessed in a fan shape rather than a straight line, so if one falls through the ice, you won't all plummet to an icy death. It is also the southernmost boundary for walrus hunting; the walrus, though extremely rare, is a popular game animal because of its valuable tusks. The Greenlandic name Sisimiut means Burrow People.

Qeqertarsuaq/Godhavn

95 *1 hr, 20 min west of Illulissat by helicopter (8 hrs, 30 min by coastal boat; reserve far in advance).*

In the Disko Bugt (Bay) is the island of Qeqertarsuaq/Disko, where the main town is Qeqertarsuaq/Godhavn. Until 1950 this was the capital of northern Greenland; Nuuk/Godthåb served as the southern capital. The task was divided because it was too difficult to rule the entire island from one town. Accessible by helicopter and ship, Godhavn is often booked to capacity by European tourists; they come for the organized dogsledging trips, as this is the only area in Greenland with summertime dogsledging.

Ilulissat/Jakobshavn

96 *45 min north of Kangerlussuaq/Søndre Strømfjord by plane.*

In the center of Disko Bay is Ilulissat/Jakobshavn, 300 km (185 mi) north of the Arctic Circle. At the tip of its fjord is the Northern Hemisphere's most productive glacier, calving 20 million tons of floes each day—equivalent, according to the Greenland tourist board, to the amount of water New York City uses in a year. For a humbling experience, take one of the helicopter tours encircling the glacier. A violent landscape of floating ice giants and dazzling panoramas, it's been inhabited by the Inuit for as long as 4,000 years. The town was founded in 1741 by a Danish merchant, Jakob Severin. Today the largest industry is shrimping, though in the winter dogsledgers fish for halibut along the fjord.

Visit the **Knud Rasmussens Fødehjem** (boyhood home of Knud Rasmussen); this Danish-Greenlandic explorer (1879–1933) initiated the seven Thule expeditions, which enhanced the knowledge of Arctic geography and Inuit culture. At the museum you can follow his explorations through photographs, equipment, and clothing. ✉ *Dkr 20.* ☺ *Daily 10–4.*

Dining and Lodging

$$$ ✕▥ **Hotel Arctic.** This modern hotel, divided into two low-lying red buildings, is in the mountains on the edge of town, and provides views of the ice fjord and the mountains. Rooms are simple, with bathroom, phone, radio, and TV. The main dining room has panoramic views of the iceberg-filled harbor and serves fine beef and fish dishes. ✉ *Box 1501, DK–3952,* ☎ *299/94–41–53,* ℻ *299/94–39–24. 40 rooms. Restaurant, sauna, billiards, meeting rooms. AE, DC, MC.*

$$$ ✕▥ **Hotel Hvide Falk.** The compact rooms in this central, moderate-size, two-story building are furnished with TVs and small desks, and have magnificent views of the icebergs and the Disko Mountains. The restaurant, which specializes in seafood—especially herring, cod, and salmon—looks out over the bay and its looming icebergs. The director of the hotel, Lars Rasmussen, is explorer Knud Rasmussen's grandson. ✉ *Box 20, DK–3952,* ☎ *299/94–33–43,* ℻ *299/94–35–08. 27 rooms. Restaurant. DC.*

Uummannaq

🄻 *55 min north of Ilulissat/Jakobshavn by helicopter.*

The inhabitants of the town of Uummannaq, on the island of the same name, maintain Greenlandic traditions in step with modern European life. Ranging from hunters to linguists, they are as apt to drive dogsleds as they are four-wheel drives. The town lies beneath the magnificent hues and double humps of the granite Uummannaq Mountain, 3,855 ft high. Because the village is also perched on uneven stone cliffs, housing largely consists of brightly painted, freestanding cottages rather than the ugly Danish barracks that line some of the larger towns.

The **Uummannaq Museum** will give you a good overview of life on the island, with photographs and costumes of local hunters and displays on the now-defunct mines of the area. Exhibits also detail the doomed 1930 expedition of German explorer Alfred Wegener, and there is also a bit on the Qilakitsoq mummies (☞ Nuuk/Godthåb, *above*), found in a nearby cave in 1977. ✉ *Uummannaq Museum,* ☎ *299/4–81–04.* ✉ *Free.* ☺ *Weekdays 8–4.*

The **Uummannaq Church,** dating from 1937, is the only stone church in Greenland and is made from local granite. Next door to it are three sod huts, typical Inuit dwellings until just a couple of decades ago.

Though there is plenty of **dogsledging** north of the Arctic Circle, the trips that set forth from Uummannaq are the most authentic, as local hunters drive; they are also the most gentle, since the terrain here is especially smooth. Visitors sit comfortably in heavy, fur-lined sleighs that tear across the frozen fjord in the hands of experienced Inuit drivers. Trips can be arranged at the Hotel Uummannaq and range from a few hours to several days of racing through the terrifying beauty of the landscape and sleeping in the shadows of towering icebergs.

Dining and Lodging

$$ ✕⊞ **Uummannaq Hotel.** This natty harbor-side hotel and brand-new extension offer bright, compact rooms with white, Danish-designed furniture. The fine restaurant serves local specialties, including polar bear, caribou, seal, and plenty of fish. ⊠ *Box 202, DK–3961,* ☎ *299/95–15–58,* FAX *299/95–12–62. 22 rooms, 10 in a nearby annex. Restaurant, bar. AE, MC, V.*

Thule

98 *2 hrs, 40 min north of Uummannaq by passenger-cargo plane, 1 hr, 45 min north of Kangerlussuaq/Søndre Strømfjord by plane.*

The northern reaches of Greenland are sparsely populated, with few hotels. The American air base at Thule, used for monitoring the Northern Hemisphere, is difficult to visit, but check with the Danish Ministry of Foreign Affairs in Copenhagen (☎ 33/92–00–00) or the Royal Danish Embassy in Washington, DC (⊠ 3200 Whitehaven St. NW, 20008-3683, ☎ 202/234–4300, FAX 202/328–1470).

Ammassalik

99 *2 hrs west of Reykjavík by plane, connecting via helicopter from Kulusuk.*

Much of the east coast is empty. The most accessible towns are Ammassalik and Kulusuk, a tiny village slightly farther northeast. Both towns welcome most of Greenland's visitors, day-trippers from Iceland. Though tours, arranged through Icelandair, are usually short—often just day trips—they are very well organized, offering an accurate (and relatively affordable) peek at Greenlandic culture and the natural splendor of the Arctic.

Lodging

$$ ⊞ **Hotel Angmagssalik.** Perched on a mountain, with a lovely view of the town and harbor, this hotel is decorated with a simple wood interior, both in the guest rooms and common areas. ⊠ *Box 117, DK–3900,* ☎ *299/98–12–93,* FAX *299/98–10–09. 30 rooms, 18 with shower. Restaurant, bar. AE, DC, MC, V.*

$$ ⊞ **Hotel Kulusuk.** This is a new hotel located close to the coast in the tiny town of Kulusuk. Located on the coast, the hotel offers some splendid views. ⊠ *Box 1500, DK–3915,* ☎ *299/98–69–93,* FAX *299/98–69–83. 34 rooms. Restaurant, bar. AE, DC, MC, V.*

Greenland A to Z

Arriving and Departing

BY PLANE AND HELICOPTER

The main airport in Greenland is **Kangerlussuaq/Søndre Strømfjord with four weekly flights arriving in the summer from Copenhagen.** Copenhagen-originating flights also arrive three times a week in summer into **Narsarsuaq,** convenient to south Greenland. **Kulusuk** is the main airport for the east coast. **Nuuk** and **Ilulissat** also serve as domestic airports. Greenland is also serviced by four new heliports in: Aasiaatt/Egedesminde, just south of Illulisat, Uummannaq, Sisimiut; and Maniitsoq/Sukkertoppen, just south of Kangerlussuaq. In late 2000 a heliport is scheduled to open in Qaanaaq/Thule, and in late 2001, another in Paamiut/Nuuk on the southwest coast.

Helicopters and small planes connect small towns. Because of Greenland's highly variable weather, delays are frequent. As with all arrangements in Greenland, confirm all flights, connections, and details with your local travel agent or airline representative before you leave home.

The most common points of departure for Greenland are Denmark and Iceland. If you're going by way of **Iceland, Icelandair** (☎ 354/505–0300) has flights from New York, Baltimore, Fort Lauderdale, and Orlando to Keflavík, Iceland, daily in summer, and **Greenlandair** (Grønlandsfly in Danish) makes three flights a week between Keflavík and Narsarsuaq in summer and winter. It's more expensive to go by way of **Copenhagen** with **SAS** (☎ 32/33–68–48), which flies four times a week in summer to Kangerlussuaq/Søndre Strømfjord. Connections are also available through **Canada**, where you can catch an early morning flight from Ottawa to Frobisher Bay on Baffin Island, then cross the Davis Strait to Kangerlussuaq/Søndre Strømfjord on **Firstair** (☎ 613/839–8840).

Getting Around

BY BOAT

The most beautiful passage between towns is by water. Every town has a harbor, where private boats can be hired for connections or excursions. Some cruise and coastal boats, as well as the privately owned *Disko,* which plies the waters of the west coast, and the M/S *Ioffe,* which sails around the east and south coasts, make frequent stops. You can only reserve through a travel agency. Boat voyages, including luxury cruises, are also available from Canada's Frobisher Bay, Norway's Svalbard (archipelago), and Iceland. Contact **Arctic Umiaq Line** (✉ Box 608, DK–3900 Nuuk, ☎ 299/32–52–11, FAX 299/32–32–11) or **Greenland Travel** in Copenhagen (☎ 33/13–10–11).

BY PLANE AND HELICOPTER

Greenlandair is the only airline licensed for domestic flights on the island. Its modest fleet of helicopters and small planes is booked year-round, so make reservations well in advance.

Contacts and Resources

EMERGENCIES

Every community has its own fire, ambulance, and police numbers and dentist and doctor, all of which you may reach through your hotel. The best way to handle emergencies is to avoid danger in the first place. Don't take risks, ask for advice, and give your travel agent and hotel your itinerary so that they can reach you in case of emergencies—or if you don't show up when you're due.

Hospital: Sana Dronning Ingrids Hospital (✉ DK–3900 Nuuk, ☎ 299/2–11–01).

GUIDED TOURS

On-the-spot excursions are available in most towns and range from about Dkr 250 for a half day to Dkr 600 for a full day, more for dogsledging, boat, and helicopter trips. Because transportation and accommodations are limited, have all details of your trip—connections, accommodations, sightseeing, and meals—arranged by an experienced travel agent, tour organizer, or airline. (It's also helpful to bring a copy of your tour contract and all confirmations.)

Tour packages range from one- to four-day east-coast excursions from Reykjavík by Icelandair to monthlong excursions, which can include sailing, hiking, hunting, dogsledging (February to May), whale safaris, and iceberg-watching.

United States: Bennett of Scandinavia (✉ 270 Madison Ave., New York, NY 10016, ☎ 800/221–2420). **Eurocruises** (✉ 303 W. 13th St., New York, NY 10014, ☎ 800/688–3876). **Icelandair** (✉ Symphony Woods,

5950 Symphony Woods Rd., Columbia, MD 21044, ☎ 800/223–5500). **Quark Expeditions** (✉ 980 Post Rd., Darien, CT 06820, ☎ 203/656–0499). **Scanam** (✉ 933 Rte. 23, Pompton Plains, NJ 07444, ☎ 800/545–2204). **Scantours Inc.** (✉ 1535 6th St., Suite 209, Santa Monica, CA 90401, ☎ 800/223–7226). **Travcoa** (✉ 2350 S.E. Bristol St., Newport Beach, CA 92660, ☎ 949/476–2538 or 800/992-2003).

Canada: Marine Expeditions Inc. (✉ 30 Hazelton Ave., Toronto, Ontario M5R 2E2, ☎ 416/964-9069). **Pedersen World Tours** (✉ 15 Wertheim Ct., Suite 402, Richmond Hill, Ontario L4B 3H7, ☎ 416/882–5470).

In Denmark, contact **Arctic Adventure** (✉ Reventlowsg. 30, DK–1651 KBH V, ☎ 33/25–32–21). **Greenland Travel** (☞ Visitor Information, *below*) also operates out of Denmark.

LATE-NIGHT PHARMACIES
If you are taking medication, bring enough to last throughout your visit. In emergencies, the local hospital can fill prescriptions.

VISITOR INFORMATION
There is a tourism office in almost every town, but brochures, maps, and specific information may be limited. Call ahead for an exact street address (a 299 access code must be dialed before all phone numbers when calling from outside Greenland).

Ammassalik (✉ Box 112, DK–3913 Tasiilaq, ☎ 299/98–13–11, FAX 299/98–17–11). **Ilulissat/Jakobshavn** (✉ Box 272, DK–3952 Ilulissat, ☎ 299/94–43–22, FAX 299/94–39–33). **Kangerlussuaq/Søndre Strømfjord** (✉ Box 49, DK–3910, Kangerlussuaq, ☎ 299/84–10–98, FAX 299/84–14–98). **Nuuk/Godthåb** (✉ Box 199, DK–3900 Nuuk, ☎ 299/32–27–00, FAX 299/32–27–10). **Qaqortoq/Julianehåb** (✉ Box 183, DK–3920 Qaqortoq, ☎ 299/64–29–13, FAX 299/64–29–87). **Qasigiannguit/Christianhåb** (✉ Box 140, DK–3951 Qasigiannguit, ☎ 299/91–10–81, FAX 299/91–15–24). **Qeqertarsuaq/Godhavn** (✉ Box 175, DK–3953 Qeqertarsuaq, ☎ 299/92–11–96, FAX 299/92–11–98). **Sisimiut/Holsteinsborg** (✉ Box 65, DK–3911 Sisimiut, ☎ 299/86–48–48, FAX 299/86–56–22). **Uummannaq** (✉ Atuarfimmut B-821, Box 200, DK–3961 Uummannaq, ☎ 299/95–17–05, FAX 299/95–14–75).

In Copenhagen, **Greenland Travel** (✉ Gammel Mønt 12, ☎ 33/13–10–11) has a helpful and knowledgeable staff. **Greenland Tourism** (✉ Pilestr. 52, ☎ 33/69–32–00) is another reliable Copenhagen-based operation.

8 THE FAROE
ISLANDS

THE 18 FAROE ISLANDS (Føroyar in Faroese; Færøerne in Danish) lift up out of the North Atlantic in an extended knuckle of a volcanic archipelago. All but one are inhabited, by 44,800 people and 70,000 sheep. The native Faroese live by fishing, fish farming, and shepherding, and carefully maintain their refreshingly civilized pace of life.

Situated 300 km (188 mi) northwest of Scotland, 430 km (270 mi) southeast of Iceland, and 1,300 km (812 mi) northwest of Denmark, the fjord-chiseled islands support little vegetation besides a bristle of short grasses and moss. The climate is oceanic: humid, changeable, and stormy, with surprisingly mild temperatures—52°F in summer, and 40°F in winter—and a heavy annual rainfall of 63 inches.

Of their 1,399 square km (540 square mi), only 6% is fertile, the rest rough pasture—an Eden for 70 breeding and 120 migratory species of birds, among them thousands of gannets, auks, and puffins. Beneath azure skies and rugged, mossy mountains, villages of colorful thatched houses cling to hillsides while large trawlers and small fishing boats stream in and out of their harbors. Religious and proud, the Faroese have built churches in nearly every settlement.

Catholic monks from Ireland were the first to settle the islands, but they died out and were replaced by Norwegian Vikings, who settled the land about AD 800. It was here that the *Løgting* (parliament) met for the first time in AD 900 in Tórshavn—where it still meets. Under the Danish crown, the islands have had a home-rule government since 1948, with their own flag and language. The roots of the Faroese language are in Old West Norse. Most people speak English, but a Danish dictionary can be helpful to the visitor, as Danish is the second language.

It's difficult for visitors to understand the isolation or the practical relationship the Faroese have with the natural world. Dubious outsiders, for example, accuse locals of cruelty during the traditional pilot-whale harvests. An essential foodstuff, the sea mammals are killed in limited numbers to reduce the islands' dependence on imported meat. The profit factor is eliminated: whale meat is not sold—it's given away to the townspeople in equal portions on a per capita basis. The hunt is also an important social bond involving both the young and the old.

In 1993 the islands plunged into a severe depression, with unemployment, formerly an unknown phenomenon, surging from less than 3% to more than 20%. Toward the end of 1996, however, unemployment was pushed back down to 8% as the numbers of cod surrounding the islands mysteriously tripled (scientists and biologists are at a loss to explain why). Tourism is also a part of this brighter picture, and is increasing at a rate of 10% to 15% yearly. Though there appears an upward trend, there is also some fear: large international oil companies believe there is oil in the region. If they strike it rich, the islands could get out of their financial difficulties and return the Dkr 4 billion they currently owe Denmark. But many people fear that the black gold will irrevocably change the face of their islands.

Tórshavn on the island of Streymoy makes for a good touring base; spend one night in Klaksvík on the island of Borðoy. The very efficient bus and connecting boat service is the best way to travel between towns (☞ The Faroe Islands A to Z, *below*).

Tórshavn

1,343 km (839 mi) northeast of Copenhagen, 2 hrs, 15 min by plane.

Most visitors who arrive on the Faroe Islands by plane begin their explorations on the largest and most traveled island of Streymoy, which, though carved by sheer cliffs and waterfalls, has good roads and tunnels. On the northern end of the island are bird sanctuaries and a NATO base. On its southeastern flank is one of the world's tiniest capitals, Tórshavn, named for the Viking god Thor. Centrally located among the islands, Tórshavn has a population of 16,000. A Viking parliament was founded here in about AD 1000, but it did not have any real legislative power until 1948. St. Olav's Day, July 29, is named for the Norwegian king who brought Christianity to the islands. Celebrations include rowing competitions and group dances in the form of a chain—a sort of North Atlantic ring dance.

The rugged **Tinganes** is a small peninsula between the east and west bays that was the site of both the old trading post and the meetings of the local parliament (*tinganes* means "assembly place"). Here you can see some of the town's oldest buildings, dating from the 17th and 18th centuries, and some old warehouses, which today house the government offices. At the end of the docks is **Skansin**, a fort built in 1580 by Magnus Heinason to protect the town against pirate attacks. After many reconstructions, it reached its present shape in 1790 and was used as the Faroe headquarters of the British Navy during World War II. Two guns from that period remain.

Down from the Tinganes is Old Main Street, lined with small 19th-century houses and crossed by twisting streets. You'll come to the slate **Havnar Kirkja** (Tórshavn's Church), rebuilt many times in its 200-year history. Inside is a model of a ship salvaged from an 18th-century wreck, the ship's bell, and an altarpiece dating from 1647.

There are very few trees on the islands. **Tórshavn Park,** a walk up Hoyviksvegur, used to be the pride of the town—it was a rare cultivated oasis of green trees in a land where storms and strong winds flatten tall vegetation. Planted around the turn of the century, the park thrived until 1988, when a storm virtually destroyed it.

Standing atop a hill, **Kongaminnið** (King's Memorial) commands a good view of the old town. The basalt obelisk commemorates the visit of King Christian IX in 1874. ⊠ *Norðrari Ringvegur, just off R. C. Effersøes Gøta.*

At the northern tip of Tórshavn is the modern **Norðurlandahúsið** (Nordic Culture House), built in 1983. It hosts an international jazz festival in mid-August and theater and concerts throughout the year. ⊠ *Norðrari Ringvegur,* ☎ *298/17900.* ☉ *Call for event schedules.*

Dining and Lodging

$$$ ✕🏨 **Hotel Föroyar.** Five minutes from Tórshavn center, this Best Western hotel has a view of the Old Town. The rooms all have TVs, refrigerators, phones, and bathrooms, and there's a good restaurant with island specialties. ⊠ *Oyggjarvegur, FO–110,* ☎ *298/317500,* ℻ *298/316019. 216 beds. Restaurant. AE, DC, MC.*

$$$ ✕🏨 **Hotel Hafnia.** Close to the pedestrian streets of town, this modern business hotel offers a good buffet and big-city ambience. The rooms vary in size, but all are comfortably appointed with TVs, telephones, desks, and private showers. The restaurant serves Faroese seafood, including local cod and flounder as well as international dishes. ⊠ *Áarvegur 4, FO–110,* ☎ *298/311270,* ℻ *298/315250. 76 beds. Restaurant. AE, DC, MC.*

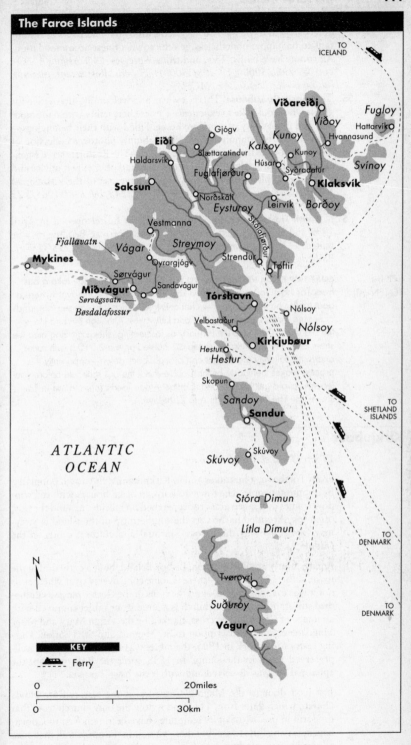

$$$ ⊞ **Hotel Tórshavnar.** In the middle of Tórshavn, this newly renovated hotel caters to those who do not need a lobby bar and five-star restaurant to be happy; nonetheless, it's the town's finest accommodation. All rooms have baths, TVs, and trouser-presses. ⊠ *Tórsgøta 4, FO–100,* ☎ *298/350000,* 𝔽𝔸𝕏 *298/350001. 53 beds. Restaurant, pizzeria, but no liquor license. AE, MC, V.*

$$ ⊞ **Skansin Guesthouse.** This is a warm and welcoming alternative for guests who would like to experience Faroese hospitality within the modesty and personality of a private home. Filled with their belongings— a watercolor of a family-owned island, family photos, a collection of old records—the house is familiar and cozy. The Restorffs serve a generous breakfast (included in the room rate) and offer expert advice and assistance in planning activities. Guests have use of the kitchen. ⊠ *Jekaragøta 8, Box 57, FO–110,* ☎ *298/312242,* 𝔽𝔸𝕏 *298/310657. 22 beds. No credit cards.*

$ ⊞ **Youth Hostel Tórshavn.** This newly built hostel opened in April 1999 and is located next door to the Hotel Föroyar. Bedding may be rented. ⊠ *Við Oyggjarvegin, FO–100,* ☎ *298/318900,* 𝔽𝔸𝕏 *298/315707. 98 beds in 2-, 4-, and 6-person rooms. AE, DC, MC.*

OFF THE   **BOAT TRIP FROM VESTMANNA TO THE BIRD CLIFFS–** You can take a bus
BEATEN PATH   from Tórshavn to Vestmanna (40 km/25 mi north of Tórshavn), where a
                  boat takes you through narrow channels from which you can see thousands
                  of nesting birds, including puffins and kittiwakes. Although the bird life is
                  the big draw, the sheep life is nearly as fascinating: sheep grazing atop the
                  sheer cliffs. In the spring the sheep are hoisted up the 2,310 ft with ropes,
                  and in the fall they are caught and brought back down—apparently this
                  process makes them taste better. Double-check the bus schedule before you
                  leave to avoid getting stranded. Contact Aldan Tourist Information in Tór-
                  shavn (☞ The Faroe Islands A to Z, *below*).

Kirkjubøur

13 km (8 mi) south of Tórshavn.

From Tórshavn, a bus takes you to Kirkjubøur, a tiny town populated by about 60 people. The townsfolk live in black houses with red window frames and green grass roofs perched on hillsides around the tiny, often fog-shrouded harbor. At the southern tip of the island is Streymay; the town was the Faroes' spiritual and cultural center in the Middle Ages.

A particularly ambitious priest, Bishop Erland, built a cathedral in the town in the 13th century—there is some controversy over whether or not it was ever completed—and the ruins of the Gothic **Magnus Cathedral** still stand. Inside the church is a large stone tablet engraved with an image of Christ on the cross, flanked by the Virgin Mary and Mary Magdalene, and an inscription to St. Magnus and St. Thorlak. During restoration work in 1905, the tablet was removed to reveal well-preserved relics of the saints. In 1538, after the Reformation, the episcopal see was dissolved and with it the town's power.

Just next door to the Magnus Cathedral is the restored **St. Olav's Church,** which dates from 1111 and is now the only church from that time still in use. Most of its sculptures have been removed to Copenhagen, leaving little to see, but there's a hole in the north wall that once allowed lepers standing outside to watch the mass and receive the Eucharist. The altarpiece is the work of the most famous painter of the islands, Sámal Mikines.

Near the church is a former farmhouse, the **Roykstovan,** which today is a museum. Legend has it that the lumber for the building came drifting to the town, neatly numbered and bundled, from the Sogne Fjord in Norway. Inside are the traditional Faroese one-main-room living quarters and a dozen other rooms. It's been in the same family for the last 16 generations, and it is here that foreign dignitaries are welcomed to the town. The large split-log building is said to be about 900 years old and is the oldest cabin in Europe.

Saksun

30 km (18 mi) northwest of Tórshavn.

Among the fjords slicing the northern end of Streymoy is the tiny town of Saksun, one of the most popular excursions on the islands. Set around a pastoral lake in the midst of a deep valley are scattered sod-roof houses with lovely views. The town also swarms with great skuas, large brown seabirds prone to low dives. As you unwittingly near their nests, you will certainly notice their cantankerous presence.

Eiði

52 km (32 mi) northwest of Tórshavn.

The island of Eysturoy, just east of Streymoy, is connected to the latter by bridge and buses. The center of activity is the town of Eiði, which lies to the northwest in a spectacular landscape. Looking northwest, you can see two 250-ft cliffs, a part of local mythology: one night an Icelandic giant and his wife came to carry the islands to Iceland, but she dropped them, giving the islands their cracked geography. Once the sun rose, the giants were petrified and transformed into the bluffs.

Due east of Eiði is the islands' highest point, the 2,910-ft **Slættaratin-dur** mountain. On the shores of the southern **Skálafjørður,** the longest fjord in the archipelago, the majority of the island's 10,500 people live.

Lodging

$$ 🏨 **Hotel Eiði.** Perched on a hilltop in a village near the sea, about an hour by bus from Tórshavn, this slightly dated hotel is small and clean, with TVs and refrigerators in all rooms; some have private bath. ✉ FO–470, ☎ 298/423456, 🖷 298/423200. *28 beds. Restaurant. DC, MC, V.*

$ 🏨 **Gjáargarður.** This youth hostel, built in traditional Faroese style, has a prime position on the north end of the island, near the ocean and the mountains. ✉ *FO–476 Gjógv,* ☎ *298/423171,* 🖷 *298/423505. 100 beds. No credit cards.*

Klaksvík

35 km (22 mi) northeast of Tórshavn.

The island of Borðoy is accessible by boat from eastern Eysturoy. On its southwest coast, nearly divided by two fjords, Klaksvík is the Faroes' second-largest town and most important fishing harbor; its fleet of sophisticated boats harvests cod, haddock, herring, and other fish. Within this scattering of islands, Borðoy, Viðoy, and Kunoy are connected by causeways. The other three islands, Fugloy, Svinoy, and Kalsoy, are accessible by passenger boat or helicopter.

Within Klaksvík, the baptismal font in the **Christianskirkjan** (Christian's Church) is a piece of carved granite thought to have been used in pagan rituals in Denmark 4,000 years ago. Suspended from the church roof is a 24-ft boat used by a former vicar to visit nearby towns; the boat—

common in Danish churches—is a symbol that God is watching over the village fishermen.

Lodging

$$ ⊞ **Klaksvíkar Sjómansheim.** Sheep graze on the front lawn of this big, white hotel; the back overlooks the colorful harbor. The staff is cheery and helpful, and rooms—request one with a harbor view—offer no-frills comfort; showers and toilets are in the hallways, but sinks are in the rooms, some of which have private baths. The restaurant serves generous portions of the homemade special of the day. ⊠ *Vikavegur 39, FO–700,* ☎ *298/455333,* FAX *298/457233. 34 rooms. No credit cards.*

$ ⊞ **Youth Hostel and Guest House Ibuð.** This youth and family hostel, the only one on the northern islands, is in a former hotel, built in 1945. It is near a ferry slip and surrounded by hiking trails. ⊠ *Garðavegur 31, FO–700,* ☎ *298/455403 or 298/457555. 28 youth hostel beds. No credit cards.*

Viðareiði

18 km (11 mi) north of Klaksvík.

The island of Viðoy is among the wildest and most beautiful of the islands, with mountains of 2,800 ft and sheer cliffs plunging into extremely rough, unnavigable waters. Amazingly, 600 people live here, many in the town of Viðareiði. Cape Enniberg, at its northernmost tip, reaches 2,460 ft; it's the world's highest cape rising directly from the sea. From the town of Viðareiði you can take a boat tour (call Tora Tourist Travel; ☞ The Faroe Islands A to Z, *below*) to see many seabirds nesting on cliff walls, including kittiwakes and puffins—endearing little black-and-white birds with enormous orange beaks. The Faroese have a remarkable relationship with the puffins, harvesting them by the thousands for food and yet not endangering their numbers.

Lodging

$ ⊞ **Hotel Norð.** In a small town of 300 inhabitants on the northern end of the island, this simple business hotel has beautiful surroundings and great bird-watching. ⊠ *FO–750,* ☎ *298/451244,* FAX *298/451245. 20 beds. MC, V. Closed Sept.–June.*

Miðvágur

18 km (11 mi) west of Tórshavn.

Vágar, the third-largest island, takes its name from its fjords, and it is cut by three of them, as well as by the Fjallavatn and Sørvágsvatn lakes, the last of which is fed by the Bøsdalafossur, a 100-ft waterfall. The main town here is Miðvágur, an excellent perch for auk- and gannet-watching.

Lodging

$$ ⊞ **Hotel Vágar.** A standard small hotel, this one is modern. ⊠ *FO– 380 Sørvágur,* ☎ *298/332955,* FAX *298/332310. 56 beds. Restaurant. AE, DC, MC.*

Mykines

48 km (30 mi) west of Miðvágar (1 hr, 15 min by boat, 15 min by helicopter).

It's rough sailing to the tiny atoll of Mykines and only manageable when weather permits. In the town of the same name, population 19, the few dwellings are roofed with sod. The town was sited here to be close to the **Mykineshólmur,** an islet swarming with thousands of puffins, which are harvested for food. You can get here by traversing the island north-ward on foot about 2 km (1 mi) from the boat landing in Søvágur.

Sandur

25 km (16 mi) south of Tórshavn, 16 km (10 mi) south of Klaksvík.

Sandoy, the fifth-largest island, lies to the south. Relatively fertile, it's named for the sandy white beaches of the town of Sandur, on its bay. Sheep graze on green hills, and the lakes north and west of town swell with auks, purple sandpipers, and great skuas. This is great walking or biking country; bike rentals are available in town.

Vágur

64 km (40 mi) south of Tórshavn.

The southernmost island, Suðuroy, is milder than the others, with culti-vated green fields at its center and mountains along the coast. Ferries from Tórshavn dock either in Vágur or the quieter village of Tvøroyri.

Lodging

$$ 🏨 **Hotel Bakkin.** This plain lodging is usually booked by fishermen and local workers. ✉ *FO–900 Vágur,* ☎ *298/373961,* 🖷 *298/373962. 18 beds. No credit cards.*

$$ 🏨 **Hotel Tvøroyri.** In the middle of town, this old hotel has simple, clean rooms, some with bath, and minimal service. ✉ *FO–800 Tvøroyri,* ☎ *298/371171,* 🖷 *298/372171. 21 beds. AE.*

The Faroe Islands A to Z

Arriving and Departing

BY FERRY

There is frequent ferry service to all islands, with the most remote areas served by helicopter as well. Once a week in summer, between mid-May and mid-September, there are car ferries from Hanstholm, Jylland (34 hours) to Tórshavn that stop in between, with calls in the Shetland Islands, Norway, and Iceland. Between mid-September and mid-May, a direct ferry departs from Hanstholm every Saturday evening and arrives in Tórshavn on Monday morning. Call **Smyril Line** (☎ 33/16–40–04) for more information.

BY PLANE

SL Visitor Cards are sold at airports (☞ Getting Around, *below*). De-lays due to heavy fog are common. **From Copenhagen** there are daily connections to the western island of Vágar that take about two hours. From there, count another 1½ hours to get to Tórshavn by bus and ferry. For reservations, call either **Atlantic Airways** (☎ 33/14–44–20) or **Mærsk Air** (☎ 32/31–45–45) in Copenhagen (call ☎ 298/311025 when in Tórshavn). Both fly year-round between Copenhagen and the Faroes and also from Billund in Jylland in the summer season, with connections available from Amsterdam, Brussels, Frankfurt, London, Athens, Nice, Paris, London, and Stockholm. Two weekly flights are also available from **Reykjavík** (☎ 33/12–33–88) on **Icelandair,** which also flies twice a week, in summer, from Glasgow and Aberdeen to the Faroes and on to Iceland. Atlantic Airways also flies between the Faroes and Iceland.

Getting Around

If you're a good walker, pack a good pair of shoes, rain gear, and plan to wander, especially as the most striking features of the Faroe Islands are outside. When you tire, board a bus; the schedules are more or less regular, and the drivers tend to be friendly toward perplexed travelers. Of course, a car is much more convenient but also very expensive to rent (Dkr 565–Dkr 815 per day). Taxis are also expensive and not as practical as being independent, whether in a car or on foot.

The main islands are connected by regular ferries; smaller ones are linked by mailboat and helicopter. The **SL Visitor Card** is a good value for exploring the islands; it affords free passage on all SL (the local transportation company) buses and ferries. Be sure to buy the card at the airport (or from your travel agent) to pay for the trip to Tórshavn. It costs Dkr 385 for four days, Dkr 600 for seven days, Dkr 900 for 14 days; it's half-price for children under 12, free for those under 7 years old. For ferries, call **Strandfaraskip Landsins** (☎ 298/314550, FAX /298/ 316000) in Tórshavn. **Helicopter Service** (☎ 298/333700) is available in Vagar. In towns, and between islands that are connected by bridges, there is regular bus service. For schedules and reservations, call **Bygdaleiðir** (☎ 298/314550) in Tórshavn.

Driving laws are the same as in Denmark. Car rentals are available in Tórshavn and at Vagar Airport. A network of two-lane asphalt roads has been built between towns, using tunnels and bridges. The roads are best on the nine main islands. Speed limits are 50 kph (30 mph) in urban areas, 80 kph (50 mph) outside. Once outside towns, beware of untethered animals.

Contacts and Resources

Ambulance, fire, police (☎ 112).

Pharmacy: Tórshavn (✉ by SMS shopping center, ☎ 298/311100). **Klaksvik** (✉ Klaksvíksvegur, ☎ 298/456055). **Tvøroyri Pharmacy** (☎ 298/371076).

In addition to the local tours offered by many hotels, two main tour operators on the islands, **Kunningarstovan** (✉ N. Finsensgøta 13, Tórshavn, ☎ 298/315788) and **Tora Tourist Travel** (✉ N. Finsensgøta, Tórshavn, ☎ 298/315505), offer angling, city, and bird-watching tours.

Bird-Watching–Cave Tours: Tora Tourist Travel runs tours to Vestmanna Birdcliffs Tour (six hours), which includes a look at bird colonies and nearby caves.

Boat–Fishing Tours: Tours of Nolsoy and Hestur (Kunningarstovan) leave from Tórshavn harbor and include coastal sailing through the Kapilsund strait and along Hestur's west coast to see puffins and other seabirds. The three-hour trips are aboard the 50-year-old wooden schooner *Norðlýsið* (*Northern Light*), and guests may even get a chance to do some fishing.

Sightseeing Tours: Tora Tourist Travel organizes a tour to Gjógv, the northernmost village on Eysturoy (five hours), including a view of mountains and a local village.

The helpful brochure *Around the Faroe Islands,* is published by the tourist board. In Copenhagen, call the **Faroese Tourist Board** (✉ Hovedvagtsg. 8, ☎ 33/14–83–83). The **Danish Tourist Board** (branches in Denmark and abroad) can also supply information.

Klaksvík Tourist Information (✉ N. Palsgøta, FR–700 Klaksvík, ☎ 298/ 456939). **Aldan Tourist Information** (✉ Gangin, FO–100 Tórshavn, ☎ 298/316055).

9   PORTRAITS OF DENMARK

DENMARK AT A GLANCE: A CHRONOLOGY

ca. 10,000   Stone Age culture develops in Denmark.

ca. 2,000   Tribes from southern Europe, mostly Germanic peoples, migrate toward Denmark.

ca. 500   Migration of Celts across central Europe impinges on Denmark's trade routes with the Mediterranean world. Trade becomes less economically crucial because of the growing use of abundant iron.

ca. 770   The Viking Age begins. For the next 250 years, Scandinavians set sail on frequent expeditions stretching from the Baltic to the Irish seas, and even to the Mediterranean as far as Sicily, employing superior ships and weapons and efficient military organization.

830   Frankish monk Ansgar makes one of the first attempts to Christianize Sweden and builds the first church in Slesvig, Denmark.

1016–35   Canute (Knud) the Great is king of England, Denmark (1018), and Norway (1028).

1070   Adam of Bremen composes *History of the Archbishops of Hamburg-Bremen,* the first important contemporary source for Danish history.

1169   King Valdemar, who was acknowledged as the single king of Denmark in 1157 and undertook repeated crusades against the Germans, captures Rugen and places it under Danish rule, signifying the beginning of the Danish medieval empire. It culminates in 1219 when Valdemar marches to Estonia and builds a fortress at Ravel. In 1225, Valdemar, after being kidnapped by a German vassal, is forced to give up all his conquests, except for Rugen and Estonia, in exchange for freedom.

1282   At a meeting of the Hof, or Danish Parliament, Danish king Erik Glipping signs a coronation charter that becomes the first written constitution of Denmark.

1370   The Treaty of Stralsund gives the north German trading centers of the Hanseatic League free passage through Danish waters and full control of Danish herring fisheries for 15 years. German power increases throughout Scandinavia.

1397   The Kalmar union is formed as a result of the dynastic ties between Sweden, Denmark, and Norway, the geographical position of the Scandinavian states, and the growing influence of Germans in the Baltic. Erik of Pomerania is crowned king of the Kalmar Union.

1479   University of Copenhagen is founded.

1520   Christian II, ruler of the Kalmar Union, executes 82 people who oppose the Scandinavian union, an event known as the "Stockholm bloodbath." Sweden secedes from the Union three years later. Norway remains tied to Denmark and becomes a Danish province in 1536.

1534   Count Christoffer of Oldenburg and his army demand the restoration of Christian II as king of Denmark, initiating civil war between supporters of Christian II and supporters of Prince Christian (later King Christian III).

1611–16   The Kalmar War: Denmark wages war against Sweden in hopes of restoring the Kalmar Union.

1611–60 Gustav II Adolphus reigns in Sweden. Under his rule, Sweden defeats Denmark in the Thirty Years' War and becomes the greatest power in Scandinavia as well as northern and central Europe.

1660 Peace of Copenhagen establishes modern boundaries of Denmark, Sweden, and Norway.

1754 Royal Danish Academy of Fine Arts is established.

1762 The duke of Gottorp becomes czar of Russia and declares war on Denmark. Catherine, the czar's wife, overrules her husband's war declaration and makes a peaceful settlement.

1801–14 The Napoleonic wars are catastrophic for Denmark economically and politically: the policy of armed neutrality fails, the English destroy the Danish fleet in 1801, Copenhagen is devastated at the bombardment of 1807, and Sweden, after Napoléon's defeat at the Battle of Leipzig, attacks Denmark and forces the Danish surrender of Norway. The Danish monarchy is left with three parts: the Kingdom of Denmark and the duchies of Schleswig and Holstein.

1849 Denmark's absolute monarchy is abolished and replaced by the liberal June Constitution, which establishes freedom of the press, freedom of religion, the right to hold meetings and form associations, and rule by Parliament with two elected chambers as well as the king and his ministers.

ca. 1850 The building of railroads begins in Scandinavia.

1864 Denmark goes to war against Prussia and Austria; the hostilities end with the Treaty of Vienna, which forces Denmark to surrender the duchies of Schleswig and Holstein to Prussia and Austria.

1914 At the outbreak of World War I, Germany forces Denmark to lay mines in an area of international waters known as the Great Belt. Because the British fleet makes no serious attempts to break through, Denmark is able to maintain neutrality.

1917 Danish writer Henrik Pontoppidan is awarded the Nobel prize for literature.

1918 Iceland becomes a separate state under the Danish crown; only foreign affairs remain under Danish control. Sweden, Denmark, and Norway grant women the right to vote.

1920 Scandinavian countries join the League of Nations.

1929–37 The first social democratic governments take office in Denmark, Sweden, and Finland.

ca. 1930 The Great Depression causes unemployment, affecting 40% of the organized industrial workers in Denmark.

1939 Denmark and the other Nordic countries declare neutrality in World War II.

1940 Germany occupies Norway and Denmark.

1949 Denmark, Norway, and Iceland become members of NATO. Sweden and Finland decline membership.

1952 The Nordic Council, which promotes cooperation among the Nordic parliaments, is founded.

1972 Sweden, on the basis of its neutral foreign policy, and Norway decline membership in the EU; Denmark becomes a member in 1973. Queen Margarethe II ascends the throne of Denmark.

1982 Poul Schluter becomes Denmark's first Conservative prime minister since 1894.

1989 Tycho Brahe Planetarium opens in Copenhagen; and Denmark becomes the first NATO country to allow women to join front-line military units. Denmark becomes the first country in the world to recognize marriage between citizens of the same sex.

1991 The Karen Blixen Museum, in Rungstedlund, Denmark, is founded.

1992 Denmark declines to support the Maastricht Treaty setting up a framework for European economic union. Denmark wins the European Soccer Championships.

1993 Denmark is the president of the EU for the first half of 1993. In a second referendum, the country votes to support the Maastricht Treaty, as well as its own modified involvement in it. Tivoli celebrates its 150th year, Legoland celebrates its 25th birthday, and the Little Mermaid turns 80. Denmark also commemorates the 50th anniversary of the World War II rescue of Danish Jews, in which they were smuggled into Sweden.

1995 The 50th anniversary of the end of World War II in Europe is celebrated, especially in Denmark and Norway, where May 5 marks the end of the German occupation.

1996 Copenhagen is fêted as the Cultural Capital of Europe.

1997 Copenhagen's venerable Carlsberg Brewery, one of the largest supporters of the arts in Denmark, celebrates its 150th anniversary.

THE UTTERLY DANISH PASTRIES OF DENMARK

I BELIEVE above and beyond every gastronomic specialty a country offers, there is one, just one, perfect, delicious bit or bite or drop of something or another that sums up everything the country is and ever has been. As a transplanted American living in Denmark, I long thought the country's perfect bite was the smørrebrød, or open-face sandwiches: they are practical, well designed, and small—in essence everything Denmark is. Over time, however, I have revised my theory. Today, I believe that divine bite can be found in the pastries, the Danish pastries.

Take a stroll through Copenhagen, and before long, you'll have to make an effort to pass up the bakeries, to steel yourself not to try one of the flaky sweets. But then again, why should you? A Danish is effortlessly elegant, unobtrusively hedonistic, and often packed with a surprise—an edible metaphor of the Danish experience.

Imagine this: you are walking through Copenhagen, and you happen to meander off Strøget, the store-crammed and remarkably congested pedestrian spine. Immediately, you notice the pace of the city slows. Antique shops sidle up to cafés while, a block away, rows of half-timbered houses lined with thick squares of convex windows wiggle to nowhere. At the tip of Gammel Strand, literally the old beach, you spy a lone fisherwoman in worn shawls and head scarves hawking live eel and smoked herring. You wind back to the more-than-150-year-old La Glace, purported to be the oldest confectionery shop in Copenhagen. Decorous ladies in aprons serve you a dainty china pot of coffee and light, crisp, and exceedingly Danish, pastries.

Not just any sweets these—not French, nor Austrian—and certainly not those suspicious-looking pillows of white dough injected with Red Stuff you chance to order in the United States, but the real McCoy, made in the same way since the 19th century. It makes me wonder why the Danes don't lay claim to the name, and insist upon it as an appellation d'origine.

THE FIRST TIME I had a Danish pastry, at the source, was 14 years ago, when the Dane of my affections (my husband today) introduced me to Copenhagen. A late night of debauchery had turned into an early morning amble, when Jesper and his best friend, Jan Erik, assured me that pastries would cure all of our ails. Though most bakeries don't open until 6 AM, Jan Erik went to a side door and rapped on its top window. Shady conversation with a young, flour-dusted blade ensued, and paper bags and cash were quickly exchanged. (I was never clear if it was law or legend, but in those days, most Danes believed the police enforced regular shopping hours.) Prize in hand, we strolled to Peblinge Sø, one of the

CITY'S LAKES, where we sat on a bench, drank from a carton of milk, and ate several flaky pastries topped with nuts and sugar icings and filled with marmalades and creams. As the sun rose, defining the ducks, swans, and occasional heron, I felt enormously happy just to be there.

Those who record such events mark the birth of the Danish pastry sometime at the end of the 19th century, when Danish bakers went on strike, demanding money rather than room and board as payment for their work. Their employers replaced them with Austrian bakers, who brought with them the mille-feuille, or puff pastry, which they learned to make from the French. Once the Danes were back at work, they adopted the continental dough, making it their own by adding yeast and sweet fillings.

It was a tradition at the time (and to a lesser degree today) for Danish bakers to travel abroad to add to their repertoire. This pastry cross-pollination helps explain why the yeast-risen puff pastry is called *Kopenhagener Geback,* literally "Copenhagen bread," in Austria, and Danish pastry in America. Ironically, the yeast-risen pastries are still called *wienerbrød*, or Vienna bread, in Denmark.

What makes Danish pastries special is the production process, which for most bakers is still done by hand. Essentially, the dough—milk, flour, eggs, butter, sugar, and yeast—is made, then chilled. It is then rolled into a rectangle, and, unapologetically, a slab of margarine or butter is put on the center third. The two ends of the dough are folded over the butter, and the process is repeated three times, until there are 27 layers in all.

Once the dough has been rolled and chilled, it is finally shaped into pretzel forms (called *kringle*), as well as braids, squares, triangles, fans, combs, swirls, pinwheels, horns, crescents, and wreaths, and filled with *remonce*, the stupefyingly rich butter, sugar, and nut (or marzipan) combination. The word remonce only sounds French; since it was very fashionable in 19th-century Denmark to give things French-ified names, a Danish baker is said to have invented the word. Ask for it in Paris, and, no doubt, you will be met with bewilderment.

In addition to the remonce, Danish bakers also fill their pastries with raisins, fruit compotes, and vanilla and—to a lesser degree—chocolate custards. As Gert Sørensen, the chief baker and owner of Konditoriet in Tivoli, says, "The final product should be crisp on the outside, juicy on the inside."

He should know: as one of the country's most respected pastry chefs, he has been educating and enlightening generations of young pastry stars. In fact, not just anyone can be a *konditor*, as they are known in Denmark. The rigorous education takes three years and seven months, and entails basic economics as well as an apprenticeship at a bakery, making wienerbrød daily. Danes are happy to consume the schoolwork, and do so at breakfast, after lunch, or with their afternoon coffee, especially on the weekends. Copenhagen alone boasts more than 150 of Denmark's 1,400 bakeries, the latter pulling in the equivalent of $727 million annually, about 20 percent of which is attributable to wienerbrød. At an average cost of 5 kroner (roughly 91 cents), I figure that's close to 30 million pastries a year.

Trying to pick the best of Copenhagen's—let alone Denmark's—pastries is like hunting down France's best truffle. Though Denmark's pastry chefs participate in a number of national and international pastry contests (and consistently rank among the world's best), nearly every Dane has found a bakery within a five-minute cycling radius of home that they claim to be the best in the land. My own allegiance is to the bakery named Bosse, in the neighborhood of Østerbro. I often find my bed-headed self wandering there on Saturday morning to buy a bagful of pastries with names like rum snail, marzipan horn, and my husband's favorite, a rum ball, essentially the sausage of pastries, all the leftover bits rolled together and often covered with chocolate sprinkles. My own favorites include the *spandauer,* a flat swirl of dough, centered with vanilla custard, and the marzipan horn, a crispy twirl of pastry rolled up with remonce. Even though these may not be the finest pastries in town, they are the genuine article, and uncommonly Danish.

But, there's much more to Danish pastries than wienerbrød. At La Glace the windows display delicate special-occasion cakes like those for baptisms, trimmed with marzipan pacifiers, cradles, and dolls. From her original 1920 pink, green, and gold tea room, proprietor Marianne Stagetorn Kolos explains that most guests come for her layer cakes, like the best-selling *Sportskage,* a mound of macaroons, whipped cream, and caramel chunks created and named for a play performed at the nearby Folketeatret in 1891. It's a Danish custom to name confections for events and personalities, but there was a time when ordering a miniature Sarah Bernhardt, a chocolate-truffle-covered macaroon named for the French actress, was an act of courage. During World War II, resistance fighters and sympathizers recognized one another by ordering the pastry as a "radio macaroon," since it resembles an old-fashioned radio knob. The name stuck.

Close by, on a quiet cobblestoned courtyard, is the Kransekagehuset, where confectioner Jørgen Jensen makes the marzipan cakes compulsory at any Danish wedding. Using 1 kilogram marzipan to 400 grams sugar to 200 grams egg whites, Jensen molds the dough into rings of varying sizes. Once baked, they are fashioned into cones or cornucopias, squiggled with white icing, decked with paper decorations, or filled with wrapped candies.

I know the *kransekage* intimately. At our wedding years ago, Jesper and I split the difference in our Italian-Armenian-American-Danish backgrounds, and ordered two cakes, one of which was a kransekage laced with Danish and American flags, and tiny, shiny-paper firecrackers that made a polite, little bang.

"It's something special," smiles Jensen. "It's something very Danish."

—by Karina Porcelli

TIVOLI

A WOMAN IS TELLING ME about her life and her travels in a poetic English that, I am sure, despite being a native English speaker, I will never master.

"I came to Tivoli for the first time when I was five," she says in a lilting Danish accent. "My parents made me take a nap first, because they said it would be like the fairy-tales."

Erna Wahlin stretches her feet and points them high in the purple evening air. She sits next to Elly Larsen, two years her junior, at 86 years old. The downy-haired octogenarians prattle on about the quality of the coffee, the flakiness of the pastries, the way young people dress, and the magic of their beloved Tivoli.

Behind them, thousands of green, yellow, and purple lights twinkle as the first bulbs of the evening blink. The air fills with a gushing waltz that dissolves to the squeals of children as they are flung skyward in Ferris wheels and motorized swans. Coifed teens bound toward a ride, nearly toppling an elderly couple in mid-smooch. A young couple pushes a baby carriage, adangle with paper cocktail umbrellas, toward the Peacock Theater, and teenagers romance awkwardly in the corners of the Japanese Garden.

Tivoli's innocence is catching, especially on sunny days when Danes and tourists flock to its neat lanes and flower gardens to enjoy an old-fashioned amusement park with nothing Disneyesque about it. In the Copenhagen scheme of things—where mothers park baby carriages (contents snoozing) outside bakeries, where business-folk talk on mobile phones while cycling to work, and where blonds-like-only-Scandinavians-can-be blonds drink Carlsberg in public parks—Tivoli fits right in. It shares a chicken-and-egg relationship with the capital: which came first? Tivoli or Copenhagen's quixotic ways?

Tivoli still blurs the line between formal European garden and old-time amusement park. In April, when the soggy northern winter retreats and the days lengthen in hyper-speed succession, the Danes are ready to throw off the chill and celebrate. It is time for Tivoli. In the relatively short five-month season, more than four million people come through the gates—an impressive figure considering the population of Denmark just hovers over five million.

Though the number of visitors has grown, the park has not changed radically since the 19th century, when Danish architect George Carstensen persuaded King Christian VIII to let him build an amusement park. He argued the park would be an opiate for people of all classes and backgrounds, and "when people amuse themselves, they forget politics."

TIVOLI WAS ORIGINALLY BUILT on the edge of Copenhagen's fortifications, among cows and countrysides. As the city was still scarred by the bloody battles between Denmark and England (it was here Lord Nelson turned his famous blind eye, and bombed Copenhagen to bits), the park rose up like an apparition. It sprouted quirky Oriental and Moorish architecture inspired by Carstensen's privileged childhood in Algiers, where his father had been Danish Consul General.

On August 15, 1843, the day Tivoli officially opened, most visitors were enchanted by the exotic park, including Hans Christian Andersen, so inspired he wrote his tale, The Nightingale. Others, including the press, thought Carstensen foolish to encourage the social classes to mix. Danish history recalls Carstensen a braggart—a condition even modern Danes dislike. As his popularity declined, Carstensen decided to test his political and entrepreneurial talents abroad, but, eventually returned to Copenhagen bankrupt. The story goes he was not recognized when he returned to the gardens he founded, and had to enter through the turnstiles a paying visitor.

Unlike many famous amusement parks around the world, Tivoli is not in a dislocated expanse, far from the city. Rather, it is the heart of the city. The main entrance on Vesterbrogade welcomes visitors with a grand arched portal and shaded walking paths. They lead to more than 20 verdant acres, punctuated throughout with flower-trimmed fountains, covered stages, and outdoor pavilions. Not including the independently run Jazzhus Slukefter and Vise Vers Huset, a bar featuring folk music, seven separate venues offer entertainment. Performances range from children's theater to classical concerts featuring luminaries like violinist Anne-Sophie Mutter, flutist Jean-Pierre Rampal, and Denmark's own musical jester Victor Borge.

Any self-respecting amusement park has rides, and Tivoli is no exception. Its 28 rides are settled unobtrusively along its perimeter, and have always been a part of the whole, rather than a central, attraction. The roller coaster existed at Carstensen's time, along with a freak show and shooting gallery, but all of that has disappeared, and the roller coaster is, thankfully, a newer model from 1914. The rides have been built over the years—all with benign names like "The Wild Swans" and "Tubs Ahoy"— to take passengers on mildly butterfly-inducing flights. Though other parks tout coiled innards of gut-wrenching, scream-spewing, warp-speed chaos, children and roller-coaster buffs seem perfectly happy at Tivoli.

When it comes to eating and drinking, the Danes enjoy their food, whether it be a five-course meal or a paper bag of hand-picked Gummy Bears. At last count, 30 sit-down restaurants trimmed the park, plus dozens of sausage stands and candy counters for grazing. I have a weakness for the ice-cream cones: freshly baked waffles rolled and filled with triple-scoops of rich ice cream, a dollop each of strawberry jam and whipped cream, topped with the world's largest chocolate-covered marshmallow.

AS WITH MANY THINGS DANISH, there is a sense of poignancy in Tivoli. If one buys 50 season passes over the course of so many years, management will provide them season passes for the rest of their life. Carefully dressed pensioners in fine hats and heavy shoes walk as they lean against each other, then collapse on shaded benches.

Two fine ladies sip coffee and share a cigar. A grandfather and grandson totter in parallel infirmity toward a photographer, and offer compositional advice. Tivoli is their park, and Danes young and especially old, lay claim to it. I raise a skal to a man celebrating his 70th birthday.

"Have you heard they have opened a Tivoli in Japan?" I ask. He scoffs, and takes a long draw of his beer. "Tivoli is Denmark," he says. "How can you translate that?"

Insubordination and an astringent sense of humor, especially in the face of foreign authority, have always been Danish attributes. During World War II when the Nazis demanded Jews wear identifying stars, the Danish king, Christian V, put one on first, his loyal subjects quickly following suit. Later when Denmark's resistance was growing in bravery and infamy, the Germans retaliated by striking Tivoli, destroying its most characteristic buildings. Quietly defiant, the Danes built a tent Tivoli within the week, and resumed their promenades.

Things are more peaceful these days, but it appears the pace of modern life does not enter these gates. In a country where personal income tax exceeds 50 percent, and most shops close at 5:30 PM Monday through Thursday, commerce is secondary to the process of life. When Michael Jackson visited the park in the early '90s, local legend says he asked to buy it, but was politely told it was not for sale. While Tivoli glitters with fine restaurants and silver and porcelain boutiques, there are no rabid barkers waving cotton candy, no oily hucksters pushing the arcade games. Tivoli employees, Danish or not, are uniformly neat, polite, and available when needed. Rides are exhilarating, but really, there isn't a hell-raiser in the place.

The gardens enchant even those whose botanical knowledge barely differentiates between trees and grass. Radiant roses face violet thistle, Dutch tulips bow to a dapple of daisies. Their numbers astound: the park contains 864 trees and 400,000 flowers, including 65,000 tulips and 55,000 narcissi. In a single year, upwards of 135,000 new bulbs are planted. Despite their quantity, subtlety is key. The trees, including sprays of willow and bamboo, thrive in natural splendor, and are not carved into obtuse topiaries. Understatement, again, is everything.

LIFE IS NOT A PROBLEM TO BE SOLVED, but a reality to be experienced," said Søren Kierkegaard, Denmark's famed existentialist, in a rare moment of levity. So true, my Danish husband Jesper agrees, before hopping atop a giant, red plastic fish. This is the Tivoli of the weird. I have brought a group of American and British friends to visit the park, and Jesper is telling them about the now defunct flea circus of his childhood, when an old man trained a pack of infinitesimal acrobats to fling themselves across a tiny trapeze. Our friends eye him suspiciously as they stroll to one of 20 arcades, "Det Muntre Kokken," or the Crazy Kitchen, where mild-mannered men and women take out their frustrations by hurling, pitching, launching, slinging, heaving, lobbing, and slamming white tennis-size balls into hundreds of real porcelain dishes.

Nearby, in placid Lake Tivoli, elegant black New Zealand swans and plebeian ducks paddle to their huts, but, this being Denmark, some wade to their pink summer duck villa. More than mere waterfowl, these lucky ducks have few worries, though I reconsider when my three-year-old daughter begins to feed them bits of a leftover pastry. There is an altercation: a giant carp two feet long—its mouth an alarming "O"— raises its huge head out of the water and displaces a perplexed mallard.

Then it is show time at the Peacock Theater, where pantomime in the Italian tradition of commedia dell'arte, is complete with Pierrot, harlequin, Cassandra, and Columbine. Only Pierrot may speak, a result of an accident sometime around the turn of the century, when a dancer's skirt caught fire, and the audience demanded an explanation. As is typical in Denmark, the experience turned into ritual, which survives today. At the end of the performance, children on grown-up shoulders plead a few words from the elegant joker, and reward with a hearty hurrah.

Nighttime transforms Tivoli into a delicate pattern of illuminated curlicues and brightly lit archways. Electric dragonflies flutter atop the lake, and weeping willows twined with white lights tremble. Denmark is the only country outside the United States to celebrate American Independence Day, and Tivoli's midnight fireworks are decidedly not big bang, but delicate twists of gold and silver. The Barfoed fireworks family has been illuminating the park since it opened more than 150 years ago, and will do so again this year, as the sixth generation volleys just enough magic into the dusky sky. White bouquets of light rise and fall and boom, then wink to black. The audience oohs and aahs, and leaves Tivoli wanting just a little bit more.

—by Karina Porcelli

BOOKS AND VIDEOS

Books

A History of the Vikings (Oxford University Press, 1984) recounts the story of the aggressive warriors and explorers who during the Middle Ages influenced a large portion of the world, extending from Constantinople to America. Gwyn Jones's lively account makes learning the history enjoyable.

Excellent reading on Denmark includes: the works of Karen Blixen (Isak Dinesen) set in Denmark; *Pelle the Conqueror* (volumes I and II) by Martin Andersen Nexø (a novel about a young Swedish boy and his father who work on a stone farm in Bornholm under hateful Danish landowners); *Laterna Magica* by William Heinesen (a novel of the Faroe Islands by perhaps Denmark's greatest writer since Karen Blixen); and the satirical trilogy by Hans Scherfig—*Stolen Spring, The Missing Bureaucrat,* and *Idealists*. Wallace Stegner's novel *The Spectator Bird* follows a man's exploration of his Danish heritage. Peter Høeg's acclaimed novel, *Smilla's Sense of Snow,* is a compulsive page-turner that paints a dark and foreboding picture of Copenhagen and the waters around Greenland; the movie version debuted in 1997. Fjord Press (Box 16349, Seattle, WA 98116, ☎ 206/935-7376, FAX 206/938-1991) has one of the most comprehensive selections of Danish fiction in translation of any publisher in the United States.

Videos

Babette's Feast, which won the Oscar for the best foreign film of 1987, was produced in Denmark. Danny Kaye starred in the 1952 film *Hans Christian Andersen.* In fact, his crooning of "Wonderful Copenhagen" became Denmark's official tourism slogan. Disney's *The Little Mermaid* is a great way to get your kids interested in Andersen's fairy tales.

DANISH VOCABULARY

English	Danish	Pronunciation
Basics		
Yes/no	Ja/nej	yah/nie
Thank you	Tak	tak
You're welcome	Selv tak	**sell** tak
Excuse me (to apologize)	Undskyld	**unsk**-ul
Hello	Hej	hi
Goodbye	Farvel	fa-**vel**
Today	I dag	ee **day**
Tomorrow	I morgen	ee **morn**
Yesterday	I går	ee **gore**
Morning	Morgen	**more**-n
Afternoon	Eftermiddag	**ef-tah**-mid-day
Night	Nat	nat

Numbers

1	een/eet	een/eet
2	to	toe
3	tre	treh
4	fire	fear
5	fem	fem
6	seks	sex
7	syv	syoo
8	otte	**oh**-te
9	ni	nee
10	ti	tee

Days of the Week

Monday	mandag	man-day
Tuesday	tirsdag	**tears**-day
Wednesday	onsdag	**ons**-day
Thursday	torsdag	**trs**-day
Friday	fredag	**free**-day
Saturday	lørdag	**lore**-day
Sunday	søndag	**soo**(n)-day

Useful Phrases

Do you speak English?	Taler du engelsk	te-ler doo in-galsk
I don't speak ... Danish	Jeg taler ikke Dansk	yi tal-ler **ick** Dansk
I don't understand.	Jeg forstår ikke	yi fahr-store **ick**
I don't know.	Det ved jeg ikke	deh **ved** yi ick
I am American/British.	Jeg er amerikansk/britisk	yi ehr a-mehr-i-**kansk**/bri-**tisk**
I am sick.	Jeg er syg	yi ehr **syoo**

Please call a doctor.	Kan du ringe til en læge?	can **doo** rin-geh til en lay-eh
Do you have a vacant room?	Har du et værelse?	har **doo** eet va(l)r-sa
How much does it cost?	Hvad koster det?	va cos-ta **deh**
It's too expensive.	Det er for dyrt	deh ehr **fohr** dyrt
Beautiful	Smukt	smukt
Help!	Hjælp	yelp
Stop!	Stop	stop
How do I get to . . .	Hvordan kommer jeg til?	vore-**dan** kom-mer yi til
the train station?	banegarden	**ban** eh-gore-en
the post office?	postkontoret	**post**-kon-toh-raht
the tourist office?	turistkonoret	too-**reest**-kon-tor-et
the hospital?	hospitalet	hos-peet-**tal**-et
Does this bus go to . . . ?	Går denne bus til?	**goh** den-na boos til
Where is the W.C.?	Hvor er toilettet	vor **ehr** toi-le(tt)-et
On the left	Til venstre	til **ven**-strah
On the right	Till hǛjre	til **hoy**-ah
Straight ahead	Lige ud	**lee** u(l)

Dining Out

Please bring me . . .	Må jeg få	mo yi foh
menu	menu	me-**nu**
fork	gaffel	gaf-**fel**
knife	kniv	kan-**ew**
spoon	ske	skee
napkin	serviet	serv-**eet**
bread	brǛd	brood
butter	smǛr	smoor
milk	mælk	malk
pepper	peber	**pee**-wer
salt	salt	selt
sugar	sukker	**su**-kar
water/bottled water	vand/Dansk vand	van/dansk van
The check, please.	Må jeg bede om regningen	mo yi bi(d) o **ri**-ning

130

INDEX

NOTES

meget · maët · Very

NOTES

NOTES

NOTES

NOTES

NOTES

Looking for a different kind of vacation?

Fodor's makes it easy with a full line of specialty guidebooks to suit a variety of interests—from adventure to romance to language help.

Fodor's. For the world of ways you trave